Democracy's Subjections

Democracy's Subjections

Colonial Modernity and the Gendered Subject of Violence

Lyn Ossome

BLOOMSBURY ACADEMIC
NEW YORK • LONDON • OXFORD • NEW DELHI • SYDNEY

BLOOMSBURY ACADEMIC
Bloomsbury Publishing Plc, 50 Bedford Square, London, WC1B 3DP, UK
Bloomsbury Publishing Inc, 1359 Broadway, New York, NY 10018, USA
Bloomsbury Publishing Ireland, 29 Earlsfort Terrace, Dublin 2, D02 AY28, Ireland

Published in Great Britain 2026

Cover design: Grace Ridge
Cover image © Ayed Arafah

A catalogue record for this book is available from the British Library.

Library of Congress Cataloging-in-Publication Data available

ISBN HB: 978-1-3505-4523-6
PB: 978-1-3505-4522-9
ePDF: 978-1-3505-4525-0
eBook: 978-1-3505-4524-3

Typeset by Lumina Datamatics Ltd
Printed and bound in Great Britain

For product safety related questions contact productsafety@bloomsbury.com.

For my parents, Damarie and Barry Ossome
who were my first and best teachers

and

in memory of my beloved Gugu
who still walks with me.

Contents

Acknowledgements

Solitude invariably accompanies every lengthy attempt at writing, yet the very possibility of what is written cannot but be a collective one. Many individuals made this book possible in one way or another through encouragement, intellectual companionship and friendship at different times over the eight-year course of writing it. For this I thank Danai Mupotsa, Sarah Ssali, Mahmood Mamdani, Dzodzi Tsikata, Joy James, Shireen Hassim, Gyekye Tanoh, Gabi Ngcobo, Paris Yeros, Camalita Naicker, Issa Shivji, Andrea Cassatella, Samara Ragaven, Akinyi Walkowa Odinga, Athinangamso Nkopo, Crystal Simeoni, Sirisha Naidu, Busi Sibeko, Kwame Owino, Sekou Owino, Josephine Ahikire, Yosef Jemberie, Hala Al-Karib, and Selly Thiam. Andrea Cassatella read several versions of the manuscript and patiently debated me through its most contentious parts. I know that the book is better for it. Various chapters benefited from discussions in a number of forums over the years, including the Ifriqiyya Colloquium at Columbia University, the Black Women Writing African Politics collective, the Research Laboratory of Non-exemplary Sociology at Rio de Janeiro Federal Rural University and the seminar series at Makerere Institute of Social Research. Lara Foot generously made time for a wide-ranging conversation around her play *Tsephang*, to which I hope I have done some justice in retelling. I remain indebted to my students past and present: theirs is the generation that has put to us the toughest of questions yet. I am thankful for the support of my larger family, for my niece Akiru, and especially my siblings Dave, Becky and Sweetie, with whom I share a great friendship and understanding. My parents have loved us immensely through everything. My mother is a remarkable woman. She was my first teacher and it is through her eyes that I have most consistently tried to make sense of the worlds about which I write. To my late father I owe the love of ideas. He would have challenged me on every major claim of this book and I hope that these pages somewhat reflect the answers he would have expected. Three anonymous readers seriously engaged with the text at various stages and I am deeply indebted to them. My editor, Nick Wolterman, believed in the idea and supported the book with much conviction. I thank him most sincerely. My gratitude goes also to Anna Eggers and the editorial team at Bloomsbury, who graciously guided me through the publication process. To the captive subject past, present and to come who this book mourns, may this effort restore even a tiny possibility of imagining a different future.

Preface

The paradox at the core of this book – that is, the link between democracy and violence – is a problem which I began to seriously consider nearly two decades ago in the wake of the most violent elections in Kenya's history, which I had witnessed firsthand. My initial endeavour to make sense of that violence led to a doctoral thesis whose initial interest was the political economy of sexual violence in the context of elections, but which ultimately led me to a body of critical debates concerned with the limitations of the liberal democratic project in the postcolony. A number of residual questions remained unanswered in the book that emerged out of that earlier work. For instance, a focus on the nature of the state alone did not seem to adequately explain why it is that certain groups of people experienced the state as a recurring nightmare of violence and not others. What was it that explained the postcolonial state's propensity for extreme gendered violence in the name of democracy? And why had democracy been so easily co-opted as an alibi for such violence? A response to these questions seemed to require an approach that is more concretely grounded in the histories of the *subjects themselves* of postcolonial democracy. This book is my attempt to give form and substance to those subjects, issued from the vantage point of women and in the tradition of political economy.

The idea of democracy, as I approach it in this book, harbours the possibility both of critique and emancipation. The former takes a stance against liberal democracy (bourgeois representation) as being an inherently violent form of political organization in the postcolony, emerging as it does through the mere substitution of 'hitherto violent structures of exploitation, despotism and degradation' with talk of 'individual rights, civil liberties, freedom of expression' and so on, 'without any fundamental transformation in the economic, cultural, or bureaucratic domains'.[1] But this imposition does not necessarily eliminate the fundamental idea of *Democracy* as harbouring the possibility of freedom, egalitarianism and sovereignty, which liberation movements everywhere demand in its name. It is, in other words, both necessary to critique democracy's normative violence in contexts where historical, social and material conditions have not yet matured to include as many groups as possible and to recall its liberatory promise. The primary subject of such a critique (and promise) in this book is a gendered one.

In it I examine the links between colonialism, democracy and gendered violence, drawing on anticolonial[2] feminist critique as an analytical framework to argue first, that the gendered/reproductive (labour) question is a necessary condition for women's legibility as subjects of both the colonial and postcolonial state; second, that this mode of subjectivation renders colonized women as quintessentially modern subjects of the state because of the articulation between their labour and their political subjectivity; and third, that this mode of subjectivation produces a structure of governmentality that places women/gendered subjects at the centre of any decolonial/democratic possibility in the postcolonial state.

A note on the idea of a 'subject' is also necessary given its preponderant use throughout the book. The rationality proposed by the 'progress of modernity' implies the elimination of subjectivity in favour of a triumphant objectivity.[3] Yet the idea of a subject (of history, of the state, of democracy, of rights and so on) remains resilient. The sociological notion of the 'subject' that I draw on in this book is only partially indebted to Foucault's notion of 'subjectivation', through which he theorizes the internalization of rules, categories and values in a cycle of ever unfolding subordination of each individual to a power which imposes categories of perception and action in everyday life. Such categories might include gender, class, ethnicity, sexuality or race, but are *not* mere perceptions under conditions of colonial domination, where individuality is all but denied to the colonized, such that everyday life is experienced always as part of a group: as *political identity.* It is in this regard that the liberatory logics of anticolonial struggles gain power and reconstitutes the subject as also an agent of history. Furthermore, in the colonial context, the process of subjectivation is invariably accompanied by violence. The question, *who is the subject of democracy?* is generalizable to a universal subject, but is historically specific to the extent that it cannot be answered in any universal sense other than by discovery through critique of the structures, conditions and institutions that render the subject visible. Lastly, if colonialism as a process of modern domination and dispossession is already imbued with violence, then the colonial subject must a priori be understood as a *violated* subject. The 'gendered subject of violence' is, in this regard, a fundamental claim regarding a relationship between gender and violence as a mode of subjectivation.

The book's overall approach broadly locates my intervention amongst scholarly critiques of the modernist logics and legacies of colonial rule but exceeds this scholarship to deal concretely with the question of violence as the primary structure of legibility between gendered subjects (concretely theorized as *labouring* subjects) and the postcolonial democratizing state. This is a formulation which suggests that postcolonial democracy is haunted by both a history and a presence of feminist anticolonial and postcolonial struggles against exploitation and erasure, to which the state and capital characteristically respond with violence. At the same time, postcolonial democracy is confronted by the ethical responsibility against violence which the colonized place upon it. The apparent contradiction between these two positions highlights a core tension that runs throughout the book: that is, that the very possibility of democratic life is circumscribed for those that are subjectivated through democracy's violent histories and who are compelled to respond to this violence *within* the logics of democracy.

Violence and the protest/resistance against it are here conceived as the two other necessary historical conditions (in addition to labour) that historically produced the political subjectivity of women/gendered subjects in the colonial and postcolonial state. In other words, the modern political subjectivity of women/gendered subjects emerges, first, on the giving end of labour (as *labouring subjects*), second, on the receiving end of violence (as *violable subjects*) and, third, through their protest/resistance against these (as *resisting subjects* or *agents*). Together, these three conditions constitute part of a single (inseparable) logic that ultimately shapes and (re)produces the modern political subjectivity of women/gendered subjects as a *labouring-violable-resisting subjectivity*. The interdisciplinary methodology of this work – drawing on political studies, feminist political economy, historical studies and literary studies – also maps the parameters of its theoretical contributions.

Introduction

> *...theoretically and ideologically, one must relentlessly expose bourgeois democracy – and its various freedoms – as an expression of bourgeois class dictatorship but politically one must vote for bourgeois democracy against fascism and authoritarianism.*[1]

> *Decolonization, which sets out to change the order of the world, is, obviously, a program of complete disorder. It cannot come as a result of magical practices, nor of a natural shock, nor of a friendly understanding. Decolonization, as we know, is a historical process: that is to say it cannot be understood, it cannot become intelligible nor clear to itself except in the exact measure that we can discern* the movements *which give it historical form and content.*[2]

The painting on the cover of this book is drawn from the series by Palestinian artist Ayed Arafah titled 'My mother is picking cactus every day'. This particular work is titled *Mother picking cactus.*[3] The artist's note to me describes the paintings as representing 'women's struggle, resistance and patience in the Palestinian community, where ... [women are] *the greatest fundamental power* of the Palestinian liberation structure'.[4] The sturdiness of the cactus plant, its ability to endure under extreme conditions, is similar in virtue to that which women require in order to sustain the resistance: 'cactus and patience are the same word in Arabic' – *Sabr.*[5] It's meaning synonymous to another, *Sumud* – the ideas of steadfastness and perseverance that define Palestinian anticolonial resistance.[6] But what is to be persevered? What is the nature of that which is to be endured? Certainly not oppression, but faith in the possibility of freedom that for the colonized is conditioned upon struggle: 'there is...nothing romantic about these cruel conditions, nor is there anything romantic about the *absolute need* to live with patience and steadfastness to avoid utter extinction'.[7]

Liberation struggles of any kind are given to agony: '[p]icking the cactus is telling their story, in a way. Picking cactus is not nice. It causes pain'.[8] In her reading of Arafah's *Mother picking cactus*, Merucci (2021) grounds the work's significance in 'the relationship between liberation and pain', and meditating on the artist's reflections regarding what it means to be a woman in Palestine, wonders whether 'pain is emblematic of these women's stories'. In Arafah's view, 'Palestinian women are under double Occupation – [the Occupation by Israel and an Occupation by] the masculine of the community. Women are doubly resisting'.[9] Through the eyes of the artist, Merucci (2021) considers the labour intensive work of picking cacti as being a reflection of 'the link between freedom, gender and labor'.[10] Picking of cactus is 'a means of production in a society where patriarchy informs societal norms and values [and] one of the ways Palestinian women contribute their labor is through the picking of cactus plant'.[11] Yet, the plant's cultural place in that society extends women's labouring on cactus beyond the realm merely of production. It is also fundamentally emblematic of the social and cultural reproduction of a society threatened with extinction. In Arafah's words, the persistence of tradition in that context cannot be read separately from the social conditions: ... *when the chance of a good life is under pressure, it makes people stick to traditions.*[12] Holding on to tradition, Merucci writes, following Said (1992) 'is also about *not disappearing* as a community and culture'.[13] The question then that flows from these meditations, and a central one that structures my own inquiries in the book is this: what narratives of liberation are rendered visible through the centring of a *gendered, labouring subject* of history?

This is a basic question to which every generation of women seeks a response under conditions invariably dictated by their own times and exigencies. Under the conditions dictated by the anticolonial struggle, the illegitimacy of the plundering, violent state is not in question and the liberation struggle easily clarifies its objectives as being to dismantle colonial rule and establish national sovereignty and self-determination. Under the postcolonial condition, the liberation struggle is subsumed under the illusion of democracy to the extent that its objectives mirror democracy's terms.[14] This point has, for instance, been argued in relation to democratic South Africa, where the perception reigned 'that the dawn of democracy signaled a break with violence [and that] difficulties and conflicts, in a democracy, would be resolved without resorting to violence'.[15] In reality, everywhere across the continent where liberal democracy holds up its signposts (free and fair elections, rule of law, freedom of expression, human rights and so on), the persistence of violence confirms the reality that the postcolonial democratization project has not yet been able to wedge itself between the state and violence.

The gendered nature of this failure is evidenced by the protests of young women across the continent who have been at the forefront of reviving our collective consciousness regarding the brutality of the state and the perniciousness of the violence in social and political institutions. From the #MustFall movements in South Africa's recent history which rallied us around stark images of young university women's bold defiance of state and institutional power using the weapon only of their bare bodies and voices, to the #EndSars movement in Nigeria and #ShutItAllDown in Namibia, the contemporary face of defiance clarifies a gendered subject of violence, and its direction towards the state conveys both a disenchantment with the state and desire for it as a mediator of democracy. 'Mother picking cactus' – the symbolism of women compelled to socially reproduce the collective under impossible conditions – echoes the protest of young women. Resistance as gendered labour, and gendered labour as embodied speech that finally draws our attention to the gendered *subject* of violence. As I argue in chapter 6, if making sense of violence constitutes the fundamental condition for addressing it, then the nature of violence that is 'unspeakable' places into question both the law that does not have a language for it and the meaning of such violence in the context of democracy.

Democracy – that primary possibility for sublation which the late modern state has within its parameters handed to us – is burdened in equal part with the weight of the brutal legacy of colonial violence (violence that long precedes colonialism), and with the imperative of addressing the subjects of that legacy of violence. Where the nature of violence is gendered, democracy has both to 'see like a state' and to 'see like a feminist'.[16] In its statist form, it has to address itself to the generalized violence of the modern state, and in its feminist form, it has to address the particularity (the gendered nature) of the modern state. In this regard, the democratizing state is engaged in a seemingly irreconcilable struggle between two contradictory forces – on the one hand a universalizing tendency and on the other a tendency towards *difference* as a mode of control. Liberal democracy has not been able to recognize, let alone resolve, this deathly struggle between the universal subject ('natives' in general) and the subject of difference (natives in their gendered, labouring, ethnicized, sexualized and racialized particularity).[17] It is this struggle to reconcile difference and universality which I theorize in the book from the vantage point of women, as *democracy's subjections*.

Mother picking cactus is every woman who has known the burden of care where no infrastructure exists to support it. Yet history defies any generalization towards working people and tells us that the ways in which gendered reproductive labour is organized and survives under colonial conditions are going to be vastly different from the ways in which it is organized and survives under conditions where the cost of care is more evenly distributed – that is where that labour is democratized and socialized. Feminist histories also show us that conditions of unfreedom reconstitute the conditions of care and social reproduction *as coercive* and *violent*. Against colonial capitalist violence and dispossession, democracy promises redistribution – an even ground that might delink social reproduction from accumulation and violence, and return care to the domain of 'revolutionary love', in keeping with Joy James.

Yet the idea of redistribution presumes firstly, that not merely this labour, but those who undertake it, are *legible* – that is, are visible not just to the market as economic resources but also to the state as political subjects and to society as social and cultural subjects. Isn't democracy after all, inclined to offer us the possibility of overcoming ourselves in the 'economic cell form' (as mere commodities) and realizing ourselves in more *humane* form? The evidence of the postcolonial failure of redistribution sits with us today, rather ironically in the name of 'democracy'. At present, gendered labour and gendered violence function synonymously in the sustenance of empire, and the recognition of 'care' rarely now exceeds productivist arguments that consider gendered labour only in relation to its potential for profitmaking. The death of the gendered political subject is constitutive of empire: even progressive movements in our history have managed to evade this gendered subject, who today is almost completely subsumed by the masculinist tendencies that structure democracy under neoliberalism. In short, despite its historical necessity, the gendered labour of social reproduction has yet to produce *a coherent political subject* recognizable in the language of popular democracy. This book traces the story of that gendered political subject through colonial and postcolonial time. It tells the story of a historical struggle between gendered labour and the social forces that have defined (and denied) it political coherence, and therefore also the story of least one fundamental source of violence in the postcolony.

Under conditions of oppression, the reproductive labours that women perform are necessarily undertaken in the name of the care and survival of the group and as such, bear no particular distinction. It is labour that is performed *on behalf of* the collective and as part of the resistance and therefore eschews internal dissent; it is, in other words, not 'burdened' by difference. For this reason, questions of class, gender, age, sexuality, religion and ethnicity do not, for instance, feature prominently in the discourse on *Sumud*, with particular implications. The reality of any resistance whose character does not resolve its internal contradictions is likely to raise those questions afresh in the aftermath of liberation. It is also for this reason that under conditions of oppression, the idea of *gendered* violence becomes particularly vulnerable to erasure, since the violent cost of liberation work is presumed to mark the group as a whole, and the labour of resistance too, borne by the group *as a whole*. There is, in other words, no response dedicated to gendered violence alone under conditions of oppression. But gender cannot constitute an effective political question where it cannot gain coherence as a historical question. Such articulation requires visibility of the gendered labours that also grant social and political subjectivity to women. Labour that, as with all its antecedents under capitalism, requires disciplining because its control depends upon coercion rather than persuasion.

There is possibly a counterintuitive argument here, given what is at stake in articulating a theory of liberation and at the same time subjecting liberation politics to feminist critique. Furthermore, this formulation takes for granted the centrality of gendered labour in any movement towards liberation. The point, though, is to highlight the internal contradictions with which all liberation movements must grapple in order to become genuinely democratic. I examine those contradictions from the vantage point of one group that has historically sustained our collective capacity to survive oppression – *women*[18] as gendered labour – and so direct attention towards a dimension of colonial governance that has remained obscure in existing scholarship: the role of women's reproductive and care labour in stabilizing indirect rule. I show that this labor, while essential to colonial governance, simultaneously produced classed, ethnicized, racialized and gendered bodies that were rendered disposable. These bodies remain captives of colonial modernity, bearing its burdens into the postcolonial present.

Multiple vantage points of articulating a subject position of course exist, and the choice of one vantage point is invariably political. My focus on a singular historical subject – the *gendered labourer*– as the one to whom I seek to return her 'coat'[19] says as much about my own feminist positionality as it does about what I feel is at stake in liberation struggles that do not adequately account for 'secondary' contradictions, as (even) the left is wont to think of gender. The story of the 'coat' of gendered labour begins in the present, with evidence all across the Third World of violent revolts against establishment politics which postcolonial democracy has not been able to curb. Just like Euro-American democracies, the postcolonial polities – while ostensibly committed to egalitarian ideals – remain sites of both state-sanctioned and communal violence, with gender-based violence occurring at alarmingly persistent rates. The central questions the book poses then are as follows: why does the wrath against democratic failure target gendered labouring bodies? How did the postcolonial gendered subject become so violable? And how has gendered violence come to substitute other forms of subjection in modern democracies?

The harvesting of prickly pears from cactus is a painstaking and dangerous task, helped along only by the promise of the sweet fruit that it conceals. The social relations that condition that harvest are not revealed by the object of labour (the plant), but rather it is women's work (the *subjects* of that labour) that draws our attention to the plant. If the cactus were to assume the metaphor of democracy, then it is women – who in their daily determination to nourish the resistance, to provide care and to sustain the human consciousness which must accompany even the minutest of struggles – who can tell the story of the price of harvest which they alone bear in the course of daily toil. The story of the resistance waged by Palestinian women in the name of the collective is also the story of Sudanese women in the informal tea-selling trade on the streets of Khartoum and the revolution they nurtured in 2019 in the form of reproductive care for the resisting masses who camped at their feet until victory was theirs. It is also the story of countless women raped and humiliated in the civil wars of Bosnia and Rwanda – historically constituted as alibis for the nation, as boundaries of ethnic community and the family – and violated in the name of the ethnic nation and family honour.

The inability of certain subjects of violence to militate against it in their own names is deeply rooted in the invisibility and erasure of such reproductive labours that place them at the heart of liberation struggles without granting them the voice to articulate the cost of that labour. Subjection is then, in its simplest expression, the inability to experience violence, and therefore liberation, in one's own name. What one cannot claim in their own name, they cannot hold out for redress. The major claim of this book which I demonstrate throughout is that such gendered reproductive labour is deeply embedded into the logics of colonial capitalist modernity and remains captive to the postcolonial state.

The framing debates

A significant body of work has emerged, especially in South Asian studies, that examines the colonial modern state.[20] The current contribution draws on these historical debates by deploying them towards a structural critique of democracy and the decolonizing agency of gendered subjects of violence. There are also a small number of books concerned with the relationship between violence and democracy.[21] My book intervenes in those debates by examining how modern violence reproduces gender as a democratic imperative. I show this primarily through methodological fidelity to feminist political economy that is also a departure from existing theorizations. The remainder of this chapter provides an overview of the major thrust of those formative debates and ends with a brief note on the book's structure.

Our democracy – that is, of postcolonial Africa – is borne of the *subsumption* of gendered labour and the violence that accompanies this process.[22] This book addresses the postcolonial moment that continues to produce people marked as much by the precarity of their identities as by the proximity of these identities to violence. One way of understanding the subjectivities that render certain groups vulnerable to violence is by refracting them back to the violence of colonialism; that is, by viewing postcolonial subjectivities as fundamentally historical. Under colonialism, various identities (ethnicity, caste, race, gender, sexuality, class, labour) took on significance as instruments of political and social control and aided the mapping of subjugation onto the bodies of the colonized in complex ways. Key scholarly critiques have offered a lens through which violence perpetrated against the postcolonial subject could be understood against these histories.

The problem of the postcolonial state, they show, has been that of an incomplete transition which raises the imperative of decolonization,[23] and of a failure of the postcolonial state to apprehend the conditions of violence that is the legacy of its modernist colonial past.[24] In much of Africa, a core legacy in this regard stemmed from the structure of the bifurcated state that demarcated an urban 'civilized' space from a rural, tribalized 'customary' domain of indirect rule. To the former, human rights – that measure now deeply coded into meanings of democracy – were accorded; for the latter, claims for justice retained their identification with a 'pre-democratic' form of state – the tribalized enclaves to which colonialists subordinated control of the natives. What then would it mean for the colonized to claim rights in the 'democratic' form of the state?

The literature also shows the process of indirect rule as having been inescapably identitarian in nature. For gendered subjects of colonial rule, identity materially functioned as a mode of controlling reproductive labours and sexuality, and the appropriation of productive labour for the colonial capitalist endeavour. Barely remarked in the literature and a major claim in this book, however, is the fact that gendered, reproductive labour had been the condition of possibility of the political economy of colonial indirect rule. Culturally, gendered identities served as markers of nations divided into so many tribalized enclaves of rule. This process of gendering did not necessarily conform to the anatomical sex distinction,[25] but rather was articulated to the structures, conditions and institutions of rule through which gendered subjects became marked as *violable*. This is an important qualification as it allows us to analyse the structural ways in which gendered identities gradually and distinctly mapped onto the bodies of women and some men; and secondly, it overcomes the tendency in feminist literature to focus solely on men as perpetrators and women as victims of gendered violence – which fundamentally is a de-historicization of violence.

The markers most consistently applied in the colonial project of 'define and rule' were class, gender, caste, racial and ethnic differences – identities that were and still are reproduced through their interaction with contemporary structures, conditions and institutions of democratic governance, which themselves must be understood in historical terms. In this sense then, class, race, ethnicity, sexuality, religion, caste and so on cannot on their own, subject individuals to violence. It is rather through their normative ordering *as instruments of colonial modern rule* that they came to mark certain bodies as abject, unworthy, unruly, transgressive and unclean – and through which they condemn these bodies to a permanent confrontation with the idea of freedom. Furthermore, bivalence/multivalence *always* marks gendered identities;[26] this suggests both the impossibility of the liberal individual subject and complicates the determination of the identities through which the violated are interpellated and through which they experience violence. Bivalence in other words, points us towards a *structural* link between gender and violence.

Bivalence also means that women, constituted by their colonial interpellation as producers and reproducers of labour, as boundary markers of tribe, and as active and passive subjects of patriarchal control, cannot be understood in their singularity *as* women. As political subjects, colonized women were rendered visible to the state only through what they *did* (their labours), rather than what they were (as a gender group). This is an argument against a core claim of Western democracy that views its subjects of rights on the basis of what they are, rather than on the basis of the functions they perform – a formulation which ultimately would negate women's historical relationships to class, race, ethnicity, religion, caste and so on.

The liberal democratic state cannot account for this multiplicity of gendered locations and therefore necessarily (re)constitutes bivalence/multivalence of identities as excessive, illiberal and inimical to its project of democratization; to this 'incompatibility', it responds with violence. If bivalence/multivalence historically conditioned the ways in which women experienced violence, then it is impossible to understand the causes and consequences of gendered violence through a social theory that does not deal historically and materially with the structures and conditions that (re)produce identities in these ways. It is to this task of understanding the relationship between the modernist identitarian legacies of the colonial state and gendered violence, as well as its continuities in the postcolonial democratizing state, that this book turns.

My primary concern is with how the modern state appropriates and reproduces gender as social, political and cultural modes of control and of legibility to the democratizing state. If gendered violence perpetrated by and on behalf of the colonial state served the purpose of disciplining, maiming, subjugating and controlling the colonized, what might an analysis grounded in a feminist anticolonial approach illuminate regarding the particularities of gendered violence in postcolonial Africa? And what might this tell us about the purpose that gendered violence serves in the postcolonial context of democratization? Who politically, might be considered the violator, and on whose behalf is violence committed? Whereas the criminality of the colonial state withstands scrutiny, how might we think of the democratizing state, normatively configured at present as 'liberal' and violence within it as 'illiberal'? To whom does the democratizing state transfer the burden of its criminality for violence committed in the name of democracy – that is, who is the 'perpetrator' and to whom do 'victims' of gendered violence direct their claims for justice?

I approach these questions through a postcolonial and anticolonial feminist critique of the link between colonialism, democracy and gendered violence, broadly locating it amongst scholarly critiques of the modernist logics of colonial rule, but exceeding this scholarship to deal concretely with the question of violence *as postcolonial erasure* of colonial subjectivity. The existing scholarship has attempted to address the 'ambivalent relation between postcolonialism and European Enlightenment', and through an immanent critique of the Enlightenment, views 'Enlightenment [as] critique'.[27] According to this perspective, Euro-modernity as the harbinger of colonialism endows the colonized with the language of critique of their own subjugation: that is, gendered violence is not endowed with the tools to *offend* 'civilized' society prior to the event of colonialism, and neither is it an affront to democracy prior to the postcolonial period when democratization becomes *the* lens of decolonization.

The colonizer and the colonized are thus bound by these 'tools' of the Enlightenment. To this dilemma, Dhawan (2014) poses a series of questions that are worthy of reflection: 'does it suffice to critique Western operations of racist and imperialist violence, or must not the heterosexist violence in the postcolony be simultaneously contested? If, rather than being a negative practice, critique is first and foremost 'an act of love' entailing the critique of what one cannot *not* want, how is critique linked to survival?'[28] The suggestion here is that the decolonization of gendered violence – the *survival* of the gendered subject of violence – must in this sense entail (contra Lorde) deploying the 'master's tools [in order to] dismantle the master's house'.[29]

Colonial domination both circumscribed and inscribed into the colonies the conceptual language and institutional conditions under which [the colonized] would be obliged to fight for freedom,[30] thus paving the way for the postcolonial impasse wherein colonial structures and subjectivities were reinscribed in new ways in the postcolonial world – which Dhawan argues, 'inheres that we are obliged by the inescapably modern conditions of our postcolonial predicament'.[31] The challenge then lies in our ability to unsettle and subvert the mastering ambitions of the Enlightenment without a simple rejection of its claims. Furthermore, insofar as we are historically determined by the Enlightenment, it remains unavoidably one of the conditions of the analysis of ourselves.[32] To Dhawan, the challenge then relates to establishing the direction of postcolonial critique if we are to avoid reinforcing the Enlightenment's *coercive* legacy.[33] This is one of the questions that most confounds this book: that is, to whose use does a text claiming commitment to decolonization put itself by confining the subject of its analysis to Enlightenment's measures of progress (i.e. democracy, rights, justice)? Does resisting the moralist urging of democracy to install a permanent victim against a permanent perpetrator of violence hold the potential of shifting the direction of critique?[34] How, in other words, does one restore to democracy the dialectics both of history and of the present without ceding the ethical responsibility (against violence) which the colonized place upon democracy in the postcolonial moment?

We might further ask whether it is the case that we are 'inescapably modern', as Scott (2004) insists, or whether the colonized are obliged, as some anti-colonial critics have insisted, to reject the Enlightenment as a 'colonization of the mind' and instead envision decolonization as a 'return' to 'local knowledge systems' embedded in 'traditional cosmologies'.[35] The dismissal of Enlightenment-derived narratives that made history not a story of reason, progress, prosperity, freedom, liberation, secularization, equality or justice, but rather a record of imperialism, colonialism, slavery, racism, sexism, domination, genocide and exploitation, renders a complex domain of liberation politics in the postcolony.[36] The postcolonial critique of the Enlightenment is 'caught in a performative contradiction in that the vocabulary of critique is inherited from the target of its critique'.[37] It is through an engagement with these dilemmas that this book returns to the idea of democracy, as a modernist stage on which the present contestations around questions of justice, rights, equality and liberation play out. For many women, the clamour for these ideals is often marked as transgressive and met with acts of violence, or violence in more structurally determined forms.

The idea of 'democracy's subjections' that lends to this book its title, therefore, both implicates democracy in sustaining the colonizing structure and charges it with the imperative of liberating those that have been subjected to its violence.

We must enquire in this regard how democracy[38] and its preoccupation with 'non-violence' structures insurgency as unnatural and illiberal, and by implication externalizes violence as an aberration, rather than as constitutive of politics in contexts burdened by colonial legacies of bifurcated rule. What insights might be derived from a feminist critique which takes seriously women's material conditions, lived realities and historical experiences of politics in understanding violence? Stated differently, what would a lens situated in critical feminist methodology and theory reveal about the nature of violence in states so bounded by identitarian politics? *And to what extent might an anticolonial critique of violence that is necessarily narrated by the colonized disentangle Enlightenment's emancipatory claims from those held by the colonized*?

On this last point, Spivak's analogy of the postcolonial predicament in terms of a 'child of rape' is illuminating: '[r]ape is something about which nothing good can be said. On the other hand, if there is a child, that child cannot be ostracised because it's a child of rape. To an extent, the postcolonial is that'.[39] How does such a framing help us engage methodologically with the 'tools' of Enlightenment (among which 'feminism', including 'African feminism' also stands accused)? To Spivak, this requires using the Enlightenment '*from below*' – opening it to what [and who] it was obliged to exclude, but not in an uncritical way.[40] Such a project would entail rethinking the Enlightenment's relationship to 'delegitimized knowledges' and their role in the project of decolonization.[41] This book's theoretical contribution is as such, also embedded in its methodological approach. It should be read majorly as a theoretical work anchored by empirical evidence drawn mainly from secondary sources. Lastly, in embracing interdisciplinarity and situating the work in the fields of political studies, feminist political economy, historical studies and literary studies, the book attempts an 'affirmative sabotage' against disciplinarity – disciplines themselves being a stubborn legacy of colonial knowledge production.

Book structure

This book is concerned with the relationship between the modernist identitarian legacies of the colonial state and gendered violence, and its continuities in the democratizing state. Chapter 1 examines the ways in which the modern state appropriates and reproduces gender as social, political and cultural modes of control and legibility to the contemporary democratizing state. A number of questions from that analysis stride the remainder of the book: first, if violence perpetrated by and on behalf of the colonial state served the purpose of disciplining, maiming, subjugating and controlling the native, how might an analysis grounded in a feminist critique of the colonial modernist project illuminate the particularities of gendered violence in colonial Africa? And what might this tell us about the purpose that gendered violence serves in the postcolonial context of democratization? Second, who politically, might be considered the violator, and on whose behalf is violence committed? Third, whereas the criminality of the colonial state withstands scrutiny, how might we think of the democratizing state, normatively configured at present as 'liberal' and violence within it as 'illiberal'? And to whom does the democratizing state transfer the burden of its criminality for violence committed in the name of democracy – that is, who is the 'perpetrator' and to whom do 'victims' direct their claims for justice?

Chapter 2 grapples conceptually with the modernist constitution of violable subjects and specifically focuses on the emergence of gendered subjects in the historical modern period of colonialism. The relationship between modernity and colonialism is a co-constitutive one to the extent that violence has been definitive of both. By way of tracing various debates concerned with the question of colonial modernity, the chapter develops a theoretical outline of what might be termed as a 'gendered subject' of violence. It shows processes of gendering as marked by various forms of violence and exclusions (structural, physical and discursive) and extends beyond discursive theorizations of subjectivation towards a material focus on modernity's primary subjectivating instrument – the law, and its corollary in the colonies, *order* – and the difference it produces and instrumentalizes, including ethnic, racial, class, caste and sexuality. Colonial modernity thus translated as a 'conundrum of modernity experienced in colonial subjection' is here understood as a historical vantage point from which to account for the colonized in their world; a theoretical/methodological framing of the gendered violence in colonial society and a critique of the modern subject of violence and thus, of rights.

Chapter 3 examines the colonial administrative practices in settler colonies and, from an anticolonial vantage point, elaborates the juridical and administrative mechanisms through which colonized bodies emerge as gendered subjects that both experience violence and commit violence in the colonial and postcolonial state. A focus on the codification of customary laws shows the indirect subjectivation of women as juridical beings. In dealing with the law as a subjectivating agent as such, the chapter elaborates both the forms of acquiescence and protest through which women were interpellated by the colonial state through the regime of customary law.

Chapter 4 examines the challenges which the reproductive structure of the colonial political economy, predicated on captivity, poses for democracy. The idea of captivity is central to an understanding of the stabilization of native rule and colonial dominion over land and labour, yet it remains marginal in the literature, perhaps owing to the gendered conditions that make it possible. My basic concern in this chapter is to elaborate the relationship between colonization and captivity. Inspired in part by the figure embodied in Joy James's 'Captive Maternals', I argue for a reconsideration of what gendered violence *does* for democracy. While undoubtedly gendered, James's captive subject is not reducibly female: the 'womb' that nurtures and insulates colonists is generated and maintained through violence against both women and men. Why then, do women and men survive colonial captivity so differently? What explains women's enduring vulnerability to gendered violence even in the postcolonial democratizing state? My response to these questions is through a re-examination of the effects of various social techniques and administrative regimes through which colonized women and men were coerced into the structures of the colonial political economy as reproductive labour. As that analysis renders apparent, democracy's claim of minimizing violence does not withstand scrutiny when examined against the gendered structures which colonial captivity enacts.

Chapter 5 turns to a critique of women's interpellation as ethnic subjects in the liberal democratic state – that quintessential inheritance of late colonialism – through an examination of the politicization of ethnicity as the basis of native control under colonial rule, and its subsequent depoliticization through the liberal discursive turn towards women's rights and gender politics in the postcolonial state. By marginalizing ethnic identification to a relation outside of human rights and democratic institutions, liberal democracy also de-institutionalizes the social relations of gender, race and class, which were/are central organizing social forces of ethnicity in the colonial and postcolonial state. The nature of the problem that this poses to democratization is this: where they can no longer be enacted by the state as an instrument of control, deeply entrenched gendered and ethnic institutions have tended to function in *statist form against* their own gendered subjects.

Chapter 6 is grounded in an empirical analysis that strings together a critique of postcolonial gendered violence through two artistic interventions: the award-winning South African play titled *Tshepang: The Third Testament*

(2003), which deals with the unspeakable trauma and violence of rape, and the documentary *India's Daughter* (2015), based on the 2012 Delhi gang rape and murder of twenty-three-year-old 'Nirbhaya'. Both interventions enjoin us to consider the ways in which certain bodies enter into the public sphere and raise historical questions regarding the idea of 'consent': that is, what is entailed when our lived bodies are fundamentally contradictory to our juridical being. The chapter also considers how liberal politics of recognition are modified when those who seek redress against sexual violence cannot 'speak', let alone appeal to the courts (i.e. are illegible in their juridical constitution), but rather have to appeal to the public as the only channel through which to gain visibility to the state's organs of justice. In the final chapter I return to the book's central conceptual idea of 'democracy's subjections', in a critical reflection on the dilemmas and contradictions which the colonial encounter and its subjugative orders produce for the postcolonial democratizing state.

1

Gender in Colonial History

Who is the subject of feminist history in general, and who is the gendered subject of Third World feminist history? Both are questions which decolonial feminism invariably encounters in seeking to define its meaning, relevance and location in the tradition of anticolonial and decolonial theorization. Gendered subjects are historical subjects to the extent that they appear *both as an invention of colonialism* and as occupying the unique position of *not being translatable outside of (or being specific to) the political, cultural and economic structures and contexts* in which they operate. In other words, gendered violence in the colonial milieu has to be understood distinctly from the gendered violence that is perpetuated in the context and name of democracy, although a structural legacy certainly binds the two contexts.

In this sense, the colonial archive is burdened by the legacy of its object/aims, and its dehumanizing effects have to be confronted. As cultural scholars are beginning to ask, how do we decolonize the colonial archive which is built upon the denial and erasure of the histories of the colonized? One means of doing this is by building anew the archive of the colonized, by taking the voices and narratives of the colonized themselves as 'primary texts' to reconstitute what they know about themselves,[1] and to shift the terms of the debate between the colonizer and colonized. This includes subjectivating sections of colonized society that remain marginal in our liberation histories. In this endeavour, women as gendered labourers are my primary interlocutors.

The event of colonialism laid bare the profound psychosis and violence through which colonialism produced its *native subject*, who would become the primary subject of democracy in the postcolony and the putative panacea for postcolonial violence. But the end of colonialism has not brought in its wake an end to violence. Far from it. Postcolonial violence has instead found a new subject – or more accurately – renewed the colonial preoccupation with an old subject: *the gendered subject*. No longer legible through the lens of native subjectivity,[2] gendered subjectivity compels an analysis that locates its victims both in the milieu of the colonial modernity that produces them *as violable* and in the contemporary period of democratization that validates this violability through a liberal machinery that is perniciously at odds with the postcolonial condition, precisely due to its refusal to account for gender in its historicity.

This historicity – the specific form that democracy in the postcolony shores up for us – arises in part from the fact that industrial capitalism's revolutionary subject (Marx's proletariat) has merged in the late capitalist period with the peasantry, surplus populations and 'captive maternals',[3] to produce a much more complex subject of modern violence. A labouring subject, who unlike the coerced one under colonial domination, is now fully endowed with rights although not yet emancipated from the immiserating conditions of their existence. Marx did critique this combination of democracy and capitalism as an inherently unstable form of organization of society thus: 'only the political form of revolution of bourgeois society and not its conservative form of life',[4] 'only a spasmodic, exceptional state of things . . . impossible as the normal form of society'.[5] One must confront the ever-present threat of implosion and violence which this fundamental instability harbours.

My intervention is to revisit the link between democracy[6] and violence, which is no longer a tenuous one and is now more widely acknowledged even by liberal and mainstream theorists of democracy.[7] Yet the literature remains divided on whether this violence is a contemporary problem attached to the nature of democratization in the postcolonial state, or a historical problem produced by the particular form of the colonial state. Key scholarly critiques locate the problem of postcolonial violence in an incomplete transition of the state – i.e. one which deracialized without de-ethnicization – as such producing the imperative for decolonization and democratization;[8] and on the failure of the postcolonial state to apprehend the conditions of violence that are the legacy of its modernist colonial past.[9]

These 'conditions of violence' have primarily been theorized as a legacy of the bifurcated structure of the colonial state that demarcated an urbanized 'civil' space (with entrenched racial difference), from a rural, tribalized 'customary' domain (with entrenched ethnic difference) as the mode of indirect rule. Feminist scholarship has gone further to highlight the equally historical nature of difference on the basis of gender, extensively illustrating the centrality of gender and gendered violence as an organizing mechanism of colonial domination and control.[10] I both draw on and depart from these earlier debates by showing that gender had been the *condition of possibility* for the bifurcation and stabilization of the colonial state and, relatedly, develop a theory of gendered violence in the postcolonial democratizing state.

The colonial state was liberal within certain limits. In its economic form, the colonial state was an extension of the nineteenth-century regime of liberal competitive capitalism that had been ushered in the industrializing north. Combining exploitation in the European core with colonial expropriation in the periphery, this regime tended to leave workers to reproduce themselves 'autonomously', outside the circuits of monetized value. It also created a new bourgeois imaginary of domesticity: it elaborated the ideal of 'separate spheres' even as it deprived most people of the conditions necessary to realize it.[11] In its political form, it instituted 'civilized society', laws and jurisprudence modelled on the modern European legal regime. The limits that emerged in relation to the repugnancy clauses that formed the basis of the customary legal regime, and that were reserved for native governance, expressed both the economic and political constitution of the state as a structural articulation.

Beyond those limits, the colonial state took on a specific form within which the particularity of its modernity emerges. Late colonialism departed from the earlier European conquests in two fundamental ways: first, whereas the latter had been preoccupied with establishing dominion and sovereign power over native peoples, under late colonialism, European sovereignty is no longer in question – its mission instead is the stabilization of its sovereign rule over the colonies.[12] This raises the question regarding what it is that a theoretical and methodological approach to empire as a 'necessary and continuing part of the history of the modern state'[13] renders visible in relation to liberalism's complicity in the violence of empire. What would such an approach illuminate in relation to the (female) subjects, written out of liberal subjecthood yet normatively conscripted by its violence in the expansion and stabilization of empire? Indeed, as Lata Mani too has observed, indigenous women were neither the objects nor the subjects of liberal reforms; rather they were the ground on which European and national battles were fought for competing visions of empire and modernity.[14] To whom, as such, does the 'illiberal', gendered subject of democracy turn for narration if not the foundational logics and violent constitution of empire that produces the conditions for their subjugation?

Second, the colonial state reproduced and mediated difference around race, ethnicity, sexuality, gender and caste as the basis of its stabilization. Gender relations were particularly troublesome and contradictory in the ways in which they entered the realm of colonial control. For instance, Stoler (2002), drawing on Javanese colonial housekeeping manuals from the 1920s and 1930s, writes that 'it was in the disarray of unwanted, sought after and troubled intimacies of domestic space that colonial relations *were refurbished and their distinctions made*'.[15] The moral coding of intimacy was a primary concern in colonial policy, and its unwitting casualties, invariably native women. In fact, the colonial standards by which one was classified as 'European' were 'based not on skin colour alone but on tenuously balanced assessments of who was judged to act within reason, affective appropriateness, and a sense of morality'.[16] The liberal basis of the colonial state is in this sense clear. The primary relationships, however, that mediated the colonial enterprise were highly dependent on a racializing logic that was also explicitly gendered:

> European manhood in the colonies, whether measured by 'character and civility or by position and class, was largely *independent of* the presence of European women'.[17]

In other words, it is native women who lent credence to the racialization of the subject population (the native) as distinct from the colonizer. European relations with native women both exposed what was not civilized (colloquially, 'going native') and demarcated a domestic/private realm that putatively exceeded the administrative arm of the colonial state. The question thus extends beyond the 'discrepancies between prescription and practice of civility' and the 'racialized regimes of truth' that concealed these discrepancies,[18] to the more fundamental question regarding the implications of centring women in the historiography of the colonial (and postcolonial) state. Beyond confirming the gendered nature of the state, 'the exclusions it enabled and the violence it condoned',[19] how is our critique of violence modified by tracing its function in the constitution of the political question of the native in relation to the 'private' domesticated domain: that is, violence as mediating the relationship between native and gender identities?

The gender question in the native question

The primary dilemma facing the colonial state had been how a white minority seeking territorial and administrative control could exercise power over an indigenous majority. This problem of stabilizing alien rule was '[i]n colonial discourse. . . politely referred to as "the native question"'.[20] The resolution of this question, I show, carried within it the structural underpinnings of another question – a *gender question* – with manifestations extending well beyond the colonial state. My argument here is *not* that colonial rule produces gender (cf. Oyĕwùmí 1997), but rather that the primitive accumulation which the colonial state undertook on behalf of empire raised the imperative of political stabilization of the colonies (the native question), whose resolution led to the fragmentation of native consciousness along so many lines – racial, ethnic, caste, class and gender. As such, gender did acquire the status of *political identity* under colonial governance and was henceforth to be approached as a *political problem*. The evidence suggests that across the settler colonies, the resolution of the native question proceeded through and led to the production of an even more insidious one; a gender (or woman) question.[21]

In Zimbabwe, for instance, from the mid-1910s, colonial officials frequently argued against legislative measures to promote female emancipation, claiming that such actions interfered with 'native custom'. Writing in 1924, the native commissioner of Chipinga contended that 'dangerous ground would be trodden unless we have support of the native'.[22] The native, of course, was presumed to be male, and 'native custom' was what male elders claimed it to be.[23] The attitude of the state towards women's rights was 'highly ambiguous and contradictory'.[24] Having based their system of colonial administration on the manipulation of indigenous authority structures, using local leaders to implement state policies, colonial officials could not afford to let those structures be undermined by agents outside their control.[25] Their fundamental concern therefore, was 'safeguarding the domestic authority of African male guardians'.[26] But women drew on the same customary regime in protest and subversion:

> The refusal of women to marry their appointed partners, their desertion of unwanted husbands, and their flight to missions, mines, farms, and urban areas posed a serious threat to African male authority, and consequently, *to the entire system of indirect rule*.[27]

The colonial state punished women not for the labour for which they were migrating from rural to urban areas to perform – including farm work, petty trade and prostitution – but rather for complaints brought to them about women's 'disobedience' by native male elders, against which colonists legislated through ordinances such as the Native Marriage Ordinance in Rhodesia, through which 'the marital status and guardianship of every woman could easily be established [and] unmarried women, or at least those whose unions were not recognised under the Native Marriages Ordinance, could . . . be identified and forced to return to the rural areas'.[28] Across the African colonies male elders made similar demands, to which colonial authorities responded in like fashion: their primary objective in doing so was in 'guaranteeing the success of indirect rule'.[29]

But women's offensiveness was not merely because 'they were rebels who undermined patriarchal authority and flouted the laws of the colonial state'.[30] The control and regulation of women's productive and reproductive labour was fundamental to the colonial enterprise: I have argued elsewhere that reproductive labour was the *condition of possibility* of the political and economic resolution of the native question, without which stabilization of the colonial state would have been untenable.[31] This claim is indirectly made in earlier literature:

> In South Africa, the resolution of the native question was fairly unambiguous: As the economy became industrialised, it gave rise to "the colour problem," at the root of which were "urbanized or tribalized natives." [The point, however] was not that racial segregation ("territorial segregation") should be done away with. Rather it was that it should be made part of a broader "institutional segregation" and thereby set on a secure footing: "Institutional segregation carries with it territorial segregation." The way to preserve native institutions while meeting the labour demands of a growing economy was through the institution of migrant labour, for "*so long as the native family home is not with the white man but in his own area, so long the native organization will not be materially affected.*"[32]

Colonists were quite clear in their belief that the primary evil of colonial occupation lay not in 'white employment of native men', but rather in the failure to preserve the native organizational structure *within* the 'tribal jurisdiction': it was 'migration of the native family, of the females and children, to the farms and towns' which was to be prevented and 'abandonment of the native tribal home by women and children' the mischief most threatening to the system of white domination and exploitation.[33] Stated differently, it was impossible to control the native – his time, his labour, his product and mind – without establishing control over the native's social, cultural and domestic domain. Yet the problem was much more than that territorial segregation rendered racial domination unstable because 'the more the economy developed, the more it came to depend on the urbanized or detribalized natives' as Mamdani (1996) has argued.[34] A more serious problem for colonial domination lay in the fact that although formally preserving native institutions as a separate (and subordinate) domain, the system of 'identity' and 'differentiation'[35] upon which native institutions were maintained depended on *reproducing* structurally entrenched *difference*.

The racialization of natives and the tribalization of ethnic communities were processes that accumulated difference far beyond the domain of political rule, for they also necessarily reinforced a sub-stratum of power relations that was negotiated and maintained on the basis of social and cultural arrangements. Whatever popular power eluded native institutions, they were compelled to forcefully assert by establishing and sustaining tribalized domains of rule. The outcome of diverse ethnic groups was ethnically organized local powers which in the postcolony, manifested as so many civil wars.[36] As historical manifestations of colonial rule, these ethnic wars offered two possible futures: an authoritarian one or an emancipatory one.[37] While the former continues to be a feature associated with the tribalized, traditional realm of politics, the latter is presumed to be evidenced by democratization. Yet these dual possibilities were held out only for those who straddled both the traditional and civil realms: those who could be 'civilized', so to speak – a possibility that existed only for the *subjects proper* of colonialism; for *men*. Contestations for freedom, however, exceeded this bifurcation – an acknowledgement that can be inferred from the intentions of colonialists, who decreed a single order defined by the 'civilized' laws of Europe. In this order,

> [n]o "native" institutions would be recognised. Although "natives" would have to conform to European laws, only those civilized' would have access to European rights. Civil society, in this sense, was presumed to be civilized society, from whose ranks the uncivilized were excluded. The ideologues of a civilized native policy rationalized segregation *as less a racial than a cultural affair*.[38]

This reconstitution of segregation as cultural (thus presumably not a political project identifiable with the colonial state, in contrast to race which was so) in fact concealed the very political nature of the gendered exclusions that formed the basis of the native policy upon which indirect rule was stabilized. The very fact that men emerged as the agents – political subjects – of indirect colonial control suggests that a gendered process of differentiation had been fundamental to the resolution of the native question. The obvious implication of this idea and the task that faced colonial administration was to *show* that native policy was indeed 'cultural'; an endeavour whose outcome would demarcate and define the relationship *not* between colonizer and colonized, but between colonized men and colonized women. This was the resolution proper of the native question, which generated gendered politics that were at the same time tribalized and disarticulated from race. Women, subjected to this gendered, tribalized realm of colonial domination as such, could not articulate their injury in the racialized, 'civilized' language of rights as though subjected under civic authority. Their claims and struggles were primarily shaped and modified by their interaction with native authority. It is within that realm that we need also to locate and understand colonial responses to women's claims, as disciplining and sanctioned by the colonial state, and thus invariably violent. The 'decentralized despotism' thesis indeed implies the instrumentalization of violence whose primary casualties *within that realm* of colonial domination were the gendered subjects of rural tribal authority: of indirect, modern power.

At the heart of my argument then is also a concern with colonized identities: that is, the nature of subjections produced by colonial modern power where rule by difference produces the native question, the response to which produces a gender (or 'woman') question. It is from this historical basis that I seek to understand the modern gendered subject of violence, for and against whom postcolonial discourses of democracy and rights are mobilized. In the immediate post-independence period, the lingering native question directed the task of postcolonial nationalism towards deracialization as its marker of liberation. The present accumulated task of democratization is, on its part, primarily directed against ethnic identity (detribalization). Both of these tasks, however, confirm the constitution of the native on the basis only of their ethnic identity. The conceptual notion of democracy's subjections then, also critiques the dehistoricization of the native in their (re)constitution as democratic subjects, and by implication, the gendered biases/erasures manifest in the postcolonial project of democratization. It is in the interstices of these biases that I locate and analyse the contemporary problem of gendered violence.

The 'woman question'

Colonial historiography reveals a preponderance of the woman question, which as I show in Chapter 2, was justified within certain notions of modernity and nationalism. Some of the scholarship shows that the woman question loomed large in the nineteenth century and was concerned 'not as much with what women wanted, but rather with how they could be modernized'.[39] In addition, it underwrote nationalist anticolonial strategy, with evidence that 'nationalism did in fact provide an answer to the new social and cultural problems concerning the position of women in "modern" society – an answer that was predicated *not on an identity but on a difference*[40] with the perceived forms of cultural modernity in the West'.[41]

As such, to insist that women had posed a question to the colonial state – to insist at all on a 'woman question' – is to assert that women *produced* certain problems for the colonial state to which it was compelled to respond.[42] After all, it is within the imperial project that, for the first time, the oppression of women becomes a precondition for the subjectivation of (colonized) men as political subjects of the state. This stood in historical contrast to the rational European male figure of Western liberalism whose political subjectivity emerges in singularity and in spite of white women. Colonized women, in contrast, attain significance in the imperial project, and as the literature shows, the concern with their modernization was merely a façade behind which 'the real battles of colonialism were waged'.[43] The historiography both highlights colonized women's indirect relation to empire and raises underexplored questions regarding the disproportionate nature and function of violence that they experience in the course of imperial legitimation, given their calculated erasure.

'Women', McClintock writes in her important study of empire, virtually 'vanish from the affair of empire, and colonized men are feminized by their association with domestic servitude';[44] 'imperial domesticity' she argues, was '. . . a domesticity without women'.[45] The interchanging of race and gender is a particularly striking feature which she highlights thus: '[while] in scenes set in the Victorian home, female servants are *racialized* and portrayed as frames for the exhibition of the commodity, in advertising scenes set in the colonies, African men are *feminized* and portrayed as exhibition frames for commodity display. Black women, by contrast, are rendered virtually invisible'.[46] While the political question of the native rested on race, its cultural component depended on an intervention into the gender dynamics of the colonies: 'domestic ritual became a technology of discipline and dispossession'.[47]

The breadth of this intervention is referenced in a number of other studies. Lorcin (2012), for instance, highlights a paradoxical situation in the colonial context in which the domestic/private space was also a political space when it came to the issue of race.[48] The link between modernity and women was equally interesting: 'whether colonial women were actually "modern" or not did not matter . . . [t]hey were held up as *exemplars of modernity* to the local population of the colonies in which they lived'.[49] Also serving this link was the use of the condition of women as a signifier of progress,[50] where settler women 'were positioned as exemplars of modern womanhood in relation to the colonized peoples', a paradoxical relation given that they could only access this narrative of modernity *within* the colonies: 'when held up to the values and behaviour of the "new woman" of the metropole, settler women . . . were, more often than not, traditionally minded with regards to gender relations and family "ideology"'.[51] The concept of the modern settler woman, Lorcin argues, was shaped by the colony rather than the metropole.

This location of white women's modernity within the colonial milieu functions significantly as an acknowledgement of the colonies in and of themselves as autonomous sites in which modern power is articulated to the peculiarity of historical place and time. That is, as sites in which the modern subject might be understood as a product of their total social, political and cultural context, and therefore necessarily as produced in the interstices of colonial violence and struggles in resistance to colonial domination. The anticolonial question that is posed here then is this: how might we, in accounting for the colonial problem space, understand subjects of rule that emerge primarily in relation to the colonial event – that is, whose constitution (as political subjects) is *unthinkable* outside of this historical space of colonization? This is especially so because the question of colonialism compels us to engage with the particular ways in which modern power modelled on a western semiotic alters or affects the colonized.

My interest, however, is not with the colonial modern lives of settler women,[52] but rather with the disavowed modernity of colonized women – with their putative location not only in a 'traditional' realm in which they are predominantly understood in relation to the native question, but primarily too, in the public realm in which they produce a political problem – the 'woman question' – for colonial rulers, even as their political subjectivity is denied. Even though colonized women had not been the *subjects proper* of colonial rule, they did experience its constitutive, administrative and disciplining violence in both indirect and direct ways, mediated by the customary regime of native governance and laws. The colonial regime of (customary) law stood at the cusp of modernity: on the one hand as a modernist response to the native question and on the other, as a tool that subjugated women in relation to a discourse of 'backwardness' – inimical (repugnant) to liberal personhood, and impossible as subjects of modernity. Many of the repugnancy clauses did touch on the private domains of native existence, a fact which raises the need for an extensive critique of the relationship between these 'inner' domains and the substantive law. Repugnancy is shown in the literature as having primarily targeted the private domain,[53] and exclusions on the basis of repugnancy highlighted liberal ideas around human rights, morality, and common law, and moulded modern subjecthood against these notions.[54]

Colonized women might in this regard be shown as being the *quintessential modern subjects*, precisely because their political subjectivity, more than that of colonized men and white women and men, emerges primarily in relation to the modern disciplining violence of the colonial legal regime, specifically customary law, such that colonized women are not a priori constituted as subjects (of the state) outside of this invention. Though not explicitly, other scholars have argued in a similar vein about colonized women that

> [t]heir self-hood or subjectivity cannot be separated from the specific historical and political conjunctures that constituted their world. Colonization and orthodox religion prescribed and proscribed the limits for . . . women.[55]

Violence mediated this relationship between women and the colonial state: '[t]he authorities in charge of enforcing custom, so-called customary authorities, were sanctioned by the state and backed up by state violence'.[56] The modernist nature of this violence was concealed within the bifurcated logics of colonial authority, built on a dual system of civil juridical law and the customary legal order, both of which were exclusionary. While in a modern state, civil law is supposed to guarantee the rights of all citizens in civil society, in colonial civil law, however, 'the regime of rights was limited and partial. Citizen status was not conferred on all ambits of civil society. The primary exclusion was based on *race*'.[57] In a similar fashion, 'the customary order excludes from itself the tribal outsider. Each native tribe had its own customary law, and each had an outsider'.[58] This process of racialization and tribalization corresponds with the political dilemma of colonists, the native question, but does not explain the political economy of colonial rule, the condition of its stabilization that is congealed within it. This condition, as I show, can be articulated as a gender/woman question that has political, economic and social dimensions and implications for democracy.

The economic and social dimensions of the woman question have received significant attention in the literature, mainly in relation to the migrant labour economy that pertained in settler colonies and the need for social reproduction upon which it was anchored.[59] The political dimensions of this question, however, raise a different set of concerns to which the literature has not adequately responded. The first is juridical: women's struggles in the colonies were directed against laws that enforced restrictions on movement, forced displacement, taxation and forced labour, each of which defined the nature of their citizenship within the colonies and ordered their legibility as subjects of the state. Second is the question of identity: colonial legislation depended on the demarcation of natives along the lines of class, ethnicity, caste, sexuality and gender, each of which produced an identitarian dilemma whose resolution (decolonization and democratization) carries within it the threat of violence – as class struggle, civil war, gendered violence, etc. The political economy of indirect rule thus accounts not only for the 'classes, class exploitation, force, and violence'[60] within which the colonial state concealed its economic motive, but also for the ways in which this economic motive aligned with the reproduction of the native in their politicized form as ethnicized, gendered and racialized. In other words, these legacies produced both *violable* and *violating* subjects who arrive at the contemporary period with contradictory interests in the democratizing state and are its major interlocutors. What is at stake with asserting the quintessential modernity of gendered subjects is that analyses of the violence they experience have to deal concretely with their imbrication *within* the very structures, conditions and institutions of democracy through which liberation is claimed.

Democracy's subjections

> Only the most naïve of questions are truly serious. They are the questions with no answers. A question with no answer is a barrier that cannot be breached. In other words, it is questions with no answers that set the limits of human possibilities, describe the boundaries of human existence.[61]

What radical possibilities,[62] if any, does democracy summon in response and relation to the imperial and colonial subjugations that haunt its liberal form? We know from the literature that class and race consciousness did effect limits to political enfranchisement in the colonies. Yet while the native ordinances through which men were enjoined to the colonial state did not extend to the direct control of women, the labour ordinances did target women's productive and reproductive labour resources and time, albeit not directly because the colonial state denied formal recognition to women's role in sustaining its structure of extraction.[63] The colonial response to women is as such inaccurately translated in direct relation to the state, but rather should be viewed in relation to the substantive ways in which women experience the state at its margins, as well as their resistance to it.[64] Women's relationship to the colonial state became most apparent through their actions of resistance to impositions of the colonial state that were exercised on its behalf by African males.[65] As such, to pose a structural question regarding how it is that the colonial state governed women is also to respond, in part at least, to the question regarding *how it governed indirectly.*

The questions posed to the postcolonial project of democratization have so far subsumed the subjectivity of women within the subjectivity of the native. But while native subjectivity and gendered subjectivity were co-constitutive, the state's response to women highlighted the limits of the law and in fact pushed it beyond the boundaries of its liberal roots in empire and application in the colonies. The language of *culpability* that was espoused by colonists exposed these limits. Thus, for instance, women could be punished for disobeying formal orders but could not be criminalized under the rubric of statutory law/legal formalism. Marina Santoru, writing on colonial Kenya has shown that to colonists, the punishable 'crime' committed by some (women) was their support for the *Mau Mau* movement, rather than any single action carried out on behalf of the movement. The Emergency[66] made it possible to punish the decision of women to join the movement, but punishing actual crimes was a secondary matter.[67]

We might then pose the following questions: what does it mean to be deemed punishable but not criminalized?[68] And what to make of the fact that injury against women was attributed to their 'unruliness', 'indiscipline', 'permissiveness', 'seduction' and so on, interpreted in ways that meant that women could be subjected to punishment in the form of further bodily harm and injury, but could not seek redress as juridical subjects of the (colonial) state? The law, both civil and customary, was the colonial state's primary instrument of subjectivation, and the fact that women were not its subjects proper suggests that women's relationship to the state needed to be understood on the basis of the concrete locations from which they were being subjected to its disciplining power. Indeed, the prosecution under statutory law of rape cases involving natives, which I elaborate in Chapter 3, reveals a colonial logic that was more articulated to the control of reproduction than to criminalization per se, of rape. Native women *qua* women simply did not matter that much, but as reproductive/labouring bodies, they were central to the colonial project.

As Chatterjee notes, empire was 'not an abstract universal category floating around in some transcendental global space [but rather] is embodied and experienced in actual locations'.[69] The narratives through which we make sense of empire and of the production of difference within it must necessarily then also be situated and concrete, drawing on actual historical events rather than deriving from conceptual abstractions. The production and/or instrumentalization of difference was fundamental to the stabilization of colonial rule, and difference was a primary basis upon which internal solidarities of the colonized were checked. This is in part because the administrative function of the bifurcated state, which was exercised towards political control, concealed a deeply structural problem of colonial domination. As the colonial project introduced commodity production and the accompanying regime of migrant labour, the class dimension of the bifurcated state became important and its effects very clear. It brought into focus the political project that the colonialists had: to contain these class-based mobilizations that it was producing, which it achieved through the entire project of native administration where civil laws did not apply, and where gender and ethnic solidarities undermined class consciousness.

These processes from above (the law) and below (the coercive force of native administration) were violent, and both were modern in their nature. The question of gender, however, complicates our understanding of modern colonial violence: that is, given that gender does not gain autonomy as a locus of colonial control, it is its articulation to other domains of colonial rule that constitute our understanding of the modernist character of gendered violence. The claim I have already put forward, that women ought to be considered as the quintessential modern subject, draws on the fact that their production as political subjects proceeds primarily on the basis of their identification with domains of rule that become politicized in the colonial modern milieu (and in the postcolonial state). These domains were most prominently ethnicity, class, race and caste – categories that had been the primary regulatory mechanisms of colonial law. It is in this regard that we must focus on the rendering of ethnicity, of class, of race and of caste as gendered – that is, as primarily mediated through gendered processes.[70]

This formulation bears at least two major implications for the contemporary practice of democracy. The first relates to the relationship between democracy and the modern phenomenon of the nation-state. Three major features continue to define nationalism: autonomy or liberation from external constraints to pursue one's own ideas of freedom; unity where internal divisions of race, caste, ethnicity and gender are erased; and reconstitution into a single historical territory and identity. Women occupy a peculiar position in this process: on the one hand they are abstract citizens in the eyes of a law that is quite formal and indifferent to their specific needs, and on the other hand their identity is continually evoked in distinct and substantive ways as preservers of the nation.[71] This attachment of gendered identities to class, caste, ethnicity and race constitutes the woman question (which has historical origins), and which is reconstituted in new ways within the postcolonial democratizing state. But the impulse of the liberal democratic form of the state has been to repudiate difference, which in essence is also a renunciation of the woman question and the violence through which it was constituted.

The second implication relates to the ways in which violence structures claims to the state as demands, and the claimants as illicit. It is the language of *protest* that historically has most structured feminist power and claims against the colonial state, within the anticolonial resistance, and in the democratizing state. Protest signals the marginal, obscured, existential and structural locations of its subjects. Protest is also encumbered by violence on all sides – on the side of its subjects (as the will to freedom) and on the side of its object (as the will against the state), and internal to itself. It is the form of power that most compels recognition by the state and around which democracy is currently organized. Historically, the state could confine both women and men as gendered subjects to a domesticated depoliticized sphere. The literature demonstrates that men could exit that sphere as either waged labourers or as administrators of customary law. Neither of these avenues of escape were available to women – as captives, women's primary recourse was through resistance and protest. It is in these ways that the state's response to women could be understood as a *political response* – that drew women into political society as subjects of politics. These modes of claiming power have continued in the postcolonial and democratizing state, primarily because women are still denied political space, but ironically shape what we understand as democratic politics.

To reiterate then the primary questions I draw on: if violence perpetrated by and on behalf of the colonial state served the purpose of disciplining, maiming, subjugating and controlling the native, how might an analysis grounded in a feminist critique of the colonial modernist project illuminate the particularities of gendered violence in colonial Africa? And what might this tell us about the purpose that gendered violence serves in the postcolonial context of democratization? Who, politically, might be considered as being the violator, and on whose behalf is violence committed? Whereas the criminality of the colonial state withstands scrutiny, how might we think of the democratizing state, normatively configured at present as 'liberal' and violence within it as 'illiberal'? To whom does the democratizing state transfer the burden of its criminality for violence committed in the name of democracy – that is, who is the 'perpetrator' and to whom do 'victims' of such violence direct their claims for justice?

Furthermore, to the extent that the language of rights remains central in our thinking about modern democracy, we must also ask of this 'objectivity' which (liberal) human rights claims, who is actually included in its ambit. Who is constructed as deserving of rights, and how does this construction proceed? Who/what is excluded or suffers? And how does this inclusion/exclusion binary render what is then considered as 'reality'? In short, what casualties are produced out of the normative framing of human rights as they operate within liberal democracy?[72] The antagonisms and tensions arising out of the ensuing battle between the nation-state and its different (constitutive) components have been part and parcel of rendering the versions of human rights that become admissible in the discourse of democracy, and which rights do not. To cite Dhawan, 'it is not so much the colonial "origins" of the norms of human rights or democracy that compromise their "validity," but much more the *normative violence* that is exercised on those who violate the hegemonic definitions of these norms'.[73] The normative ordering of rights in the postcolonial world in this regard retains myriad reflections of the colonial ordering of personhood and subjecthood against which many contemporary feminist emancipatory struggles organize.

At its core, democracy represents a life and death struggle between the idea of justice and that of citizenship.[74] The acknowledgement of an injustice is at the very least premised upon the affirmation of one's humanity. This is not necessarily the case with citizenship, which is at best a *legal* confirmation of belonging within a sovereign national/regional boundary, and which while dispensing with rights and liberties, is at the same time premised upon denial of the claims of those subjects that do not cohere with the political objectives of the sovereign entity. The subjects of justice and the subjects of rights are in this regard, inimical, united only by the violence against which they both clamour for democracy. Furthermore, the structures, institutions and conditions upon which citizenship is constructed map onto the historical crevices of gender, class, race, ethnicity, sexuality and nationality, none of which can be understood apart from the constitutive violence through which they become amenable to the production of citizens and subjects. I deal in this book, with one aspect of these crevices, placing gendered citizenship at the centre of an analysis that asks how it is that we might understand the constitutive force of gendered violence in the colonial state, and how this historical (gendered) subject of violence experiences the liberal democracy that manifests under late capitalism. A central question for the gendered subject of violence is then, whether justice is even a possibility within capitalism. And secondly, whether an understanding of the nature of the crises and subjections that are produced by colonialism and which survive in the postcolony can illuminate a basis for truly democratic postcolonial societies.

2

Colonial Modernity and the Gendered Subject[1] of Violence

Between patriarchy and imperialism. . .the figure of the woman disappears. . .into a violent shuttling which is the displaced figuration of the 'third-world woman' caught between tradition and modernization.[2]

Modern empire was not an aberrant supplement to the history of modernity but rather its constituent part. It will continue to thrive as long as the practices of the modern state-form remain unchanged.[3]

The modernist constitution of violable subjects and the emergence of gendered subjects in the historical modern period of colonialism are processes that demand conceptual clarity. Such conceptualization might begin from the relationship between Euromodernity and colonialism, which is a co-constitutive one to the extent that violence has been definitive of both. By way of tracing various debates concerned with the question of colonial modernity, I seek in this chapter to develop a theoretical and conceptual outline of what might be termed a 'gendered subject' of violence. Through a focus on modernity's primary subjectivation instrument – the law and its corollary in the colonies, *order* – as well as the difference it produces and instrumentalizes, including ethnic, racial, class, caste and sexuality, I show processes of *gendering* as marked by various forms of violence and exclusions (structural, physical and discursive). Colonial modernity thus translated as a 'conundrum of modernity experienced in colonial subjection' is here understood as a historical vantage point from which to account for the colonized in their world; a theoretical/methodological framing of the nature of (gendered) violence in colonial society; and a critique of the modern subject of violence and, thus, also of rights. The chapter should also be read as primarily concerned with the *contemporary* question of gendered violence.

A significant body of scholarship has already gone into theorizing 'the predicament of colonial modernity' – as haunted by its birth through the

Enlightenment within which 'freedom and domination [were] deeply entangled'.[4] Most significant scholarship on the Enlightenment either ignores colonialism or treats it as marginal to the putatively more 'significant' issue of recuperating the Enlightenment.[5] More recently, some of the scholarship in political theory that has attempted to address the connection of the Enlightenment to European colonialism[6] has sought to provide a corrective to what they claim is a misrepresentation of the Enlightenment's epistemological investment in imperialism.[7] So, against critics of the Enlightenment who identify a universalist agenda that eschews difference and Otherness and deploys doctrines of progress and emancipation to justify the subjugation of non-European peoples, defendants of the Enlightenment ideals of rights, justice, secularism, rule of law, democracy, and cosmopolitanism see it as championing the cause of the disenfranchized.[8] To them, it is the 'liberal turn to empire' that displaced eighteenth-century theories of cultural diversity in favour of notions of European superiority and native 'backwardness'.[9] They also hold that, despite a commitment to the values of equality, human dignity, freedom, the rule of law and self-government, their investments in discourses of progress and civilization led liberal political philosophers to support imperial projects.[10]

As 'historians of the present',[11] postcolonial scholars are called upon to reflect on 'what present it is that the past is being reimagined for'.[12] Our histories of the past should be strategic interrogations of the present as a way of helping us to envision the possibilities for an alternative future.[13] This is especially so if we take seriously the claim that the tragedy of colonial modernity has been that colonial power circumscribed the conceptual and institutional conditions under which [the colonized] were obliged to fight for freedom.[14] This paved the way for the postcolonial impasse, wherein colonial structures and subjectivities were inscribed in new ways in the postcolonial world, which Dhawan argues, 'inheres that we are obliged by the inescapably modern conditions of our postcolonial predicament'.[15] If this is to suggest that the gendered subjectivities with which we grapple have been hard-wired into the structure of the postcolonial state and the fabric of postcolonial society, wherein then lies the possibility of critique and indeed, of overcoming them? What possibilities does postcolonial feminist critique as a weapon of criticism provide for the criticism of colonial modernity (which in fact, provides feminism with its tools of critique)? What political questions does subjectivation on the basis of gender, racism, sexism, homophobia, ethnicity and class – colonial modernity's enduring legacies, not freedom, autonomy and rights – raise for those invested in a politics of emancipation?

Dhawan (2014) argues that the challenge is to unsettle and subvert the mastering ambitions of the Enlightenment without a simple rejection of its claims, and draws on Foucault's recommendation that we recognize that insofar as we are historically determined by the Enlightenment, it remains unavoidably one of the conditions of the analysis of ourselves.[16] To this challenge, Dhawan responds that '[i]f the former slaves have become conscripts of the Enlightenment, reinforcing its *coercive* legacy, the question is what is the direction of postcolonial critique?'[17] Furthermore, in Scott's (2004) argument, we cannot *not* be conscripts of the Enlightenment (even though we are in a subordinate place within it).[18] Certain anticolonial critics reject the Enlightenment as a 'colonization of the mind' and instead envision decolonization as a 'return' to 'local knowledge systems' embedded in 'traditional cosmologies', and a kind of 'left universalism'[19] that is putatively opposed to the Eurocentrism which they insist inescapably haunts modernity. They call for the dismissal of Enlightenment-derived narratives that made history not a story of reason, progress, prosperity, freedom, liberation, equality or justice, but rather a record of imperialism, colonialism, slavery, racism, sexism, domination, genocide and exploitation. Against this position, Scott raises the question regarding what connection exists between, on the one hand, the 'indispensability' of Enlightenment to the resistance of domination and, on the other hand, the costs of Enlightenment thinking.[20] The postcolonial critique of the Enlightenment is as such 'caught in a performative contradiction in that the vocabulary of critique is inherited from the target of its critique'.[21]

It is within this constraint that I grapple thematically with liberal ideas of democracy, as the modernist and contemporary stage upon which historical contestations around questions of justice, rights, equality and freedom play out. For the historically excluded, the clamour for these ideals is often remarked as transgressive and met with acts of violence, or violence in more structurally determined forms. At the same time, the identitarian nature of colonial subject formation means that for the colonized, any notion of justice, rights and equality must respond concretely to inequalities and injustice rendered through gender, ethnicity, class, race and caste identities. This suggests that struggles for democracy ought to be critical of attempts to recast colonized identities in the language of excess, as has been standard practice within modern liberal discourse.

The relegation of these identities as 'excessive' ought at the same time to be understood as paradoxical, given the implication that rejecting 'colonial' identities would also mean a rejection of modernity itself. As Kwon (2015) argues, the tension arises

> . . .not because there exists an internal contradiction between coloniality and modernity, but from the fact that such a contradiction was produced and

> imposed discursively and continues to undermine our understanding of the true *intimacy between coloniality and modernity.* What are actually constitutive and coeval (coloniality and modernity) have been discursively and hegemonically severed and forced into a contradictory relationship (physically and politically) as if they were incompatible and not coeval. . .[a] rhetorical move [with] dire consequences for those lives most burdened by it...[22]

Rendered simply as 'the experience of modernity in colonial subjugation',[23] the notion of colonial modernity implies a shared legacy between the colonizer and the colonized that is nonetheless disavowed by the colonizer with particularly devastating implications 'for the lived experience of the colonial modern subject and their legacies',[24] and bears within it the threat of violence because '[t]he *refusal to recognize the modernity of his or her experience* violently impose[s] impasses and antinomies deep into the fabric of that life. The fundamental contradiction or impasse that the colonial modern subject [is] forced to negotiate on various levels, bodily, psychically, linguistically, and politically [may be characterized] as a 'conundrum of representation'.[25] It is then in this paradoxical relationship between the production specifically of gendered subjects and the inability of democracy to apprehend the identitarian nature of their claims (i.e. their relationality with class, caste, ethnicity, race), that I locate the question of violence.[26]

Any serious methodological approach to this dilemma necessarily enjoins both the violable and the violated in a structural critique of violence: that is, unlike the singular non-relational liberal subject of the Enlightenment, the modern subject of violence has to be understood as co-constituted, on the one hand, by liberal subjecthood and on the other, by the colonizing violence through which the colonizer produces and institutionalizes *difference* between himself and the colonized. In the postcolony, democracy thus necessarily addresses itself to a subject that is both rights-bearing and custom-bearing; both violated and violating; both liberal and deeply invested in the Enlightenment's language of rights – and revolutionary; disavowing the Enlightenment through the language of violence.

Accepting the interconnectedness of the colonial and the postcolonial, the methodological approach of this book draws from a theoretical engagement with major interventions in the legal, political, social, and cultural milieu of the historical/epochal period of colonialism, to which it brings a feminist political economy lens in an attempt to give coherence to the gendered character of the colonial modern state. I consider seriously the possibility of employing the 'master's tools' in an 'affirmative sabotage'[27] of the master narrative of modernity by examining it primarily from the vantage point of colonized women. Even as passive subjects, white women are acknowledged in the corpus of literature narrating modern subjecthood. But what are we to make of colonized, racialized women, who while inescapably interpellated into the modernist logics of the state (as non-juridical, labouring beings) – and in fact may be thought of as the *quintessential modern subjects* – are denied modern personhood (as political subjects)? The fact that modernist subjectivity is distinctly marked both by its juridical and political nature demands attention to the basis of this disavowal, for how are we to account for violence against those *not* considered as *violable*? Or rather, whose violation remains illegible to formal legal structures? The question of establishing who was violable and who was not was key in the stabilization of empire. The production of this violability (through the native question) *as difference* is, in this regard, central to our understanding of the colonial modern subject, against whom we might consider the role of violence.

Imperial violence and the peculiarity of its subjects

The violence of imperial expansion was such that it had to deny the capacity of colonial subjects to participate in political life. The debate was conducted not in the language of political rights, but in terms of their 'character'.[28] The hierarchical structures through which modernity discursively sought collaboration in the colonies were such that '"moral worth" was viewed not simply in the capacity for self-rule, but in the exercise of power over others, which served as a criterion for political office and participation'.[29] In all this, the tenuous relationship between anti-imperialist thought and Western feminism was apparent to the extent that the latter never questioned the infantilizing discourses that also marked colonized women as 'irrational', 'dependent', 'backward' and 'unrestrained'.[30] Yet even while Western women too were not spared such infantilization within Europe's own borders, they were key in mediating European male colonial power over colonized males – the subjects proper of colonial rule – as their own subjectivity was conditioned on narratives of their perceived vulnerability to the violence of colonized, racialized men ('*swart gevaar*'/Native danger/'Black Peril'/ Shakespeare's Caliban). The power relations inherent in these narratives placed white women beyond the reach of black men at the same time as racialized, colonized women became incarcerated by/through them.[31]

The nature of this incarceration, however, is masked through a historiography that has failed to centre – and therefore can deny – the extent to which violence against Black and Brown women mediated the encounter between the colonizer and the colonized. But what does a retelling of these histories, such as I attempt here, do? What is it that an insistence on reconstituting history from a different vantage point – as experienced by those at its margins – accomplish if it is not to collapse into a form of romanticism? Is it merely an acknowledgement that rectifies the heavy 'dependence on the writings of European observers' in representation of the colonized, as for instance CLR James seeks retrospectively to do in the (2000) preface of his seminal (1937) work, *The Black Jacobins*, in which he argues that were he writing today, he would 'write *descriptions in which the black slaves themselves*, or people very close to them, describe what they were doing and how they felt about the work they were forced to carry on?'[32]

Or is the invocation more than a moral one – that is, one which sieves through the demands of a 'history from below?' And in any case, which (gendered) subject, do we seek therein to bring to life? Is it, again as James (2022) retrospectively finds, the 'subaltern insurgents of the . . . revolution' to whom insufficient attention has been paid in the course of a (Eurocentric) writing of history?'[33] Do colonized women even fit into the mould of the subaltern figure, whose very definition Spivak (1995) observes, entails 'immobility', whereby 'the cultural space of subalternity is cut off from the lines of mobility producing the class- and gender-differentiated colonial subject?'[34] In Spivak's evocation, subalternity should refer only to those 'spaces out of any serious touch with the logic of capitalism or socialism', not to be confused with 'unorganized labour, women as such, the proletarian, the colonized, [. . .] migrant labour, political refugees etc'.[35]

Dhawan (2007) in this regard draws an important distinction between subaltern spaces and marginalized space: one does not *claim* subalternity, but rather seeks by every means to escape it.[36] The marginalized, on the contrary retain a constant relationality to power, within which they assert claims, act, resist and are constantly reconstituted as subjects of that power. The 'margin' co-constitutes the centre in a dialectical relation of reproduction in a way that subalternity simply does not. Power functions both positively and negatively at the margins in a way that it does not within subalternity, which is always negated by power.[37] The very notion of subjectivity is in fact, impossible to think where clear lines of mobility do not exist. A marginal(ized) subject is nonetheless still *a subject*, in a way that subalternity cannot permit those so bounded within it. Colonized women are to my understanding as such, more usefully considered from within a marginal rather than a subalternized space. Writing women out of history (or more accurately, confining them to its margins) does not mean they were not conscripted by, or actively shaping modern (colonial) history in significant ways. While violence against the subaltern may take a gratuitous form, visited upon those 'who may be killed but not sacrificed,' the violence that structures the relationship between the colonizer and colonized – and that between the colonized themselves – ought to be read as sanctioned (disciplining), albeit not authorized (an impossibility, given empire's illegitimate status).

While Empire's liberalism presumes a bifurcation between the domains of the 'public' and 'private' and discursively sustains this split, a reading of colonial practice from the vantage point of the colonized challenges the notion of the public as the site of politics and the private as its opposite. This point is illustrated in literary texts that have dealt with the gendered existential crises which the colonial situation produced. There is, for instance, a poignant dialogue in Ngugi wa Thiongo's earliest work, *Weep Not, Child,* that precedes the decision of one of its main protagonists, Ngotho, to join other African men in a general strike against the colonial regime. In that chapter titled 'Fear and Anger', the man yells at his younger wife, Nyokabi, 'I must be a man in my own house!'; to which she responds, 'Yes, be a man and lose your job! And then we shall all starve!' To which Ngotho responds: 'I shall do what I like. I have never taken orders from a woman . . . This strike is important for all black people. Why must I work for a white man and his children?' But Nyokabi persists, 'What if the strike fails? Tell me that!' To which Ngotho responds: 'Shut up!' and slaps Nyokabi's face.[38]

Set in the height of the Emergency period[39] in colonial Kenya, this dialogue may be read as an allegory of the ways in which violence and power mutated downward from the realms of labour and land in which black men wielded little to no control, to the family/household where this lack of agency and frustration was being translated in the language of a violent, anti-woman patriarchal power. In the novel, Mr. Howlands, Ngotho's white master whose land he works, is admiring of Ngotho – of his physical strength, his skill and ability to turn a good crop, and is at the same time conscious of and threatened by his power – a power he increasingly seeks to subvert the more that Ngotho's political consciousness as a landless peasant grows. Through this master–slave dialectic, wa Thiong'o shows how colonialism structures both the nature and possibility of claims which colonized men can make. The only thing that binds Ngotho to his master is the land – the basis also of *Mau Mau's* claims for freedom – the material basis of his power as husband (and father), and of his self-recognition as a 'man'.[40]

The colonial denial of the legitimacy of Africans' claims and relationships to the land apprehends patriarchal power by refracting it back onto the colonized themselves. In this regard, we must deal with the subjectivities produced through this refraction by prying open the world of the colonized too, as opposed to the predominant focus on subjectivation as a response to colonial rule. The primary colonial relationship had been between colonialists and African men – native women's experience of colonial violence was mediated through this relationship, and primarily so in the domain of the family/household. Anticolonial feminist critique of colonial violence therefore necessarily takes as its starting point this domesticated realm of reproduction and resuscitates it as a site also of political (as well as class) struggle – one in which subjective identities like gender, ethnicity and class are co-produced and reproduced. If that be the case then one way of making sense of violence is to see it as a product of the structural disjuncture between the domesticated realm and the 'public' realm of politics – as a manifestation of an imagined barrier between the public and the private.

Schler (2004) has illustrated the effect of such 'untranslatability' in her analysis of birthing and reproduction practices in colonial Cameroon as studied from the perspective of a western-educated Duala man, Stephen Ekalle (1947) on the one hand, and two French doctors, Olivier and Aujoulat (1945) whose study preceded Ekalle's, on the other.[41] Schler's analysis of the reports of the French doctors unsurprisingly reveals a racist and sexist bias in their interpretation, and more interestingly, a concession that African women were suspicious of and indifferent to European medical practices: African midwives . . . 'were neither convinced that Western medicine offered an attractive alternative, nor were they willing to relinquish control over an area where women operated autonomously'.[42] What the report did not show, however, was 'a sufficient explanatory *framework for African women's objectives in their rejection of* western medical care'.[43] For this insight, Schler turns to Ekalle (1947), who in contrast suggests that the seeming resilience of this local (midwifery) approach is partially attributable to the allocation of birthing to the separate social and cultural sphere of women.[44]

Ekalle (1947) argued that these practices associated with pregnancy de-emphasized an individualist reading of the roles of women and men in the reproductive process: 'Women were not merely individual reproductive agents, and their bodies were not seen as independent from their community',[45] as such suggesting their corporeal interpellation into the *community*. Yet at the same time, Schler (2004) argues, it is not enough to situate reproduction within a social and spiritual context since:

> the hierarchies of power within this social sphere *must also be considered as factors determining the actions of women*. There existed a patriarchal system in which women depended on their reproductive capabilities for their social standing, and any problems arising with reproduction or fertility greatly increased a woman's vulnerability within the community. Social rejection and isolation were not the only consequences of infertility and miscarriage. *Women were also subjected to physical violence.*[46]

The suggestion here is that women's resistance, both in response to and in relation to violence, exceeded a reading of such violence as being acts directed towards anticolonial transgression. Such a reading is narrow and abstracted from the actual lived contexts of women's reproductive labours, and underrates the significance of the 'intramural' spaces within which women waged struggles and sought to define their own visions of liberation. As Schler (2004) finds through her study of colonial Cameroon, 'colonialism established multiple sites at which two systems of patriarchy converged, with varying consequences for women. Faced with limited autonomy, women acquiesced, subverted, defied and disengaged. The strategies they chose were *both dictated by external control and regardless of it*'.[47] Instances such as those illustrated in the colonial contexts of Kenya and Cameroon suggest that the willful displacement of women's experiences onto masculinist (modernist) readings of the colonial state (and anticolonial resistance) often had the effect of distorting the nature of women's relationship to colonialism (and therefore, to its violence), or altogether writing them out of anticolonial histories when their actions did not conform to grand narratives of resistance.

There is, nonetheless, a substantial body of feminist work that has attempted to locate women concretely in the colonial economy as political subjects (in their own right) through the questions of labour and land, although these works still predominantly respond to the question of violence from the point of view of the colonizer rather than the colonized.[48] More specifically, they are concerned with the ways in which violence against women was instrumentalized in the service of colonial rule and do not deal with the foundational question of *subjugation*: that is, the processes that aided the constitution of gendered labour as an instrument of colonial domination. Given that even women's 'public' participation in anticolonial politics – through resistance to the colonial appropriation of their productive and reproductive labour – was never fully considered as 'politics proper', analyses that begin from this public sphere misrepresent and mask the objective conditions that underwrote women's anticolonial struggles.

And although colonialists (and their missionary counterparts) did seriously engage the domestic, 'traditional' realm as a site of women's subjugation, their primary objective had been to deny the political potency of this domain as a site of intense contestations and debate among the colonized, and as a site around which various identities including class, ethnicity, gender, race and sexuality were being consolidated. The cost of this denial was a serious underestimation of the political significance of women's negotiations and actions inside their communities and households. As Sheeba (2002) too, confirms in the Indian context, the 'women question' that loomed large in the nineteenth century was concerned not as much with what women wanted, but rather with how they could be modernized.[49] It is, however, behind the façade of emancipation that the 'real battles of colonialism' were waged.[50] The 'women's question' was part of a very different political agenda, serving among others, to further ideas of the nation and culture.[51]

Multivalence of the modern subject of rights

Part of the problem with this Euromodernist construction of a 'woman question' relates to its inability to apprehend multiple/simultaneous subjectivities (what might be termed as multivalent identities) – and therefore the failure to account for violence which women experience on the basis of their multiple roles and interpellations into society. I have already argued in the introduction that the proximity of certain women to violence cannot be abstracted from the materiality of their existence. In a context where identities become politicized, this materiality is itself highly mediated by certain proximities. For instance, to gain proximity to the ethnic nation is to escape poverty: that is, it is by conforming to the values and interests defined by the nation that one perceives of the possibility of emancipating themselves from an immiserating existence. The nation in this regard supersedes the state, exposing one of the pitfalls of the nation-state formulation: a fundamental irreconcilability between the modern liberal ethos of equality under the law (enforceable by the state) and conditional equality through ethnic allegiance (enforceable by the tribe).

Women caught at this intersection cannot, for instance, be both female and Luo or female and Kikuyu, and so on. While women appear as the modern subject of rights, their 'other' identities are taken (in liberal thought) as being anachronistic renderings of tribalized, racialized, identities, external to the regime of rights. One might recall in this regard, Arendt's (1968) interpretation of the rise of stateless peoples in postwar Europe as 'the transformation of the state from an instrument of the law into an instrument of the nation':[52] the inadmissibility of the nation into the state, or the impossibility of reconciling difference within the ambits of the modern (nation) state.[53] A primary question that this study thus (re)poses is this: what does this 'either/or' position entail for women? In what ways are exclusionary forms of citizenship reproduced where multivalent identities at the same time appear as inimical?[54]

Intersectionality theory has come closest to a response to this question, although still diverges in significant ways from the notion of multivalence.

A lengthy consideration of its major claims is as such, necessary. Kimberlé Crenshaw's now seminal (1989) article offers a critique of the tendency to treat race and gender as mutually exclusive categories of experiences and analysis, and argues that antidiscrimination cases tended to focus on the most privileged group members, marginalized those who are multiply-burdened and obscured claims that could not be understood as resulting from discrete sources of discrimination. She showed in one of the court cases reviewed that in rejecting the plea against discrimination of 'Black women', the law insisted on the separation of 'purely' race claims from sex claims – as such denying the possibility that Black women could be discriminated against as 'Black women'.[55] In Crenshaw's argument, the court's refusal to acknowledge that Black women encounter combined race and sex discrimination

> implies that the boundaries of sex and race discrimination doctrine are *defined respectively by white women's and Black men's experiences*. Under this view, Black women are protected only to the extent that their experiences coincide with those of either of the two groups.[56]

Crenshaw further takes the view that because of its intersectionality, 'Black women [are]. . . the class of employees best able to challenge all forms of discrimination'.[57] This broad statement raises more questions than it answers regarding the paradigmatic utility of intersectionality, precisely because it is built upon a presumption that stabilizes certain forms of oppression for Black women (the triad of race, gender and class), without illuminating *how* it is that Black women find themselves permanently located at that intersection, and not so with Black men or white women. Stated differently, in intersectional theory, Black women cease to be *historical* – and thus political – subjects: in Foucauldian terms, they emerge as eternal and transcendent subjects of juridical and philosophical discourse – that is, always already carrying the possibility of harm on the basis of these three identity markers over which they have no control.[58]

What is left out of our purview are the specific historical trajectories through which women emerge (or that demand women's appearance) at the 'intersection' as either female, or Black, or both. In other words, it is not enough to simply highlight discrimination, but rather to also ask what it is that different forms of discrimination *do* at particular historical conjunctures.[59] This could also be posed as a question as such: *when* does identity normatively defined – as Black, female, queer, etc., become political (identity), shaped by race, class, ethnicity, gender, sexuality and so on? Intersectionality theory has not responded adequately to this question, failing as it does to illustrate the shift from its normative identitarian basis to a political one.[60]

Furthermore, intersectional theory can be criticized for lending itself too neatly to liberal individuality, for which rights are sought as resolution, rather than *group* oppressions which do not lend themselves neatly to a liberal rights discourse.[61] While it elaborates the ways in which various identity categories might intersect to oppress a person, or how individuals experience oppression, its liberal individual subject – modelled upon (or more accurately, in opposition to) the White, male, European subject of the Enlightenment – does not offer the means of understanding the socialized nature and generalized form of oppression – and thus, the condition (context) of its possibility. For instance, a Black female worker's experiences of oppression cannot stand in for an analysis of the struggles of Black women as part of the working class, precisely because oppressing black women on the basis of class would not be possible without the concrete formation of an *exploited class* as a whole.[62]

The distinction between 'oppression' and 'exploitation' here matters: gender, race, ethnicity and sexuality, which are historically shaped by the division of labour (whose explanatory framework is provided by class analysis), foreground the question of exploitation as distinct from oppression, and the two are not reducible to one another. Highlighting oppression/subordination without reference to exploitation becomes a purely cultural or ideological matter – for why should white women and men (including Black men) act oppressively towards Black women if they had nothing to gain from it?[63] As such, intersectionality at best deals with the *effects* of multiple oppressions, but does not offer an explanatory framework for addressing the root causes of social inequality.[64] In its historicity, the notion of exploitation offers the latter, since it is not separable from the structures, conditions and institutions that enable it.[65]

There is, however, something more significant in highlighting relations of exploitation over and above, or alongside the oppression which women experience. While the oppressed can appeal to the law for redress – that is, are always in moral proximity with the possibility of representation, the notion of exploitation denotes a more or less permanent separation and hierarchization[66] – the negation or impossibility of representation. The primary emancipatory possibility for exploited masses then, is *through revolutionary means* – through a total overhaul of the structures of production and reproduction that fragment them. The class struggle emerges fairly clearly as the attempt by working people to engage in such systemic change and gain control of the productive forces. But the idea of multivalence that everywhere marks the colonized – such that class formation in the colonies cannot be understood separately from gender formation as well as ethnic, sexuality and caste formations – means that the subject which the anticolonial struggle (as class struggle) presently holds up for liberation is an incomplete subject.

In the postcolonial democracy, this incomplete subject invariably faces the problem of representation. Here again, Spivak's (1988) reference to those who have to grapple with the impossibility of representing themselves is relevant. For the colonized female subject, representation is assured only when various social identities (gender, race, sexuality, class and ethnicity) clamour for visibility through processes (e.g. multiparty elections, judicial complaints) that reproduce them as *political identities*. This reconstitution of social identities as political identities shapes women's encounters with violence, since the process itself of reconstituting and stabilizing an identity *as a political identity* is often fraught with violence. That women require political subjectivity in order to be legible to the liberal state is to be taken for granted. But the limitation of liberal governmentality is its inability to read women beyond the single marker of *gender*, and thus a fundamental inability to apprehend the violence that women encounter on multiple fronts as people who simultaneously bear identities as markers of ethnic nations, as working people and as members of racialized and sexual communities.

The challenge, therefore, that multivalence throws at democracy is to represent women in their historical complexity as simultaneously gendered, racialized, ethnicized and classed. Yet, 'both as object of colonial historiography and as subject of insurgency, the ideological construction of gender *keeps the male dominant*. If, in the context of colonial production, the subaltern has no history and cannot speak, *the subaltern as female is even more deeply in shadow. . .*'[67] To speak then of a 'female subject' of violence is an oxymoron that retains this erasure, as it represents an essentialized reading of violence – the idea that women face violation on the basis only of their biological sex/gender. Conversely, to speak of a 'gendered subject' of violence is to highlight a *structural process and relationality* in the colonial production of violence against women.

'The colonial idea of women'

How then, did the colonial state govern women? It is possible and indeed, necessary to pose this as a question separately from that which simply asks how the colonial state governed; that is, how it responded to the native question that faced it as distinct from the European modern nation-state out of which it had been born. Women, after all, had not been the subjects proper of the colonial state. As such, to place them within the realm/purview of governance, and to in fact insist that they had posed a question to the colonial state – to insist at all on a 'woman question' – is to assert that women *produced* certain problems for the colonial state to which it was compelled to respond. Writing on colonial India (specifically, Bengal), Partha Chatterjee (1993), for instance, attempts to locate the women's question in the claims of nationalism, arguing that 'nationalism did in fact provide an answer to the new social and cultural problems concerning the position of women in "modern" society, and that this answer was posited *not on an identity but on a difference*[68] with the perceived forms of cultural modernity in the West':[69]

> the relative unimportance of the women's question in the last decades of the nineteenth century is to be explained not by the fact that it had been censored out of the reform agenda or overtaken by the more pressing and emotive issues of political struggle. The reason lies in nationalism's success in situating the "women's question" *in an inner domain of sovereignty*, far removed from the arena of political contest with the colonial state. The inner domain of national culture was constituted in the light of the discovery of "tradition."[70]

Chatterjee, in other words, locates women in a space between the colonial state and its nationalist counterparts, viewing the so-called women's question as having been not so much about the specific condition of women within a specific set of social relations, as about the political encounter between a colonial state and the supposed 'tradition' of a conquered people – a tradition that was itself produced by colonial discourse. It was colonialist discourse that defined the tradition that was to be criticized and reformed. In demarcating a political position opposed to colonial rule, nationalism thus took up the women's question as a problem *already constituted for it*: namely, as a problem of tradition.[71] Yet while constituted through this singularity of tradition in the realm of political control, women as economic subjects turned out to be much more difficult to control and contain within the public/private, or rural/urban, bifurcation.

Luise White's (1990) work on the ways in which prostitution became part of rural accumulation is illuminating in this regard. White's major intervention is to show, through an analysis of prostitution as wage labour, that women had in fact remained beyond the control of the colonial state.[72] The argument she develops is a fairly complex one. A central contradiction of colonialism had been the way in which it mobilized and utilized wage labour: they could create and recruit a wage labour force, but they could not maintain it, meaning that the *conditions* of wage labour had to be reconstructed over and again, necessitating regular return to the countryside to replenish its labour force:[73] the political economy of social reproduction under colonial state bifurcation. In the townships and cities, the relationships which supported this process between men and women, or landlords and tenants, were illicit. White (1990) as such argues that 'if we see this central contradiction as a relationship that *included* women . . . we see that the situation of the maintenance and reproduction of the work force was *beyond the reach of the state*'.[74] It is in this realm of reproduction where the limits of colonial control became most apparent. And in this realm, White places the figure of the prostitute to the service of a narrative counter to ones that have sought to deny the relationship between women's labour and colonial control of native populations.

How could colonialists control the illegal work that took place within the colonies if they could not control their cities? In Nairobi, for instance, this lack of jurisdiction did not come from ignorance of women's illicit work but rather from *contact* with it.[75] The relations between European men and prostitutes were revealing of the character of the individuated service occupations: while there was differentiation in the trade, this differentiation was defined by women's labour form rather than by race or class. That is, the poorest of male migrants could receive the same services for which European males paid dearly. The labour form (a question of sexuality) is what explained women's ability to control and direct sexual relations regardless of the amount they earned from them: 'Illegal sexual relations were ungovernable: sexual access to prostitutes – whatever its cost – did not mean the ability to regulate their behaviour'.[76] Even more significantly as White shows, the work of prostitutes brought them into close contact with, and gave them increased access to all the accoutrements of respectability, including associations with Europeans, secure accommodation and legal documentation.[77]

Yet (women's) need for recognition remained in practice, a figment of European imagination: the imperatives that had driven women from the countryside to urban areas had more to do with the need for survival and accumulation in the face of colonial dispossession than with formalization of their labour practices. The limits of the colonial modern state's bifurcated power between legality and illegality, were rendered apparent ironically not by the male subjects who experienced the full coercive force of the state (and were therefore forcefully interpellated into its mechanics of control), but by those (women) who in the first place had been identified with 'tradition', and thus outside of the realm of direct colonial supervision. The 'illegality' that marked the relations between European men, African men and women has, however, also to be understood as voluntary. In White's findings, prostitutes 'used jobs, housing, and associations with European men not as a way to begin legitimate enterprises or enter the legal labour force, but as a way to make their prostitution more efficient and profitable. They incorporated legal documents and secure housing into their labour process; *they did not change the nature of that labour*. Prostitutes in Nairobi did not wish to abandon prostitution to join the ranks of respectable society – many did not make such a distinction – they wanted to become rich'.[78]

The sense of autonomy that prostitutes in Nairobi were able to summon in relation to the colonial authorities belies the idea of a singular 'native' subject as the binary opposite of the colonizer, but rather compels a recognition of the fragmented ways in which natives experienced the colonial state. Furthermore, what might we make of the fact that the colonial state had been unable to exert its control over the realm of social reproduction? Or of its ineptitude in checking the autonomy of African communities in the spaces where Africans had 'established, negotiated, and controlled, with their own ideas about property, family, loyalty and their own relationships?'[79] The city, White (1990) writes, had always been beyond official regulation, an outcome she attributes to the complex negotiations between prostitutes and their customers, which reproduced men's labour power when and where the state and private enterprises did not, and in doing so, constrained colonial control.[80] This 'inaccessibility' of the city is ironically rendered most visible through the lens of gendered relations.

Women's work in prostitution, or attempts to control this labour, also exposed the tension between colonialists and African nationalist groups. Female labour was contested. From the late 1940s in Kenya, for instance, the colonial state increasingly commandeered women for forced labour, and at the same time the growing number of African welfare associations began to demand regulation and control over prostitutes' work and behaviour.[81] This policing, however, was being done by both women and men, who debated the nature and extent of sexual relations alongside race relations. These debates and colonial and African responses to them, exposed another shortcoming of the colonial logic of bifurcated rule: that is, its premise upon the separation of a domain of politics proper and that of the reproduction of political subjects. Unanticipated were instances where the two collapsed and constituted a singular domain of the production of politics and resistance. Again, in colonial Kenya

> most [African welfare associations] sought to control women's behaviour with the aid of the colonial state; the state continually dismissed such requests, which suggests that it had not penetrated post-war urban life and how little it knew of African concerns. The group that did not seek approval, Mau Mau, struggled separately in the forest to define gender, marriage, and women's and men's

> work. Indeed, Mau Mau's armed citizenship of shared domesticity and warfare households were reproduced without – and this was yet another affront to the colonial state – *any houses at all*.[82]

So long as the colonial state, through its modernist bifurcated logic, could deny public/political subjectivity to women, it could also harness this same logic towards strengthening patriarchal bonds of domination – another form of native control. Chatterjee indeed (1993) critiques the denial of women's public political agency, inscribed in the spiritual/material, home/world, private/public, sacred/profane, feminine/masculine dichotomies, although refutes the liberal impulse to see this as a merely traditional patriarchal conception of gender roles. Rather, he sees the colonial situation and the ideological response of nationalism to the critique of tradition as having introduced an entirely new substance to these terms and effected their transformation. For Chatterjee, this inner sanctum *became the primary point of interaction between the nationalist project and modernity*: 'the ideological framework within which nationalism answered the women's question'.[83] It was 'not a dismissal of modernity but an attempt to make modernity consistent with the nationalist project'.[84] If colonialism was the modern state's exceptional form, nowhere was this more evident than in the limits of its encounter with anticolonial resistance. While the 'world' had been where European power challenged non-European peoples and by virtue of its 'superior' culture, had subjugated them, nationalists asserted European failure to colonize the inner, essential, identity of the East, which they viewed as laying in its distinctive, and superior, spiritual culture:

> Here the East was undominated, *sovereign, master of his own fate*. . .No encroachments by the colonizer must be allowed in that inner sanctum. In the world, imitation and adaptation to Western norms was a necessity; at home, they were tantamount to *annihilation of one's very identity*.[85]

The extent, however, to which the colonial state was in reality able to intervene into this private sanctum is by now well documented in the literature,[86] although this literature mainly proposes economic imperatives as the basis of vitiating the home/world divide. The economic subjectivation of women was clear from the early years of colonialism, and their resistance as the basis of anticolonial struggle is also well-documented. What is discernible from that literature is not so much the nature and power of the colonial state, as women's responses to changes that were taking place at the level of family/household/community that compelled their responses in ways that deepened the identification of women with gendered and sexualized labour forms (and later, citizenship). This, however, does not illuminate the conditions that made possible this 'violation' of the codes of domesticity. Had colonialists exercised a strict moral code with regard to the 'place' of women, then any violation of the private/public would invariably have invited violent responses to deter rather than control them. Along the same vein, women's natural reaction to control would have been resistance.

But in a move away from the dominant literature that normatively reads women's actions as resistance to the colonizing pressure,[87] we are rather called upon to think of the 'variety of ways in which norms are lived and inhabited, aspired to, reached for, and consummated'.[88] To Saba Mahmood, this requires an exploration of the 'relationship between the immanent form a normative act takes, the model of subjectivity it proposes, and *the kinds of authority upon which such an act relies*'.[89] Accordingly, she finds that the activities such as those of the (women's) mosque movement/piety movements she is analyzing seldom engage those institutions and practices that are commonly associated with the realm of politics, such as participating in the electoral process, making claims on the state, or using the judicial system to expand the place of religion in public life.[90] This, she argues, makes it easy to ignore the political character of these movements and for their activities to fall off the political radar – to be confined outside of the realm of 'politics proper' – even considered as apolitical in character.[91] In other words, the impossibility of seeing 'politics' where there is no resistance. To Mahmood, this characterization is a gross political and analytical mistake, because of the immense transformative power of movements such as these, which in many cases, exceeds that of conventional political groups. She thus locates the political efficacy of these movements in the function of work they perform in the ethical realm – i.e. 'those strategies of cultivation through which *embodied attachments to historically specific forms of truth* come to be forged'.[92]

Extrapolated to our current analysis, reading the actions of colonized women as predominantly articulated to 'resistance' is to place them in direct relation with the colonial state, of which they had not been the subject proper, and further, it is to read the actions of the state as a direct response to women's activities. While this does not preclude an understanding of women's actions as political acts (i.e. as responding to power), presuming women's subjectivation as related to the mode of rule rather than to the material processes/relations that mediated their relationship to the colonial state dehistoricizes these subjugative processes and renders them unavailable for our analysis of the present.

The colonial response to women

It is one thing to speak about the native question – the control of the native, rule by difference, the bifurcated state model – a core political question that preoccupied the colonizer. It is a question posed from above. But it is quite another thing to speak about the identitarian nature of colonialism – which is the point at which difference (gender, ethnicity, sexuality, age, caste and class) is put to the service of rule by difference. This, it might be shown in distinct ways, is the point at which the political economy of colonial domination gains most significance, for it is inconceivable that the instrumentalization of difference could have proceeded through an interaction between colonists and only one half (male native) of the colonized population. In other words, the condition of possibility of colonial power and the bifurcated mode of rule could only be posed as a question, and was necessarily answered from below – grasped 'through institutions immediately and actually present . . . that ensemble of institutions, the deracialized regime of indirect rule . . . best conceptualized as a subordinate but autonomous state apparatus'.[93]

The pragmatism of colonial laws is visible from the nature of responses to changes in native populations, and the need to maintain order. The beginning of colonial rule had been marked by a combination of forces ostensibly predisposed towards improving the position of women, even if the reasons did not relate necessarily to women.[94] Institutions such as polygamy and bride-price were viewed (in the settler-missionary alliance) as allowing 'the native male to live in sloth and idleness, and therefore as being at the root of colonial labour problems'.[95] The need to abolish custom was concealed in the discourse of alleviating the 'sufferings of the native woman', but which in reality, settlers saw as interfering with the object (labour) for which they had claimed the colonies.[96] Space was soon ceded to customary authorities – those officials of the local state whom out of pragmatism, colonial authorities became increasingly content to let define the substantive customary law.[97] The law had at its core the aim of safeguarding and 'enforcing the exigencies of power',[98] against which any custom considered to be 'repugnant' would not be enforced.[99] The repugnancy clause distinguished between civil and criminal law, and early on, focused on setting limits on the latter, and was concerned with social control and the exertion of power. Civil law dealt with relationships between individuals, and set practical limits in matters such as slavery, mutilation, polygamy and bride-price: they were, however, 'subordinate to political considerations, and for that reason, they were always negotiable'.[100]

The colonial attitude towards women was in these ways, ambivalent and often contradictory, and importantly complicates our reading of the ways in which colonialism reconstituted the native. Contra Chatterjee's argument that the colonial modern had revealed a split between the public and the private as already highlighted above, Mamdani maintains that the public/private split was blurred under indirect rule:

> The distinctive feature of indirect rule colonialism was precisely that colonialism took command of the private realm, redefining custom, and thereby shaping the terms within which subjectivity of the colonized would be produced. Herein lies the significance of the change from custom as social to custom as colonial law. In the premodern period, custom was a set of norms and conventions that regulated gender and generational relations. As such, it was part of the community. Under colonialism, custom became customary law. More than just observed, it was enforced. The authorities in charge of enforcing custom, so-called customary authorities, were sanctioned by the state *and backed up by state violence.*[101]

The gendered nature of the violence of the colonial state has to be understood in these indirect, mediated ways, as do the subjects of its violence. This is an argument regarding the inadequacy of approaching gendered subjectivity from the vantage point of the (colonial) state. A view from below, from the vantage point of the natives, is necessarily a structural one. That is, if we consider the conditions under which the decentralized political process of defining and ruling the native subject unfolded, then we must also of necessity consider that it is not possible to think of gendering as a distinct process or imperative: it was already articulated in the definition and demarcation of a private sphere. Customary law had after all, not been 'about guaranteeing rights [but rather . . .] about *enforcing custom*. Its point [had not been . . .] to limit power, but to *enable* it'.[102] Customary law, in other words, was both an acknowledgment of power as *residing within* the localized domains of the native and constituted the point at which colonialists actualized control over the native.

The argument has been made, for instance, that ideas about domesticity had very political purposes for colonial settlers and governments on the one hand, and for African women on the other.[103] African male authorities, who needed the labour of African women for agriculture, and colonial officials, who saw an opportunity to placate African men, were concerned about maintaining control over African women.[104] The colonial government, Ranchod-Nilsson (1992) argues, 'bolstered the patriarchal control of African male authorities over their wives and daughters in an effort to maintain a form of indirect rule that relied on "traditional" household authority structures'.[105] This argument is based on shifts in the colonial political economy and shows how legal innovations on the part of colonialists located women in the public at some points, and relegated them to domesticity at others, but *left intact* the gendered subjectivities that these shifts produced.

Examining the colonial context of Southern Rhodesia, Ranchod-Nilsson shows that the control of women remained a central issue for both the state and African male authorities until 1930 when the government enacted the Land Apportionment Act (LAA), which established the basis for the racially segregated, unequal distribution of land rights that remained unaltered until independence.[106] The effect of these laws was drastic: although Europeans made up only approximately 3 per cent of the population, the LAA gave them control over more than half the land in Southern Rhodesia, almost all of it located in the most fertile areas. The result was that

> after 1930, access to land was greatly restricted for Africans and control of women's labour did not guarantee sufficient levels of production. In short, the reproduction of poor peasant households could no longer rely on female agricultural labour but depended also on cash remittances from male migrants. The main issues of contention between colonial officials and Africans thus shifted *from the control of African women to the control of land*.[107]

These processes deepened the social and political differentiation among the natives. The production of difference through law was, however, not unique to a singular context: in Mamdani's (2012) argument, 'not only were they inscribed in law, it was in the nature of modern power that they were enforced through law. The law was constitutive of these distinctions . . . If the premodern was informed by an assimilationist logic, the modern colonial was informed by a segregationist logic'.[108] The fact that such laws did not directly target women, but rather severed the social and material basis of any claims they might subsequently have made on the colonial state is worth noting. While massive land dispossession compelled men into wage labour through the compulsion to create a stable urban labour pool and thus guaranteed men some form of mobility, the effect on women had been the opposite – segregated and confined without being freed of the burdens of social reproduction.

The corollary to this was a fundamental destabilization of household and communal relations. As Ranchod-Nilsson writes again of Southern Rhodesia, the limited access to land meant that day-to-day survival became increasingly difficult and that the household negotiations over resources and labour intensified.[109] Ironically, this period was also marked by a more intense focus and regulation of women's bodies and activities attached to them. For instance, 'an examination of civil cases concerning domestic matters such as divorce, child custody, return of *lobola* (bride wealth) or household goods, and seduction indicates that during the 1930s the increased economic difficulties . . . seem to have greatly intensified domestic struggle'.[110] The government later abandoned its highly centralized structure in favour of a more decentralized administrative approach known as community development, constituted through women's clubs that matched European women with rural African women putatively to 'stimulate development in the Tribal Trust Lands (TTL)',[111] but which in reality was a drive towards the 'housewifization'[112] of African women. The overriding justification for this development was to address the 'backwardness' of African women.[113]

This new arrangement was assured at least in part by the repugnancy laws. African women were, after all, restive and politically responsive to the changes to their domains of production, reproduction and community that were brought about by colonial dispossession and disciplining of labour. How do we understand the stabilization of this new regime apart from the powers granted to local administrators that determined what went against European morality and what did not? What we see is a contested terrain in which women were formally and systematically excluded from formal administration but still informally subjected to the colonial regime through the mediation of African men, often in violent ways. The colonial regime of (customary) law stood at the cusp of modernity: on the one hand as a modernist response to the native question and on the other, as a tool that subjectivated women in relation to a discourse of 'backwardness' – inimical (repugnant) to liberal personhood, and impossible as subjects of modernity. Where customary law was not codified, Mamdani (1996) writes that

> local initiative was invariably greater. In the settler colonies there was greater interest in codification; in free peasant economies, this interest did not surface until after the Second World War. It is in the latter that, subject to the repugnancy clause, customary authorities came to have a disproportionate influence in shaping the substantive law.[114]

Many of the repugnancy clauses did touch on the private domains of native existence – apart from the exception that was established in relation to rape cases – a fact which renders critique of the relationship between these 'inner' domains and the substantive law, necessary. This is the focus of my critique in the chapter that follows. The arrangements in law and order through which the state sought to govern the fluid domain of (social) reproduction substantively marked the nature of women's transition into the postcolony, and are a defining characteristic of present contestations and conflicts in relation to women's gendered personhood. What then would it mean, in the post-colonial and democratizing state, for women to claim rights as liberal subjects when their codification through the law retained identification with many elements of tradition and custom?

The 'woman's question' as expressed in the colonies has profane origins in imperialism. And while the regulation of women's bodies and sexuality in gendered ways predates colonialism, the form this takes in the colonial modern period cannot be distinguished apart from the imperatives and questions that drove the colonial enterprise. Be it 'civilization' (moral ambition), economic (primitive accumulation and the social reproduction of labour power), or political (the native question and the maintenance of order), gender has appeared enmeshed within the strategies and tools employed by empire to achieve the ends of the colonial state. Was the agency of women a premodern one, and therefore untransmutable to the logics of the colonial state, or does Scott's thesis hold here too, making it impossible to understand the gendered subject of violence (and responses thereof) outside of the colonial modern signifier? This chapter makes the latter argument, that while women had not been the subjects proper of the colonial modern state, the centrality of the reproductive domains which they occupied indirectly subjectivated them as juridical beings. This still does not mean that they could be considered as subjects of the colonial state, but were nonetheless subjected to its modernist techniques of governance and control. To insist therefore, on a 'gendered subject of violence' is to argue that gendered social relations (of both production and reproduction) were a core terrain on which the colonial state ordered colonized society – and to argue as well that violence was constitutive of the *reproduction* and *stabilization* of these social relations between natives and the state.

3

Customary Law and the Gendered Constitution of Violable Subjects

> *If the production of the past is the stuff of history writing, the securing of a future is the domain of law making. Between the two, there is a strategic alliance: law identifies agency in the present and in history.*[1]

How might we make sense of the colonial archive as a constitutive source of the gendered bodies that experience violence and that commit violence in the colonial and postcolonial state? The codification of customary laws[2] indirectly subjectivated women as juridical beings, as such rendering the law, both statutory and customary, as a battleground for women's emancipatory struggles. My focus in this chapter is not as much with the laws themselves as with the forms of acquiescence and protest through which we might make sense of women's incorporation into the structures of the colonial state through the regime of customary laws. The chapter reproduces the gendered subject of violence as a historical figure by placing them in relation to, as well as in contestation with the political, social and economic dynamics of the colonial state and its compulsions to demonstrate its modernity. In it I trace a tension between the juridical and the political character of women's subjectivation, and their objectification as sources of social reproduction.

My concern is with how to deploy formal colonizing instruments (law) towards the task of decolonizing subjects who were marginal to them but who are nonetheless deeply implicated in their disciplinary logic and ongoing relevance. How do we discursively reconstitute a subject whose identity is constituted through the language of violence, without re-inscribing their violability? These questions guide my consideration of the relationship between the colonial customary legal regime and the gendered subject of violence. The primary analytical lens is to approach the law as a subjectivating agent, with a focus on both the forms of *acquiescence* through which women as gendered labourers were formally interpellated into the colonial state by the regime of customary law and *protest* as the informal modes that reinscribe women in the law. The concern at the core of my analysis is how we might understand the political questions posed by women as reproducers of the native population, as 'communities who know what it [is] like to be on the outside, to be surveilled yet not seen, spoken to yet looked down upon'.[3] How, in other words, did women respond to colonial power from the juridical margins that they occupied?

Customary laws were a predominant feature of the colonial legal system, but the regulation of social relations had been undertaken through indigenous legal systems that were 'customary in origin and type' prior to the arrival of colonial rule in Africa.[4] Although varying with different colonial powers, in general each power first introduced its own legal system or a variant of it 'as the fundamental and general law of its territories and second, permitted the regulated continuance of traditional African Law and judicial institutions *except* where they ran counter to the demands of colonial administration or were thought repugnant to "civilized" ideas of justice and humanity'.[5] This duality generally established the framework of colonial legal administration and governed the application of customary law in the various colonies.[6]

The 'repugnancy clause' or the 'repugnancy doctrine' was especially significant in the reconstitution of customary laws and defining their limits. Repugnancy was established whenever 'native laws and custom prevailing in the area of the jurisdiction of the court or binding between the parties' were found to contravene 'natural justice, equity and conscience,' or were 'incompatible either directly or by necessary implication with any written law for the time being in force'.[7] The interpretation of what constituted repugnancy to statutory laws was thus random and discretionary – there was 'no generally agreed criteria by which the tests were applied'[8] other than a view held among its executors that 'where a custom fails to conform to the values of advanced societies, such customs should be taken as having failed the test of repugnancy'.[9] For those natives who found themselves at the margins of custom, for those who historically had experienced the heavy patriarchal suppression of custom, repugnancy provided an unprecedented avenue for recognition.[10]

English statutory laws remained supreme, and repugnancy to 'natural justice, equity, and good conscience' could be interpreted to mean one of three things: 'repugnant in relation to substantive law; repugnant in relation to procedure; or repugnant in relation to the degree of punishment'.[11] Lastly, 'when a rule of customary law fail[ed] the test of repugnancy, such rule fell outside the scope of *enforceable* law, and therefore was denied the status of law'.[12] In these ways, repugnancy clauses did not derive consent from society such that what was transformed from custom into law could be read as reflecting the interests of colonists as well as implying some instrumentality in relation to the groups and issues which *did* become subjected to, and therefore, subjectivated by the accepted law.

But the significance of repugnancy clauses compels more expansive consideration than in mere relation to what it *prohibited*, for prohibition feeds into the discourse of the oppressor, illuminating the object rather than the subject under restriction – establishing the punitive rather than the constitutive aspect of law. From the vantage point of its subjects – that is, those who were brought into social and political visibility through its various enactments – the doctrine of repugnancy also invites us to consider the *human and embodied labours* that fed empire and reproduced it, for these were the substantive subjects of the law. Regarding a different historical context, Saidiya Hartman writes that '[t]he sexuality and reproductive capacities of enslaved women were central to understanding the expanding legal conception of slavery and its inheritability'.[13] In other words, that the law could be read as an accurate reflection of the imperatives of production, social reproduction, and profit-making that drove the forceful incorporation of women's reproductive as well as productive labour as chattel into the slave economy. A more nuanced point, however, is the one she makes regarding the inheritability of the institution of slavery – a veiled caution that the mere abolition of slavery would not end the captivity of reproductive labour that it required:

> reproductive labour not only guaranteed slavery as an institutional process and secured the status of the enslaved, but it inaugurated *a regime* of racialized sexuality that continues to place black bodies at risk for sexual exploitation and abuse, gratuitous violence, incarceration, poverty, premature death, and state-sanctioned murder.[14]

Stated differently, the colonizing regime of law and the regime of racialized and sexualized labour that was instituted and authorized by it were one and the same. Any liberation struggle aimed towards dismantling the exploitative regime of gendered labour that had subjugated women would therefore also need to confront the authorizing laws, as such casting the law as a substantive battleground for feminist liberation in the postcolonial state, and democracy as its surrogate. This is because capitalism's need for gendered, racialized labour has not abated, and within this reality, the 'systematic violence needed to conscript black women's [reproductive] labor' remains a feature of late capitalist accumulation that is largely authorized through legislation.[15] This chapter then elaborates, through a materialist analysis, the juridical *power* which the colonial state exercised in order to sustain its imperialist ambitions as well as its legacy in the postcolonial democratizing state.

My conception of juridical power wades reluctantly into Foucauldian territory to the extent that I am persuaded by his theorization of power not 'as an institution, and not as structure; neither [as] a certain strength we are endowed with; [but rather] as the name one attributes to a complex strategical situation in a particular society . . . relations of power as not in superstructural positions, with merely a role of *prohibition* or accompaniment, [but as having] a directly productive role, wherever they come into play'.[16] My interest in this regard, is in a reading of power from below, in elaborating the relational character of juridical power – its presence or force evidenced by the resistance to it – based on the assumption that resistance (in all its various forms) can exist only 'in the strategic field of power relations'.[17]

But a distinction of the colonies from the historical context of late industrial capitalism in which Foucault is writing is necessary because in the latter context, the imperative of control and governmentality presupposes a 'free' labouring subject. The political legitimacy of even the most exploited industrial worker is taken for granted and validated in that context: class struggle presupposes this free subject, and remains silent on slaves and modernity's 'Others'. By contrast, the colonies are faced with a native question which grants political validation and civil rights only to a white minority class, a reality which modifies the basic parameters of any liberation struggle that has workers at its core (to the extent that every colony is faced with a labour question). In the colonial capitalist context, *captivity* is the fundamental condition of the labouring subject, whose productivity and reproductive capacities are derived only through coercion and violence. The state's coercive legal instruments are both direct (statutory) and indirect (customary), such that cultural power (in its relation to statutory power) defines and constrains every modern mechanism of control. That cultural domain was marked through and through by gender.

In the colonial context, sex occupies a central space in constant relation to the politics of the reproduction and supply of labour, which was a fundamental requirement of capitalist accumulation and thus, a preoccupation of colonists. The literature is awash with evidence of women as having been juridically subjectivated on the specific basis of their *reproductive identities* rather than merely on the basis of their gender (i.e. as women). Women gained visibility to the law in relation to the reproductive labours that they undertook both on behalf of the colony and their communities. In colonial jurisprudence, women are recorded as 'prostitutes', 'domestic workers', 'mothers', 'wives', 'daughters' and 'concubines' – their subject status related to the kind of labours that they performed, rather than what they normatively were (women). This is the argument I elaborate throughout this chapter. The apparent tension that the colonial structure of juridical subjectivation produces in the postcolonial democracy is related to a fundamental contradiction between the individual subjectivity that is envisioned in liberal constitutionalism (whose intervention is primarily political recognition), and the labouring subject produced by colonialism (whose claims also include social redistribution). I examine the ways in which maternal logics constituted gendered/reproductive labour in the juridical realm of colonial governance, and the implications for justice in the postcolonial state for those so incorporated into the state. Germaine to this chapter is also a commentary on method.

Colonial 'Accumulation of Women'

Economic dependence on women's productive and reproductive labour long predates colonialism. Early anthropological texts show as much. For instance, writing of life on the Gold Coast at the end of the seventeenth century, Bosman (1967) has raised the problem regarding the connection between polygyny, economy and the position of women. He notes that each man marries as many wives as he pleases, but is 'commonly contented with a number betwixt three and ten'.[18] Among the rich men who were associated with this practice, Bosman wrote condescendingly that

> two wives were exempted from labour, the chief wife who looked after the household and another who was consecrated to his god (*obossum*). The other were obliged to till the ground and plant millet yams, whilst the man only idly spends his time in impertinent tattling...and drinking palm wine, which the poor wives are frequently obliged to raise money to pay for, and by their hard labour maintain and satisfie [sic] these lazy wretches their greedy thirst after wines.[19]

The 'accumulation of women' for economic purposes has also found extensive treatment in the more contemporary literature,[20] with evidence that in places where agriculture is dominated by women, wives did command a high bride price (Boserup 1970). Other studies also establish a link between hoe agriculture, women's role in the economy, and high incidence of matrilineal institutions (Baumann 1928). The general thrust of the historical literature is that it was because of women's role in production and distribution that they were valuable to men who try to accumulate women in polygynous marriage (Goody 1973; Heath 1958). There were some exceptions to the general association between hoe agriculture, female farming and polygyny, and Goody argues that 'the attempt to relate them directly to one another appears to take a too restricted view of the 'economic' role of women', adding that '[t]o try to measure this purely in terms of the contribution to agricultural or trading activity neglects the important role of women in food preparation, the production of children and in sexual gratification'.[21] Furthermore, land scarcity was hardly the problem in precolonial societies, which featured extensive farming and low densities: rather, 'labour bec[ame] the dominating factor in the economy' thus shifting women's roles from producers of food to producers of children.[22] Goody here does not overcome the functionalist association between women's social status and social reproduction, which defines modern capitalist society.

The ability to accumulate women is invariably linked to women's *ability to reproduce*, and reproduction in turn, exposes society's propensity for violence. For instance, a demographic survey by Audrey Richards and Priscilla Reining in Buganda in 1952 found that '31.6 per cent of women over 45, all of whom had had some marital experience, reported childlessness, and this cohered with a 1948 census finding that 24 per cent of the older women in Buganda were childless'.[23] Linking this data to sterility, which seems to have been prevalent over a fairly long period, Richards and Reining (1954) argued the link between childlessness and 'a rather high degree of instability . . . with respect to personal marital relations . . .' (1954: 403). Violence, in other words, was linked to a fundamental problem which infertility announces: the inability to control women's *reproduction of* labour (and not as much their sexual reproduction, which is an irrelevant consideration as far as fertility is concerned).

These logics and economies of reproduction overdetermined in these ways, the subjectivation of women into the canon of colonial customary laws. Richards (1964) noted the 'submissive and obedient' conduct that was expected of wives in traditional Ganda households, arguing that the woman 'was a minor at law in that she was under the control of her father, her brother, or her husband as regards the conduct of court cases'.[24] Wealth and status, however, held the possibility of conferring upon women some power that allowed them to subvert patriarchal norms: '[i]t is true that old-time princesses were said to have acted like men, to have received the deference due to men, and to have been referred to by male titles'.[25] This suggests that economic power may have provided avenues to *some* women, for social and political autonomy, although such avenues would likely have been jealously guarded.

The social organization of indigenous societies also seems to have determined the position of women within them, and therefore their legibility in matters of law and politics. Throughout the course of my research for this chapter, I was struck by how little of the histories of women in precolonial society has actually been recorded in major historical texts – in the non-feminist historiographies. Where women are minimally referenced, for instance, in A.T. Mason's *Nandi Resistance to British Rule, 1890–1906,* they are (without exception) mentioned merely as nouns – nameless, faceless actors in the theatre of politics and therefore impossible to trace in the archives of state formation.

In other major texts supposedly concerned with elaborating the histories of whole societies, such as John Tosh's *Clan Leaders and Colonial Chiefs in Lango: The Political History of an East African Stateless Society, c.1800–1939,* not a single index documents the presence of women in the political and social milieu of that society. Interestingly, both Nandi and Lango were acephalous societies, and this seems to have been a distinguishing factor in the documentation of women. Further afield, precolonial Igbo society similarly had decentralized political organization, with authority placed in the hands of the king or all-male council of elders and title holders, but there, feminist historiography shows that *certain* women such as the oldest daughter of the lineage, royal women, priestesses, and heads of women's organizations, did wield important political power and authority (Chuku 2009). The stories of ordinary peasant and working women are largely absent in narratives of acephalous traditional societies.

On the other hand, and without exception, women's social and political organizations in precolonial and early colonial society are substantially documented among societies which had already established indigenous chiefly hierarchies, such as the Ganda and Gikuyu of East Africa, both of which had structures that were well suited to colonial needs. Two logical conclusions emerge from the foregoing. The first is a simple observation that the absence of women in the literature documenting acephalous societies might suggest the insignificance of women's political roles in those societies. Through similar logic, women's visibility in the literature of more hierarchical and centralized traditional societies would suggest that the roles which women played in them would have been too significant in the overall ordering of those societies to minimize or ignore. Among the Ganda, for instance, Richards (1964), hints at the political ways in which the naming and recognition of (Ganda) women functioned in defining the overall social structure of that society:

> Women were . . . traditionally *under the authority of other women*;[26] in the larger polygamous households of wealthy men in the past, all women, whether wives or concubines, lived in disciplined communities of their own. The three senior wives of the Kabaka and of important chiefs had fixed titles which *reflected those*

> *used by political title holders at the king's court.*[27] Beneath them the women of the household were arranged in order of precedence, each with specified duties and well-marked status, even if all were under the supreme control of the male household head. In true Ganda style they used the precedence titles of chiefs – *mumyuka, ssaabaddu,*[28] and so forth – to indicate the relative status of one wife to another. The *pattern of state organisation was also reproduced in the palace enclosure* by the giving of office (*kitongole*) titles to royal wives.[29]

There seemed to have been independent lines through which Ganda women could exercise authority since traditionally, women's authority was confirmed in household arrangements but also then structured the ordering of the state of Buganda. It is also significant that the monarchy mapped its own internal arrangements around that of the state (its populace), and not vice versa, suggesting its role in stabilizing the state. Furthermore, in a society where 'fertility was highly correlated with rank [and] polygyny made chiefs enormously more prolific than peasants',[30] the mere fact that polygamy was the preserve of men that bequeathed them with the power to reproduce bloodlines, wealth and labouring bodies renders visible the economic imperative that was attached to marriage.

An even more interesting point is that the titles given to *wives*, which equated them to chiefs, indicate a political function that was institutionalized through marriage. While it is male power that confers title on women (and which therefore supported the authority of women over the household), it is women as bearers of title that give life and meaning to this 'honour' through substantive enactments within society. While one's marital identity as a 'wife' would no doubt grant them authority within the family/household, their identity as a 'chief' explodes the boundaries of the household and extends women political recognition into the realm of broader society. I am arguing here a political function: endowing wives with title, no matter how normative these may have been, both *socially* stratifies women internally among their gender peers, as well as implies a *historically gendered formation* in the administrative structure of that society.

That the superiority which Baganda claim over the northern tribes of Uganda is often that those tribes 'have no chiefs and therefore, according to them, no government'[31] further suggests the necessity of political stabilization which hierarchical societies such as Buganda aspired towards. The significance of a social stratification system – a 'class system' in everyday terms – is that it is 'a society's way of applying its values to the behaviour of its members so as to call forth their efforts on behalf of agreed ends. A social stratification system says: '[t]hese are the activities to which it is worth devoting your life and these are the rewards which are held out to you in return for performing them well'.[32] British colonial administrators did not seek to undermine these customary systems that had embedded gendered modes of social stratifications within them. Rather, the peculiarity of colonial modernity was to map onto the customary, a statutory legal structure through which repugnancy re-subjectivated women by way of various exceptions targeting crimes against them, as I show below.

Yet, the fact that hierarchical and centralized traditional societies did interpellate women in these ways did not provide sufficient conditions for the incorporation of women as modern subjects in the same sense as the colonial modern state did. The distinction is to be found in the colonial mode of gendered incorporation of its subjects, which links women's subjectivation as political subjects to violence. Highly centralized precolonial societies may have functioned in statist form but did not have recourse to modern law as a subjectivating agent – an instrument which the colonial modern state did marshal through customary law to establish juridical dominion over natives. As such, despite the fact that the requirement for women's/gendered reproductive labour is common to both precolonial and colonial modern society, the *legislation* of labour which the colonial modern state mandates through its invention of customary law provides a legal basis for enforcement, which implicitly authorizes violence as a coercive mode of reproducing colonial capitalist society. The codification of customary law – the law as a coercive instrument of the state – thus mediates the reconstitution of women both as reproductive labour necessary for the stabilization of colonial economy and as political subjects of the state through the exception.

The approach was different in non-centralized societies where the colonial imposition of governance structures would have interfered with the organic development of indigenous organization. As Tosh (1978) writes on the administrative reconstitution of Lango in Uganda,

> [t]hroughout British tropical Africa, native administration between the wars was organized along three lines; in both centralized and acephalous societies, appointed chiefs *with executive and judicial authority* were the norm. On several significant points of detail, however, the system in Uganda was distinctive. This was because in Buganda, at the centre of the Protectorate, the British found an indigenous chiefly hierarchy which, with some adjustments, was well suited to colonial needs, and which they then extended throughout Uganda. The details of administrative organization in Lango were determined in the first instance by this 'Ganda model'.[33]

The model being imposed, in other words, conformed to the modernity of the colonial state – its peculiarity being in the invention of colonial customary laws which it confirmed and easily adapted from existing customs in centralized societies, and replicated them elsewhere where centralized states and chiefdoms did not exist. Interestingly, this colonial replication of the modes of governance found amongst organized kingdom states as well as in decentralized ones did carry within them the possibility of reconstituting women as political subjects especially where no record of women's political authority existed. This is not to argue that women's roles had not been important or recognized prior to colonialism,[34] but rather to make a point regarding their *re-subjectivation* in the language of modernity. Colonial government did after all, seek to undermine sources of power and authority that did not conform to Euro-modern norms. Customary coding was one avenue through which colonized women did emerge through and within the modernist logics of colonial governance as modern subjects of the state.

The colonial state also accumulated women as *economic* subjects, and it was in that sphere that women most closely encountered the state and its regulatory violence. This is in part because the new colonial economy was more favourable to men than to women. In Nigeria, for instance, training for the management of newly introduced technologies was preserved for men and boys, who were also employed in the Native Courts, the transport industry, in the mines, the Christian missions, and expatriate trading companies. Women's access to Western education was limited by its dual-gender structure that emphasized domestic science training for girls and leadership and technical instructions for boys.[35] Furthermore, 'access to the newly introduced British money also favored men more than women through the male-dominated cash crop economy and the colonial gendered employment policy that discriminated against women. Colonial economic policy also favored men more than women in access to land, extension services, high-yielding palm seedlings, fertilizer, demonstration farms, oil presses, kernel crackers, pioneer oil mills, cassava graters, loans, and other innovations and new technologies that put men in a position to dominate the export and local economies of the region'.[36] These advantages allowed men to penetrate and control what had previously been female economic spheres, and in these ways, 'most . . . women were pushed to the informal and petty sector of the colonial economy'.[37]

Women's reaction to these interventions into their social domains proved catalytic. Chuku (2009) writes that Igbo women responded to the erosion of their position in the political, social, religious, and economic spheres during the colonial period through a variety of distinctly female political mechanisms:

> boycotts, strikes, sit-ins, sleep-ins, and protest demonstrations against male authorities. During this period, women's anger was focused against the colonial government, missionaries, foreign trading companies and their Igbo

> agents. Some of the women's wars against these authorities included the 1916 demonstrations over the colonial control of marketplaces, the 1925 Nwaobiala Movement to restore societal order and preserve Igbo heritage, the 1929 Water Rate Demonstrations, the 1929 Women's War, the Anti-Tax Demonstrations of the 1930s, Price Control and Produce Inspection Protests, and the Pioneer Oil Mill Demonstrations of the 1940s-1950s. The colonial authorities usually responded harshly to these uprisings, but the women never gave up. In the end, the colonial authority prevailed [although] women were able to achieve some successes in both the economic and political arenas.[38]

Some of the women took advantage of the opportunities unleashed by colonialism, foreign capital, and mission education to become successful entrepreneurs. The fact that the 1929 Women's War seemed to have catalysed a substantive transition for some women into the ambits of colonial governance, and that women served in the newly reorganized local administration following the war is worth remarking. There had been other Igbo women who served in the colonial native administration, but their tenure came after the Women's War of 1929. Most of these women served in the Native Courts within the areas where the Women's War had taken place, and their incorporation into colonial structures seemed to have been a pacification tool.

Although female vis-à-vis male membership in these local administrative councils was minimal, some of the scholarship describes the presence of women in the hitherto all-male colonial system as a 'major development'.[39] After 1929, women also began to play a greater role in the selection of new chiefs who headed the local administration, and the 1930 Owerri Province Annual Report stated that '[p]ractically no new chief has been selected without the consent of the women of his town, and [that] he is in their hands if he wishes to keep their goodwill'.[40] Chuku (2009) rightly argues against regarding these few political appointments 'as evidence of the colonial government's effort to protect and promote female political power and authority in Igbo region. Rather, one can categorically state that colonialism undermined Igbo women's political power'.[41]

Consigning women's incorporation into the edifice of colonial government to the contradictory status of a 'major development' does not however, address the necessary question that this response by the colonial state raises: that is, why would the colonial state subordinate its primary weapon of maintaining law and order – *violence* – to modes of social control that depended on the incorporation of those (women) who were marginal to its political project? The literature suggests that the incorporation of women would not have been imaginable prior to the war, thus suggesting that the transition of women into the political imagination of the state was rendered possible only through *the event of violence*. In other words, that violence itself *constitutes the condition of possibility* of women's subjectivation and legibility as political subjects of the state.

This is an argument that exceeds the biopolitical idea of reading such modes of incorporation of women as constituting the security apparatus of the state.[42] Rather, my intention is to preliminarily pose a question I explore in Chapter 4 regarding what it is that violence *does* in the colonial situation – an analytical shift to understand gendered violence away from its gratuitous manifestations in contexts of slavery. The Women's War illustrates an often obscured but significant insight into the colonial attitude towards women: that retaliation for revolt by means of direct violence against revolutionaries would undermine the civilizational narrative that was constructed around saving colonized women. This did not prevent the state from *provoking* violence and granting it legitimacy through the recognition and incorporation of women into its structures – only from granting to women the status of legitimate subjects of violence and therefore of redress.

Neither has the postcolonial framework of democracy succeeded in escaping this trap. From women's marches in Nairobi and Namibia demanding an end to femicide, to young women baring their bodies to police brutality on the frontlines of the #FeesMustFall movements in South Africa and the #EndSars movement in Nigeria, the state has characteristically pacified women by reconstituting itself as a *police state*. By unleashing its law enforcement machinery in ever greater numbers ostensibly to 'protect' women and girls. But the law-and-order response of the state to gendered violence suggests a fundamental difficulty at the core of postcolonial democracy which is evidenced by its failure to respond to women *as political subjects* of the state – women as legitimate subjects of democracy. Belated innovations by the colonial regime to bring women into the framework of administration of customary colonial power thus seemed to be a ploy to undermine women's power wherever it was visible, and could not have empowered them.[43]

Customary Law and Subjects of Repugnancy

> Strategies of endurance and subsistence do not yield easily to the grand narrative of revolution, nor has a space been cleared for the sex worker, welfare mother, and domestic laborer in the annals of the black radical tradition.[44]

It has been argued of the repugnancy clauses, whose function had been to mark the limits of customary laws, that colonists pointed to 'a desire for connections with a wider legal and political world that custom simply [could] not provide'.[45] In other words, it was through acts such as extending the boundaries of the exception that the colonial state confirmed its sovereign authority over the colonies. It is through rape and sexual assault that we 'encountered a limit sphere of human action that is only ever maintained in a relation of exception...the sphere of the sovereign decision, which suspends law in the state of exception and thus implicates bare life within it'.[46] It is a sphere that confirms to the colonized body its indispensability and its absolute negation. As the elaboration below of the boundaries that established repugnancy shows, women's bodies and the demarcation of modernity based on crimes against them proved absolutely essential for defining colonial modernity, as well as subjectivating women into the juridical state in very specific ways as threatened *and* dangerous bodies, thus warranting a kind of 'protection' that would demand future regulation by the means of both law and order.

A moral approach marked the colonial attitude towards native women, both on the part of the colonists and of native men. Sexuality and the moral discourses which framed it emerged as a domain of struggle that defined women as sexually deviant even as the necessity of the labour of prostitution for the stabilization of the male native migrant labour force was defended by colonists. The law was ambiguous on moral questions surrounding women's sexual lives, and granted significant scope to native men through native authorities to decide such cases. This could have been one basis for consolidating the 'male deals' that constituted the relationship between colonists and native men. The law, however, was unequivocal in its intervention into sexual violence cases against native women and in that domain, it established an exception.

The shape which customary laws took established an antagonism between the colonial modernity of women (which accorded to women some recognition in statutory law), and the cultural constraint of customary laws which denied them political legibility. In colonial Kenya, for instance, Robertson (1997) provides material to interrogate the basis of the tolerance that colonial officials displayed for prostitution, on the one hand, and the hard stance it took in relation to sexual violence on the other. Those (women and men) viewed as 'undesirables' by the administration in Nairobi continued to be deported to the reserves, 'but neither prostitutes nor traders were greatly harassed in the 1930s'.[47] It was rather African authorities that made many attempts to stop women's trade to Nairobi in the 1930s to such an extent that the Nairobi Native Advisory Council asked that the rigorous pass law of 1921 be extended to women for this purpose.[48] As Robertson writes, 'the fact that African men but not women at this time were restricted by pass laws must have caused considerable resentment and heightened concern over women escaping men's control'.[49] While for colonists, the reproductive labour economy that was fed by prostitution remained central to the colonial endeavour of native control and could be defended, for native men whose cultural bases of control were being undermined through the increasing urbanization of women, control was re-established on the basis of a morality which they could freely adjudicate:

> Like local courts in Ghana and Zimbabwe, the Nairobi Native Tribunal, established in 1930, spent much of its time on adultery cases, which "in deference to native law and custom" the British authorities *allowed to be criminalized* so long as a fine was the punishment. The . . . Local Native Tribunals dealt with a steady stream of cases in which men sued each other for enticing away their wives or daughters.[50]

The exception seemed to have been offences of a *sexual* nature against women – that is, violence that would have created ambiguity regarding the monopoly over violence, which the colonial modern state wielded through a sovereign claim over the colonies. It was the *direct violation* of women that came under statutory (modern) adjudication, not the gendered economies of violence which defined the colonial situation in general:

> The DC left the adultery cases to the Native Tribunal, but rape and indecent assault were tried as *criminal offences under British law*, not subject to customary law that treated women as property and compensated men for property damage or loss.[51]

This ought to be apparent as being through and through, a liberal subjectivation of women; no doubt reactionary but nonetheless having the effect of having rendered women as subjects of the state. The colonial state furthermore, seems to have been establishing, through its statutory ringfencing of *direct* forms of sexual violence (rape and indecent assault) its own monopoly over violence. That prostitution and adultery did not exceed the realms of customary adjudication suggests a deliberate delineation between its modern subjects and its 'traditional' ones; between harms that threatened to undermine colonial political authority over natives and those culturally defined harms that insulated the state and exposed the 'backwardness' of traditional authorities and therefore consolidated or justified the bifurcation of the colonial state between the rural and urban realm.

The criminalization of rape this early on would also undoubtedly have signalled to women an idea of the (colonial) state as the ultimate authority of reference in as far as their 'protection' was concerned. The contemporary appeal to the state as the main arbiter of rape on behalf of women has in this regard, its antecedent in the colonial state. The regulation of gendered violence within the sphere of statutory law under the ruse of 'protecting' women masked a relatively obscure fact: that because gendered violence was one of the avenues through which repugnancy in customary laws constituted statutory law through the exception, *gendered violence did constitute at least one condition of possibility* for the constitution of statutory law. The quest for gender justice in postcolonial democracies would as such need to confront the question regarding the (gendered) violence which the colonial state embedded in statutory law.

The juridical subjectivation of women through the statutory recognition and adjudication of rape by the colonial state is not without irony, since the colonial state by its very methods of establishing social control and realization of its economic imperative via primitive accumulation *is* violent. The abrogation of juridical authority over matters concerning sexual violence would have alienated women from their kin communities and deepened the need by traditional authorities to retain some control over women's productive and reproductive labour – not an entirely irrational reaction given the patriarchal crisis which colonization had already visited upon native men. Yet this control also likely provided unwarranted cover for the colonial state's own patriarchal attitude towards women – a contrived distinction between two interlinked realms of gendered violence (modern and traditional) that set the stage for women's contemporary appeal to the democratizing state to adjudicate sexual violence, and in neglect of the customary domains that did and continue to engender violence against them.

This historical appeal that established for women a liberal individualist subjectivity in relation to the state through the crime of rape took shape through a distinct shift in the adjudication of rape away from customary to statutory domains of authority. Kanogo (2005), for instance, writes of colonial Kenya that 'throughout the 1920s, 30s, and 40s sexual violation of adult and juvenile females received increasing government attention [and that] the 1930s were particularly replete with court cases on rape charges. Women could seek redress in formal courts [and] communities increasingly enlisted the official sanction of the colonial state'.[52] The juridical implications of the shift from intramural resolution or 'social diffusion' of sexual violence – from the 'traditional communalization of culpability and litigation, whereby *clans* were the litigants in cases of rape . . . in contrast to the colonial process, which *individualized litigation and responsibility*' – demands scrutiny.[53] It is, after all, a significant observation that the colonial state made every effort

> to eradicate the communal interest in the issue and to attribute personal responsibility for sex-related offences. [That]…litigation reconfigured the punishment for rape in a manner that attempted to *bring the legal personhood of the women to the fore.*[54]

The attribution of personal responsibility for sexual violence to the perpetrator juridically subjectivates women in opposition to a defined perpetrator rather than to the *colonising structure* that requires violence. This is a fact that fundamentally undermines any anticolonial aspiration, that must necessarily focus on the structures of violence as a whole. The move to displace criminality onto 'problem people'[55] rather than acknowledging the structures that produce problems for people, generates adversarial relationalities among the colonized themselves and reconstitutes the colonising structure as an *adjudicating* and benevolent structure that *finally* recognizes victims of violence.

Colonial contexts elsewhere have been confronted with a similar dilemma, as Tanaka (2002) shows in his critique of the gendered manifestations of Japan's colonial misadventures in Korea during World War II. In her foreword to Tanaka's book, Susan Brownmiller generally establishes the gendered subject that emerged through 'a highly organized trafficking system during the Pacific War run by the Japanese Imperial Army, secret police, and local "labor recruitors" using the ruse of legitimate jobs for good pay'.[56] For the sole purpose of serving Japan's war effort, 'girls and women taken from country villages, or hijacked in broad daylight on city streets, became a human cargo that was transported to barracks on frontline posts, jungle airstrips, and base camps, where the captives remained in sexual servitude until the war's end'.[57] Although the establishment of the comfort women system was sanctioned at the highest level of state,[58] culpability for these crimes remained with the soldiers:

> Crimes against POWs were in most cases carried out under orders, and soldiers could easily endanger their own lives by disobeying orders. The exploitation of comfort women, also a serious crime against humanity, was, however, *a matter of personal choice*, and in this sense, those Japanese men who chose to avail themselves of this facility undoubtedly bear personal responsibility for the crimes that they directly committed against the comfort women they used. Considered purely from a viewpoint of the "motive for the crime," personal responsibility in this situation is far more serious than in instances in which soldiers acted under orders to commit atrocities.[59]

Several groups of Asian women were victims of the Japanese, including Koreans, Taiwanese, Chinese, and Filipinas. Dutch women were also taken from internment camps in Java to serve in the comfort stations, and there was 'enforced military prostitution of large numbers of Eurasian (Dutch-Indonesian) and Indonesian women that began in 1943. Here, Tanaka (2002) establishes an exception: 'Dutch military authorities subsequently vigorously prosecuted those Japanese responsible for the exploitation of *Dutch* women, but not those who similarly victimized Eurasian and Indonesian women'.[60] The US and other Allied forces also failed to prosecute Japanese who had committed crimes against Asian women, despite the fact that they had accumulated ample evidence of the system of military sexual slavery.[61]

Collective punishment was deemed necessary only for sexual crimes committed against European women – crimes committed against European *power*. At least one thing is implicit in this formulation: that a distinction seems to have been drawn between racialized and gendered subjects of violence – between those (white women) whose rights were established by sovereign power and those (colonized women) who rights were established through patriarchal power. A distinction also between legibility to the state through its *political* form and legibility through its *social* form. Only through its latter form could the state plausibly establish an exception.

Similarly, within African colonies, it can be shown that rape – *social* violence – had constituted the *exception*: it established repugnancy through one of the most violent of means, as evidence of the barbarity of the colonized and therefore, solid justification for the moral intervention of colonists. In other words, the arrogation of the crime of rape away from customary adjudication into the domain of statutory law *made modern juridical subjects* of colonized women and established a further basis for colonial domination in general. If the domain of customary authority was the primary domain for the political control of natives, then the transfer of rape adjudication from that domain into the domain of statutory law suggests a depoliticization of the issue of sexual (gendered) violence by the colonial state.[62] Furthermore, that it is the crime of rape that brought women directly into the purview of statutory law, and therefore control of the state, is significant. Crudely put, acts of (sexual) violence preceded women's legibility to the state, and thus constituted a primary condition for both original and *sustained* legibility in modern law.[63]

Nietzschean *ressentiment* must here, enter our discourse regarding the sustained occurrence of sexual violations against women despite the extensive legislation that today exists to defend us against sexual harm.[64] That is, that we ought to consider the reasons that contemporary (liberal) democratic society has not been able to do away with, or modify, this colonial condition of women's legibility to the state. At the very least, the implication is that if injuries sustained in the nature of rape constitute the basis of political recognition in the state, then this constitutes a *political necessity* which is uniquely shouldered by gendered subjects of violence. In other words, gendered violence as a basis for political recognition provides an alibi for ever greater regulation and legislation of gendered bodies and lives.

Colonial society was fundamentally structured (and fractured) by violence, a reality which the anticolonial project must, to paraphrase Fanon, recognize as its mission to undo, and when it does, either betray or fulfil this task of eliminating the necessity of violence which seems so hardwired into processes of subject formation as undertaken by/within the colonial modern state. And so, an endless cycle of *ressentiment* that is built into recognition of rights claims by the state, in which the clamour for democracy is considered as offering the best possible means for redress. The postcolonial democratizing state is burdened from the onset with a punitive approach to justice which necessarily undermines the historical basis of claims. In other words, individual culpability obliterates the political basis for justice. Where the state cannot claim responsibility for violent society, those who experience its modern violence are cast adrift, permanently in search of a perpetrator that they might hold up to the state for prosecution, all in the name of exercising a 'democratic right' to redress.

Juridical vs. Political Subjectivation from the Margins

> If a small burglary is likely to improve his legal position, at least temporarily, one may be sure he has been deprived of human rights… For then a criminal offense becomes the best opportunity to regain some kind of human equality, even if it be as a recognized exception to the norm.[65]

Arendt's subjects above are they who suddenly find themselves stateless, those 'new refugees [who] were persecuted not because of what they had done or thought, but because of what they unchangeably were – *born into the wrong kind of race or the wrong kind of class*'.[66] Those, similar to the native subject trapped in the colonial situation, whose conditions of existence did not permit them to abide by the law because colonial customary laws had been invented not to protect the native but rather to reconstitute natives as governable subjects of the colonial state – at once located at the margins of civil law, stereotyped as law breaking, criminalized through such stereotyping, and therefore deemed punishable at will. The colonial situation that 'prevented [native subjects] from being law-abiding' was in part realizable because their personhood was linked not to the basic quality of being individually human in the world, but to the *collective* nature of their subjectivation: that is, as belonging to a class, race, gender, sexuality, caste, or ethnic group that in reality constituted the basis of control by the colonial state. For the colonized, legibility to the state was achieved through the group, not as individuals.

Through this group logic, the stage was set for a fundamental irreconcilability in the postcolony, between the liberal human rights canon that interpellates people as individuals, and the anticolonial/liberation demands that are directed, necessarily through the collective, towards the democratizing state. History accurately tells us that group claims invariably undermine individual claims, primarily because any articulation of intra-group violence tends to undermine the progressive façade of the group – that is, chips away at the moral basis of its political project. If, as I have already argued in Chapter 1, the characterisation of gendered violence follows ethnic, class, gender, caste, or racial logics,[67] then it logically follows that the juridical subjectivation of women who experience sexual violence (through, for instance, anti-rape legislation) would contradict their political subjectivation as members of the group. In this regard, a fundamental problem facing the postcolonial democratizing state is the dilemma of reconciling its juridical and political ideas of justice.

This tension is demonstrable in the colonies, where juridical narratives concealed 'exceptional elements of intimacy' due to the need to formulate jurisprudence along tangible lines of evidence of the modernity of the colonizing regime.[68] In the context of colonial Kenya, Luongo (2010) studies the case of a witch-murder trial, *Rex versus Ali Mwinyi*, 'in which domestic dramas underlay (alleged) occult acts of violence'.[69] Both the prosecution and defence concealed the fact that the initial act of bewitchment which led to the murder for which the accused, Ali Mwinyi, was being persecuted also included an incidence of male rape. To Luongo, the case reveals 'how colonial jurisprudence regarded the African household as an imaginary space in which violence occur[ed] as both normalcy and criminality'. More significantly, the case shows how acts of sexual violence could be fetishized, alienated from the material/cultural milieu of native life, to the extent that 'witchcraft' was one of the few available categories for talking about intimate violence among close associates in domestic spaces. Witchcraft as a discursive category was much more available to natives than either rape, the only legal classification overtly addressing violence in the arena of the intimate, or 'unnatural offences,' the primary legal classification for dealing with sex (consensual or otherwise) between men'.[70] The occult was intangible, and so were the cultures that framed it.[71]

This case foregrounds a problem that would likely face any evidence-based legal system (as was Kenya), which would demand 'operational categories that are readily discernible, neatly bounded, and subject to *stable* formation'. But in the colonies, where 'governmentality in the criminal sphere centered on the state's claim to a monopoly on the legitimate exercise of violence,'[72]

> [a]uthorities reinforced this claim discursively, consistently juxtaposing the "rationality" of modern, state-centered legal systems with the "repugnancy" of backward, local "customary" laws. The state took an instrumental view of violence when assessing its subjects' behaviors and wielded instrumental violence through punishments such as flogging and hanging. Both routinized and ad hoc state violence also took a mundane variety of forms.[73]

It is necessary at this point to pose the question regarding the function which violence *did* in fact serve in the colonies, and whether some distinction can be drawn between the use of violence in the colonial context and its use in other modern states of their origin. Here again, Luongo (2010) is instructive in identifying a fundamental contradiction between the approaches of the local customary legal domain and the state in how each dealt with violence. According to her,

> [w]here[as] the state sought to create categories of "punishable people" and to discipline them via confinement and/or violence, most local juridical systems… sought to identify and punish, *sometimes through juridical violence*, "categories of dangerous persons" apt to perpetrate violence against bodies, spirits, and psyche. Yet, many of the sorts of social [offenders], such as witches, who fell into 'categories of dangerous persons' identified by local communities often did *not* qualify as practically punishable in the eyes of the state. In the legal interstices created by the state's emphasis on instrumental violence, *local forms of juridical violence often superseded the state's dictates.*[74]

Excesses emerging from the traditional realms of colonized society did not threaten the state's power enough to warrant bringing such violence under its direct control. It ought to be striking that 'the conflict concerning the state the most was that over who retained the right to legitimately wield violence':[75] and in this regard, that rape clearly was defined as one such conflict. In colonial Kenya (as in other colonies), the Kenya Legislative Council elevated rape to a capital crime in 1926 thus rendering the Kenya High Court the 'sole provenance for persecuting rape'.[76] Such interventions created room for the state to 'delve into the toolbox of *lawfare*, the use of law as a weapon of domination in order to (re)assert hegemony over the use of violence'.[77] Interestingly, both Luongo (2010) and Jackson (2002) the latter writing in the context of Southern Rhodesia, link the highly punitive approach of the colonial state towards rape as being a response to 'Black Peril',[78] a narrative which erases black female sexuality by reifying white female personhood as threatened by black male sexuality. In other words, pointing to a different motivation for the regulation of black women's bodies.

Colonial statutory provisions on rape only clearly targeted *black women's* bodies. That colonial law, that most modern of instruments of subjectivation established its primary *civil* subject in the colonies through black womanhood is a matter of contradiction. In Southern Rhodesia, Jackson (2002) writes that 'the focus upon sexual relations between European women and African men [Black Peril], and the exclusion of relations between European men and African women, created [certain] regulatory contradictions'.[79] Most significant was that it was a concern with capitalist accumulation and *labour* that seemed to establish the criminality of violent sexual relations between men and women. The rape or attempted rape of black women by white men was not considered perilous – 'sex between white men and black women, consensual or nonconsensual (except in the most brutal case) . . . was not a criminal offense'.[80] And Black Peril could thrive even without an environment in which actual cases of black-on-white rape were rare, since the ideological foundation of that discourse was 'white supremacy and the commitment to the preservation of whiteness'.[81] African women's bodies were regulated 'for their potential to infect African men with venereal disease',[82] their potential to undermine the vitality of black male labour and the reproduction of colonial economy more generally:

> From the late 1910s, the state, mining capital, European landowners, and various categories of African men became increasingly concerned about regulating the bodies of mobile and unattached African women. In general, policy makers and spokespersons for mining and agricultural capital sought the regulation, *but not the prohibition*, of such women in urban space. They sought the regulation of their genitalia.[83]

I have already established in Chapter 2 a central contradiction of colonialism as having been its methods of mobilization and utilization of wage labour: colonists could create and recruit a wage labour force but could not maintain it, meaning that the conditions of wage labour had to be reconstructed over and again, necessitating regular return to the countryside to replenish its labour force:[84] the political economy proper, of social reproduction. I have also shown that it is the realm of reproduction where the limits of colonial control became most apparent. The figure of the mobile native women – the prostitute – established the relationship between women's labour and colonial control of native populations. In Southern Rhodesia, while African Christian leaders sought to prevent African women from traveling to towns without patriarchal consent and/or company, '[g]overnment officials and industrial capitalists . . . resisted this form of control because women contributed to the "daily reproduction" of the African male wage labour force'.[85] Prostitutes also apparently protected white women against Black Peril, providing a 'safeguard to native men's instincts'.

The laws that legislated against the rape of African women made modern juridical subjects of native women, while those that controlled their movement, sexuality, and womanhood through the concern with disease control (the '[criminalization and pathologization] of single and mobile women') made political subjects of them – the two in seemingly permanent tension. The pathologization of African women's bodies as disease-bearing distinguished them from white women, and through this racialization of maternal labouring bodies, politicized gendered labour.[86] At the same time, the criminalization of black men for the rape of black women rendered sexual violence unrecognizable without the Black body (both male and female) and the law an instrument that both affirms and maintain this relationality. A fundamental concern facing the postcolonial democratization project then, would be whether the colonized are better off seeking justice from the juridical state (concerned with an adjudication of violent *acts*), versus seeking justice from the political/politicized state (concerned with redistribution between racial, gendered, class, and ethnic groups).

This antagonism plays out in the contemporary stage of democratization through on the one hand, capitalism's insatiable demand for women's care and reproductive labour that is subsumed within discourses of 'development' that routinely deny women historical (and thus, political) subjectivity.[87] On the other hand lies the onerous burden that the state places on women to justify their demand for safety and protection from sexual harm – that is, the law's requirement for *evidence* of injury. This is similar to the colonial situation in which African women's political subjectivity could not be established on the basis simply of their being human. Rather, state interventions into black womanhood did suggest a humanity mediated not only by negation of black women's sexuality, but by the claim of ultimate control over their reproductive labour, through a cycle involving the: recognition of injury → legislation → redress → and again injury. A dialectic of violence that configures the state as both guarantor of rights and mediator of capitalist violence.

If social subjectivity be the primary means through which the governed enter into the political imagination of the state[88] then the structures and institutions *within* which people acquire such subjectivity – whether these be marriage, divorce, labour, religion, or education – would constitute arenas not only of cultural and social struggle, but also fundamentally, of struggle between the juridical form of the state and its political form. Of struggle between the state as a guarantor of rights and the state as a mediator of conflict between various competing groups and interests. In Vinogradoff's (1924) argument 'a fundamental problem in every system of law consists in settling the legal relations between the State and its members – both the individuals and the juridical persons'.[89] One might add to this the imperative in the postcolony of reconstituting the legal system as a battlefield in which the old grounds that established juridical personhood through violence give way to new grounds in which violence harbours the possibility of justice.

My concern in this chapter has been with colonial administrative practices in the colonies, examined via a critique of the juridical and administrative mechanisms through which colonized people emerged as gendered subjects that both experience violence and commit violence in the colonial and postcolonial state. Codification of customary laws reveals, among other things, the indirect interpellation of women as juridical beings – the law as a subjectivating agent as such. This analytical lens also exposes a problem which the customary law literature generally obscures: that capitalist patriarchy severs woman *qua* subject to the law from being subject of, or creator of the law. The substantial negation of woman as subject of the law is *structurally necessitated* by the material social system (capitalism) that enables modern law and human rights to *be*, and that eventually reduce her to being mainly under the law (subject to it), a condition in which she has no say in the determination of the values, concerns and frameworks under which she operates.

Her say in these values, concerns and frameworks could, in principle, protect her from forced reproductive labour, that is, from being *in fact* a sexualized object, a subject that has no possibility of free self-determination. Yet, under modern capitalist conditions, this is wishful thinking because without social reproductive labour, the material basis of the social system of which modern law is an expression, collapses. If this holds, in this framework, the conditions of possibility of modern law that structurally violates women make any legal protection of them appear as a contradiction to the keen eye. I see this as a fundamental contradiction rather than a mere ruse, typical of liberalism. It is an exclusive inclusion: formal legal equality heightened by protection on sexual matters on the one hand and substantial structural inequality on the other.

A number of other residual questions emerge out of this chapter. For instance, one might ask what it is that is *distinctive* of the modern democratic (and capitalist) state in the postcolony as both guarantor of rights and mediator of capitalist violence as far as women are concerned. Is it that the inheritance of colonial structures (women as unfree subjects because they were originally colonial subjects) alters what seems a structural aspect, namely that women *qua* women are forced into a sexualized identity and social reproduction by the modern capitalist state? Or is what one witnesses in the postcolony something *sui generis* – merely the naked logic of the modern state?

Furthermore, there remains a rhetorical and potentially theoretical tension in my declared interest in Foucault's notion of juridical power exceeding sovereignty, and the deployment of the exception in the tradition of Schmitt-Agamben as an explanatory notion for what follows. As in Foucault's governmentality, sovereignty is presupposed throughout the chapter as a power of violating and violated agency ascribable to the state and women. The question which these formulations raise is whether at all one can *resist* without invoking the concept of sovereignty, roughly understood as the power of self-determination.

Lastly, the chapter conceals a longing for the sovereignty of a postcolonial state that could effectively democratize and guarantee justice, if the tension or contradiction between its legal and political dimensions is addressed. But is the settling of legal relations possible entirely through legal means? The response to this question is not so clearly in the negative, since at issue is the foundation of the law, which is often (or always?) extra-legal, and *irreducibly political*. This means that separating and opposing the legal and the political through the highlighting of their being in tension obscures their constitutive relation at inception. More important still, highlighting that tension without bringing it back to material forces may mean the loss of analytical sharpness. It is then my intention to offer in the remainder of the book, a more explicit reflection on this suggested nexus between the legal-political-economic.

4

'Captive Maternals' and the Modern Subject of Gendered Violence

By so much as the defective eyesight of the white world rejects black women as beauties, by so much more it needs them as human beings, an enviable alternative, as many a white woman knows. Consequently, for black women alone, as a group, "handsome is that handsome does" and they are asked to be no more beautiful than God made them, but they are asked to be efficient, to be strong, fertile, muscled, and able to work. *If they marry, they must as independent workers be able to help support their children, for their men are paid on a scale which makes* sole support of the family often impossible.[1]

The ability to control violence is the ability to engage in stable living and reproduction of communities that are healthy.[2]

*Democracy inherently has a predatory tendency. . .*a predatory habit or addiction to the expropriation and exploitation *of the captive subject that is Black.*[3]

The modern subject of democracy is a captive subject.[4] And because throughout the course of modern state formation, dominion over labour and territory has been sustained through captivity, it is the case that the captive subject is also fundamentally *a labouring subject*. The demand for their labour performs many functions: it satisfies the production and consumption needs of capitalist accumulation; is deployed towards reproduction of the patriarchal culture; it sustains the daily and generational reproduction of the workers (social reproduction); and may be appropriated for the maintenance of law and order. From the vantage point of the enslaved and the colonized, this interpellation as labouring subjects is a historical continuation of a modernity that requires, imagines and renders as a permanent feature of its structure, the 'Captive Maternal' – that figure who must repeatedly encounter their fate as unfree while acknowledging their inherent fungibility: 'My country needs me, and if I were not here, I would have to be invented'.[5] Reinstating this labouring substratum into the mainstream of modern critiques of democracy – and against democracy's claims, the unfreedom and violence that is their fate – is my objective in this chapter.

The idea of captivity is central to an understanding of the stabilization of native rule and colonial dominion over land and labour, yet remains marginal in the literature, perhaps owing to the gendered conditions that make it possible. My basic concern in what follows is to elaborate this relationship between colonization and captivity. Partly inspired by the figure embodied in Joy James's 'Captive Maternals' – those whom she describes in *The Womb of Western Theory* as 'most vulnerable to violence, war, poverty, policy and captivity; those whose very existence enables the possessive empire that claims and dispossesses them' – I also argue for a reconsideration of what gendered violence *does* for democracy.[6] While undoubtedly gendered, James's captive subject is not reducibly female: the 'womb' that nurtures and insulates colonists is generated and maintained through violence against both women and men. Why then, do women and men survive colonial captivity so differently? What explains women's enduring vulnerability to gendered violence even in the postcolonial democratizing state? My response to these questions proceeds from a re-examination of the effects of various social techniques and administrative regimes through which colonized women and men were coerced into the structures of the colonial political economy as reproductive labour. Embedded in this critique is an elaboration of the historical/modernist link between the subject of violence in the colonies and the contemporary subject of gendered violence in the postcolonial democratizing state. As the chapter renders apparent, democracy's claim of minimizing violence does not withstand scrutiny when examined against the gendered structures that colonial captivity enacts.[7]

In public, Captive Maternals are by design in the minority (e.g. movement leaders, union organizers, school heads, political leaders; and other public authority figures such as teachers, policemen, doctors and social workers). Away from the public gaze, these captives constitute the masses, their struggles concealed but fundamental to the survival of both the oppressive system and the liberation struggle itself. The latter, writes Joy James, are the 'anonymous counterparts' to the former: the masses are 'the more typical "Captive Maternals" – those most vulnerable to violence, war, poverty, police and captivity; those whose very existence *enables the possessive empire* that claims and dispossesses them'.[8] Captive Maternals defy the perjury of normative gender, and can be 'either biological females or those feminized into caretaking and consumption'.[9] James makes a further striking distinction that enjoins this form of labouring with captivity, and links both to the very possibility of empire: 'it is not their victimization that marks them; it is their productivity and its consumption. Throughout history, Captive Maternals provided the reproductive and productive labour to *stabilize* culture and wealth'.[10]

This point regarding the reproductive necessity in the stabilization of empire is one I have highlighted in earlier work, although an important conceptual departure in James's framing, which I adopt in the current study, is the analytical focus on a 'gendered' subject rather than woman. This conceptual shift does not at all preclude a serious consideration of women, and my interest in women as a political category remains central to this project. In fact, drawing out a gendered relationality in critiquing the oppressive structures of empire allows us to pose specific questions regarding women's particular vulnerability to gendered violence. That is to say, if both colonized women and men are reproduced within the same violent historical structure and normative order of domination, how are we to make sense of the differential effects of their postcolonial subjectivities, which seem to draw a line between those who commit violence on the one hand, and on the other, those who experience violence? At which points in their captivity does gender determine such contradictory outcomes for the colonized? And through what processes might we understand 'gendering'?

Gender always shapes experiences of subjectivity. However, thinking gender in the space of captivity rather than of liberal individuality (the latter, the departure point of Western feminisms)[11] demands at least two important conceptual shifts. One, as I have already highlighted in relation to the problems of theorizing intersectionality in Chapter 1, is the fact that the colonized experience oppression as a group rather than as individuals. This means that the function which gender performs in this context has to be understood in relation to the structures, conditions and institutions that maintain the group as a *coherent* whole (whether it be within the ethnic, the racial, the caste, or the class structures). Second and relatedly, the function of violence in the context of captivity shifts from the objective of singularly harming the individual, towards the structural function of *maintaining the conditions* under which the (racial, ethnic, caste, gendered and class) group is reproduced and exploited. Violence is as such, a fundamental condition for the reproduction of captive groups.

For the colonized, individuality is rendered impossible by the fact that their 'conscription' denies them any choice or free will of becoming agents of any other than the group.[12] Under conditions of captivity, the group itself is the *raison d'être*, the basis of 'being let to live': it is within it that captives gain legibility to the (colonial) state[13] – as 'migrant workers', 'domestic worker', 'askaris', 'waste pickers' and so on. Group agency as a defining feature of colonialism as such presents a fundamental contradiction to the postcolonial democratizing state with its basis in liberal individualism: that is, the fact that claims issued in the language of 'rights' do not become available to everyone. Many are denied such a possibility and are thus permanently condemned to the collective.[14] These are the 'Captive Maternals'. This point is illustrable in the recognition which liberal constitutionalism grants to 'women' – the 'invention of women' – while denying the gendered labour and captive maternity that historically constituted womanhood through colonial intervention. I shall return to this critique later on in the chapter.

My initial formulation of these ideas on the relationship between the (colonial) state and gendered violence focused as well on the question of labour. My core argument then was that while women had not been the subject proper of colonial rule, the appropriation and exploitation of their productive and reproductive labour towards the reproduction of the settler colonial political economy did function to ensure that women constituted a crucial possibility of indirect rule.[15] My central concern then had been to demonstrate the colonial foundations of the violence that women experience in the postcolonial state. My earlier analysis, however, was restricted to a critique of gendered violence associated with political competitions in the specific context of multiparty politics. A very preliminary argument I put forward at the time was that the mechanisms of colonial rule needed to be understood not only politically in relation to the bifurcation of the colonial state, but also with regard to the structural dynamics that facilitated the stabilization of the bifurcated domains of colonial rule.

The stabilization of the tribalized domains of native authority was highly articulated to the productive and reproductive roles to which labouring women in the colonies were confined as the migrant cash crop economy expanded. Women's legibility as social subjects (their subjectivity) could not be understood outside of their roles within these tribalized realms. If women marked the external boundaries of those tribalized native colonies, then the often-violent processes through which their bodies and labours were controlled and regulated needed to be understood as a key basis for consolidating tribalized identities in the native reserves. In other words, as part and parcel of a process of 'ethnic mapping'[16] that dangerously marked African women's bodies, set them up as boundaries of the ethnic community and therefore also as 'soft' targets of the interethnic rivalries and violence ushered by the 'define and rule'[17] strategies that the colonial state pursued under indirect rule.

My present concern is similarly with the persistence of gendered violence in the postcolonial state. But whereas I stopped short of elaborating my earlier claim that women were central to the stabilization of the colonial state even though they had not been its primary (political) subject, my current claim is that women's (social) reproductive labour far exceeds the agency which political subjectivity alone might confer. The background question framing this claim is this: how does a state that lacks political legitimacy (the recognized right to rule)[18] in its proclaimed territory establish dominion over its putative subjects? The apparent answer is that it does so by brute force.

But the notion of legitimacy requires modification if it is to be understood in the colonial context. Since the normative basis of the colonial state's legitimacy (its right to rule) does not emanate from a consensus with colonized people, its rule, including its coercive force, is ultimately illegitimate. As the literature shows, native resistance was a predominant response to the coercive force of the colonial state, and the shift to indirect rule – the social, administrative and cultural move to 'subordinate race to tribe'[19] – was the most logical approach to the stabilization of restive populations. It is in these *social* domains of governance that the gendered apparatus of the state is rendered most apparent: those, like colonized women, that are interpellated by the state through logics primarily directed towards the social control of natives thus constitute the basis of its legitimacy. I argue in this regard that as *social subjects*, women developed a distinct relationship to the colonial state and therefore should be considered as having been its quintessential modern subject.

Viewed in this sense – indirect rule was much more than political intervention – it constituted a social intervention into native life, affecting the colonized within various social locations including class (labour), gender (sexuality) and ethnicity (identity). This historical and political interpellation of modern democratic political subjects – that is, the unique historical baggage that those bounded together by oppression and colonial violence carry into the postcolonial state – should therefore be a primary concern of democratic politics. To ignore this is to negate the modernist constitution of political subjectivity that emerged within a particular political economy of colonial rule that depended on the captivity of gendered labours, identities and sexualities. Both of these silences also therefore relegate the necessity of posing new questions to the enduring legacies of colonial modernity – new questions that better reflect our current political times and social predicaments.

My attempt in this chapter is to do precisely this: to modify an old question regarding the centrality of gendered labour in the stabilization of the colonial political economy by posing to it the additional question regarding how gendered labour mediates not just social subjectivity, but also political legibility in the postcolonial democratizing state. I do so by refracting contemporary gendered violence back to the colonial political economy, through a critique inspired by the figure and framework of the 'Captive Maternals' – who I liken to the gendered labourer that had been the condition of possibility of the stabilization of indirect rule, as their forced servitude anchored the colonial political economy in a chain of captivity that runs from the household domain of social reproduction of labour power, to industry, plantations and mines, to native administration and to imperialist expansion. An understanding of the social techniques of captivity and administrative regimes through which colonized women and men were coerced into the structures of the colonial political economy as labour constitute my analysis here. In doing so, I seek to draw a historical link between the subject of violence in the colonies and the contemporary subject of violence in the democratizing state, through the conceptual notions of difference, reproduction, captivity, fugitivity and gendered labour.

Difference and the colonial social question

That political identity is the quintessential basis and distinctive approach to colonial rule has already been convincingly argued.[20] Although Mamdani's consideration of difference is mainly as a mode of political control, the tendency towards institutionalization that he highlights broadens the scope for the consideration of difference as being also the basis of social control:

> The management of difference is the holy cow of the modern study of society, just as it is central to modern statecraft. The shift from a homogenizing impulse to a preoccupation with defining and managing difference is most evident in the transition from direct to indirect rule . . . It is under indirect rule colonialism that the definition and management of difference was developed as the essence of governance. The difference between the modern democratic state and its colonial version is this: the modern state ensures equal citizenship in political society while acknowledging difference in civil society, but its colonial counterpart *institutionalized difference in both the polity and society.*[21]

Extended to the social milieu, this last point of emphasis suggests that indirect rule envisioned a convergence whereby existing social categories would mirror the various needs of the colonizing state (i.e. wage labour, administrative and reproductive labour). The political subjectivity (consciousness) that emerged in relation to wage labourers was class; the consciousness that emerged from the domain of traditional administration was tribalism;[22] and that which emerged from the social reproduction of natives was gender. It is these emergent political subjectivities or forms of consciousness that the state would instrumentalize towards control of the native population. The *social base* thus contained within it the necessary ingredients for the manufacturing of difference – that is, for the racialization, ethnicization, classing and gendering of native society.

While some of the literature suggests a primarily political imperative behind the colonial response to the native question – that is, how a small white minority could govern a native majority – its identitarian approach suggests that colonization had to have affected colonized societies at the level also of the social relationships that were necessary for natives to survive, produce and reproduce their means of life. It suggests, in other words, that changes in the social-economic processes of labouring people were essential to the stabilization of colonial rule. For instance, as Guy shows in the South African context, 'while homesteads could no longer exist as productive, animate, communities and were now dependent on its articulation with a wider, inanimate, commodity producing system',[23] these changes, however, did not herald a complete extinction as '[the] process of qualitative change from animate to inanimate modes of production ... [did] not necessarily demand the total extinction of social and political practices which had their origins in the animate system'.[24]

The complete annihilation of these social domains was not the aim; rather, established social roles and functions were redirected towards the task of socially reproducing a colonial economy in which the labouring process (economic identity) was central. As Guy (2009) again observes of the South African colony:

> through the system of migrant labour, chiefly authority, customary law and the gendered division of labour became an intrinsic part of the South African inanimate capitalist economy. Patriarchal power, lobolo, hlonipha, the fetishization of cattle, commitment to the homestead, ubukhosi and the personal and cultural desires and commitments that go with them continued. Indeed it might be argued that *socially and individually they intensified with the personal and the social distress necessarily associated with the disappearance of the conditions and the economic system in which they were produced.*[25]

There is a fundamental contradiction here: that through the new controls, strains and restrictions that were being placed on certain social relationships and identities (e.g. gender, ethnicity, sexuality – all but the economic [class] identities that are subordinated to colonial capitalist accumulation), the colonial state essentially compels their re-emergence as political identities – that is, *politicizes* them – and by doing so, places them in permanent antagonism to the state.[26] The constitution of such governing identities is not invented in the colonies, and had previously been tested in the Euromodern context of primitive accumulation.[27] A key distinction, however, between the repression of women in the context of the European transition to capitalism and that which takes place in the context of Europe's imperialist expansion into the colonies via primitive accumulation is that in the latter, the identitarian mode of colonial rule produced racial and ethnic ideologies in addition to the gender ideologies of the modern patriarchal state.

Similar to sixteenth- or seventeenth-century Europe where men of the Church and state were enjoined in a systematic devaluation and violation of women that severed solidarity between women and men, in the colonies too, the imposition of wage labour and forced labour resulted in the 'desocialization and decollectivization'[28] of reproduction and cast a long shadow on gender solidarities. Nonetheless, the logic of racist imperialism that was 'a response inherent to the logic of colonization'[29] meant that colonized women and men remained at least enjoined through a shared experience of domination which cultivated among them a consciousness common to themselves as oppressed people.[30] Europe already had concrete experience enforcing gender oppression in its own tradition, but had not yet been faced with the racial, ethnic and caste questions *as political questions* which it would encounter in the colonies as central problems in the stabilization of empire.[31] As a tool of control therefore, gender was already Europe's most advanced ordinance against its subjects – written into the very architecture of its identity, the most modern in its arsenals.[32]

Faced with new identitarian questions in the colonies, gender would again be placed in the service of dominion as racial, ethnic and class oppression unfolded along established gendered cleavages. The reproductive realm (native reserves) that anchored the migrant labour regime marked a particular convergence of these identities in a political sense. As argued by Oyěwùmí (1997), '*the combination* of race and gender factors' in the colonies is a necessary consideration 'because European women did not occupy the same position in the colonial order as African women . . . whatever the "status" of indigenous customs, the relations between African men and women during this period *can neither be isolated from the colonial situation* nor described as a form of colonization, particularly because African men were subjects themselves'.[33] In other words, gender in the colonial context becomes politicized, even radicalized, by the colonial state itself.

This distinct position that gender occupies in the colonies is further evidenced by the fact that the colonizing structure can neither guarantee gender solidarity (between white women and colonized women), nor can it eliminate gendered identification between colonized women and men. Gender solidarity between women is rendered impossible in the colonies because colonial captivity presents only two options for the survival of the native: ethnic or racial solidarity. At the same time the solidarity that is mobilized between colonized women and men in captivity reconstitutes gender as a distinctly social *and* political identity: that is, gender is *always* articulated.[34]

This last point is an important one in considering how modern democracy and its liberal artillery of rights treats those it identifies as gendered subjects. Key to this is that articulation as described above denies colonized genders the stability of being either cultural identity *or* political identity. They are always both. Contrast this with Mamdani's argument that if one's inclusion or exclusion from a regime of rights and entitlements is based on their race or ethnicity, as defined by law, then this becomes a central defining fact for the individual and their group membership – these become *political*, not cultural identities'.[35] He further argues that it is when political identities become polarized that they become most unlike cultural identities, because whereas cultural identities tend to shape into one another (through various forms of hybridization), polarized identities offer no middle ground and *no continuum* between them. In this sense, polarized identities give rise to a kind of political difference where one must be either one or the other, but cannot partake in both. The difference thus becomes binary, *not simply in law but in political life*.[36] But in captivity – that is, ensnared in the racialization, ethnicization and proletarianization of the colonized – gendered subjectivity *is* trapped in a continuum of negotiation, neither invisible nor visible on its own, subject to constant negotiation (the condition of political life itself) as the only guarantee for the survival of those captured within its frames.

This latter consideration goes back to the heart of the modern Western state, by implicating the very basis of its democracy. The concern here is with the nature of accommodation into which the oppressed are compelled precisely because of their state of captivity. The individual subject of Western theory – indeed Western democracy itself – is rendered possible through the captivity of those whose enslavement was the condition of freedom for the captors. James's likening this process to reproduction presents the problem starkly:

> In transitioning a colony through a republic into a representative democracy with imperial might, the emergent United States grew a womb, it took on the *generative properties of the maternals it held captive*. Western democracy, based

> in American Exceptionalism, merged Enlightenment ideologies with Western theories to birth a new nation (a nascent empire) *that fed on black frames.*[37]

The realization of the nature of this dependency often results in violence against captives. This formulation provides a concrete basis for similarly considering the place of gendered violence in the contemporary context of democratization. That is, why does democracy continue to produce bodies that are violable and those that violate? One explanation for the violence against gendered captives is that they are prone to resist and therefore continually threaten the (state and patriarchal) system, and thus constantly invoke its disciplinary regime. James, however, suggests that power and predation in states of captivity is better understood as a 'leverage', rather than say, as converging at an 'intersection'.[38] By leverage, she is referring to the delicate balancing act in which the oppressed have to *engage* in order simply to survive – as well as their ability to rapture that balance given their sheer numbers and collective anger. James calls this 'conventional' or 'on-continuum' politics.[39]

It is a continuous loop of governmentality whereby those most discriminated against are forced to settle their grievances by continuously making disparate political choices which do not necessarily converge at a unified intersection of grievances for redress. In the state of captivity, James insists 'off-continuum politics that resist governance and non-profits to follow the "rabble", rebellion through boycott, protest, or even riot becomes an act of the uncivil' and is invariably quashed and/or punished as such.[40] For the oppressed and discriminated with few rights or legal recognition, the 'intersection' becomes a point of collision and not necessarily one of resolution. This is because at the intersection of oppression, gender encounters multiple competing identities and interests (difference) in ways that determine and undermine the relationship between gendered groups and the state.

In captivity, conflict is inevitable because gendered subjects cannot refuse oppression *in their own names*, and attempts to claim freedom in their own names are usually met with violence. This is because the dissenting voice is already subsumed within and appropriated by the racial, class, caste and ethnic group: their violation is invariably concealed within racism, labour exploitation, racial and caste discrimination, homophobia and ethnic fundamentalism. Gendered subjectivity thus takes on a social life that occasionally tends towards freedom, and that also occasionally raptures, not as evidence of its own propensity for violation (i.e. women are not 'uniquely rapable' because they are women), but as a response to its structural association with other modes of governmentality (ethnicity, class, race caste, sexuality) that were violently imposed on the colonized. The inheritances of colonialism inscribe gendered violence into the very core of the postcolonial state, and therefore feminist liberation as an ever-present threat to the democracy.

For those Captive Maternals – those against whom the modern state refines its oppressive instruments of governance, even their most basic of claims for freedom would likely be met by violence. Joy James considers such disciplining violence using the analogy of a seesaw: her singular insight in this regard is that any attempt by the oppressed to approach the 'intersection' is a threat to the 'balance' on which the captor/oppressor constructs their notion of democracy: to reach the intersection (the 'fulcrum') is to topple the seesaw – acts that are read as sabotage and always met with 'retaliatory violence to punish that disturbance'.[41] Intersectionality (the 'intersection') is, in other words, an aspiration that does not represent the reality of the compromises and balancing acts that constitute the daily struggles of oppressed/enslaved/colonized people in order for them to survive systems of police brutality, rape, financial exclusion from institutions of higher learning, job discrimination, unemployment and racism.[42]

Social life and the politicization of gender

> Black women as Captive Maternals historically configured as lacking morality, intellectual capacity, and ethics confront their subjugation with trauma and stolen time (like stolen lives) as central to political battles.[43]

In keeping with the reproductive function allotted to them, the fate of colonized women in captivity was also to serve as markers of the secular boundary between the colonists and the colonized: between 'backwardness' and progress; between modernity and tradition. The literature is replete with assertions that the governance of gender in the colonies had been most revealing of the shifting imperatives of empire, which from the postwar years, ranked the modernization project on the basis of the condition of colonized women. This preoccupation with the condition of women and the ensuing politicization of gender reflects the social and ethical dilemmas which the stabilization of native rule posed for colonists. For instance, direct intervention into family life was now being rationalized on the grounds that 'more thought had to be given to the place of fertility, reproduction, and family in Africans' lives' if development were to proceed.[44]

This intention in turn called for new policies for African women: the 'emancipation of African women [would] proceed, and with increasing rapidity', an urgency underlined by new developments that saw colonial administrators now 'deplore [among themselves] the status of African women in certain respects', and contend that 'it was the progress of women that would ultimately determine the evolution of African societies'.[45] That the modernization of entire societies would henceforth be pegged on the reform of colonial policy towards women was indicated, such that the consensus, for instance, among colonists in Kenya by 1950 was that 'progressive development of African Society is relative to the increase in the status of African women',[46] suggesting that from the colonial vantage point, political pragmatism was also at play.[47] But what lay at the core of this shift? Why was the status of women suddenly to be accorded such significance?

Two problems informed colonial attitudes towards women. One was political, tethered to the purpose of empire: the boundaries of what was 'civilized' and modern was measured against the harmful gender practices, such as circumcision and forced marriage in East Africa, and polygamy and *lobolo* in South Africa,[48] that colonists had enforced through traditional authorities. These practices were gradually seen as undermining colonial authority and ultimately, colonial officials in the colonies were forced to justify and temper their policies towards women.[49] But second and considered even more dangerous was the granting of 'excessive licence' to African women.[50]

This fear of 'free' colonized women, the moral anxiety they seemed to invoke, was not irrational. Women were themselves actively responding to the modernist changes that engulfed them – chipping away at old structures and conditions of their subjugation, indirectly 'excising the ideology of political modernity internalized under colonialism'.[51] As James observes, the political battles which black women take up mirror the trauma that they experience in captivity.[52] Again, history is replete with narratives of such dynamism: captivity has always compelled rebellious acts of refusal among enslaved and colonized women: the anticolonial tax revolts in Nigeria, peasant struggles against forced labour in Kenya, refusal of pass laws in South Africa, the founding of indigenous schools to counter missionary education, militant defences of the land, mothers' struggles for the release of political prisoners and many others. The significance of these rebellions was that they (re)located women within the purview of modern state power and rendered them into subjects of modern logics of social control, enforced through policing and excessive brutality against natives. In short, these acts reconstituted women as *modern political subjects*.

We might likewise consider the politicization of colonized women along the lines of Saidiya Hartman's 'counter-conducts' of the oppressed – those 'different ways of conducting the self-directed at challenging the hierarchy of life produced by the color line and enforced by the state'[53] – which in reality locate women in a primary antagonism with the civilian state, in a clamour for something other than that which the mere recognition of their 'civil rights' alone could guarantee: that is, a desire to live *with dignity*, and possibly even to thrive. These counter-conducts are legible only intramurally: the 'open rebellion' of young black [American] women at the turn of the twentieth century, their struggles to 'create autonomous and beautiful lives, to escape the new forms of servitude awaiting them, and to live *as if they were free*'[54] – this landscape of black social life could only fully be recounted through the eyes of fellow captives. It is only through the political lens of decolonial possibility that black women gain visibility also as '*sexual modernists*, free lovers, radicals . . . [and as embodying] the promise of a future world that resided in waywardness and the *refusal to be governed*'.[55]

This refusal to be governed takes on particular political significance when also understood as demonstrating the self-knowledge which black women in captivity come to possess through their lived encounters with modern power: the expectation that while power does not speak in the name of black women, it nonetheless enacts itself through their bodies. Take the example of black women's relationship to the law. Kimberlé Crenshaw's insight that '[r]ape statutes generally do not reflect male control over female sexuality, but *white male regulation of white female sexuality*',[56] suggests that the crime which is really being punished by law is the violation of white supremacist codes rather than the violation of (white) women. To this, one could add that the rape statues also reflect the non-criminalization of rape of Black/Indigenous women/girls. The presumed innocence of white women (of whiteness itself), is constituted through a racialized Other:

> Historically, there has been absolutely *no institutional effort to regulate Black female chastity*. Courts in some states had gone so far as to instruct juries that, unlike white women, Black women were not presumed to be chaste. Also, while it was true that the attempt to regulate the sexuality of white women placed unchaste women outside the law's protection, *racism restored a fallen white woman's chastity where the alleged assailant was a Black man*. No such restoration was available to Black women . . . When Black women were being raped by white males, they were being raped *not as women generally*, but *as Black women specifically*.[57]

Black women's putative irrelevance in the face of sexual injustice in reality demonstrates how rape laws situate their bodies as markers of the racial boundary. By contrast, white women appear to the law as nothing more than alibis of white male domination, and as such their positionality in relation to the law is rendered immutable. An immutable subject, a subject that does not deviate from the norm, ultimately lacks capacity to challenge that norm.[58] Black women, on the other hand, appear as living proof of the fact of white supremacy: their violation confirms that they are *not white*.

This disavowal in part relates to the fact, as Durba Mitra's groundbreaking exploration of sexuality in the lexicon of modern social thought in the context of colonial India demonstrates, that what was considered as deviant behaviour, language, ways of being, or culture of women did in fact constitute modern society from without – that is, marked the external boundaries of excess against which modernity could recover itself again and again. Interdictions against deviance were critical to modern social development from 'primitive' to modern forms.[59] The mid-eighteenth to mid-nineteenth century regulation of sexuality by the colonial state and an emerging network of elite native men 'sought to define what society should look like and how modern citizens should behave'.[60] Thus, for instance, prostitution far exceeded embodied deviance since

> [t]he concept of the prostitute was to do all of the descriptive work necessary to explain Indian social lag; it encompassed every form of social practice and sexual act that was temporally behind a modern society dominated by patriarchy. The prostitute, as a concept, could be identified and named, made commensurate and used in comparison to sexual practices across different times and places, and trafficked as a concept in the service of claims to a science of modern Indian society.[61]

Similarly highlighting the social and political significance of 'deviance' in a more contemporary period, Nthabiseng Motsemme's study of women in Chesterville, a small township in KwaZulu-Natal, South Africa, likewise reveals the materiality and effect of various constructions of gendered abject subjectivities.[62] Examining the sociology of HIV/AIDS and the mythologies that evolved around it, Motsemme explores how the notion of 'pollution' circulated in relation to the disease, and highlights the cultural and spiritual violence that was directed towards young HIV-positive women as a result. Through these narratives she shows how 'the historical violences in which [those] young women's subjectivities are embedded, have been repeatedly defined by the *targeted destruction of their socio-cultural resources*'.[63] These are the resources that ensure cultural and self-continuity, as well as 'felt safety' for women, and so the social disintegration of these resources is likely to be experienced 'as a wound'.[64] The substantive question being raised here is how injury inflicted through social forms of control modifies women's relationship to the (democratic) state.[65] What kind of subject is being held up to the state for redress when efforts to define and defend oneself against injury are routinely read as 'deviance'?

McClintock partly responds to this question in her historical elaboration of how accusations of deviance functioned (through the mechanism of fetishization) to displace onto the domain of the primitive that which 'the modern imagination could not incorporate'.[66] That which capitalist modernity could not incorporate included: 'religion (the ordering of time and the transcendent), money (the ordering of the economy) and sexuality (the ordering of the body)' – each of which came to be organized 'around the social idea of racial fetishism'. . . 'by inventing the primitive, the idea of deviance in Europe came to serve a peculiarly modern form of social discipline'.[67] It is, however, imperialism that enacts the colonizing power of such fetishization, its effectiveness as a strategy for domination and captivity:

> The invention of *racial* fetishism became central to the regime of sexual surveillance, while the policing of *sexual* fetishism became central to the policing of the "dangerous classes," both in Europe and in the colonies. Colonized peoples were figured as *sexual* deviants, while gender deviants were figured as *racial* deviants. "Fetish-worshippers" in the colonies and sexual fetishists in the imperial metropoles were seen as the visible, living evidence of evolutionary degeneration. Identified as atavistic sub*races* within the human race, fetishists were, all too often, seen as inhabiting an anachronistic space in the linear time of evolutionary progress, warranting and justifying conquest and control. In this way, the imperial discourse on fetishism became a discipline of containment.[68]

In the discourse of modernity, ascriptions of abjection therefore, do not merely function as a disavowal of women, nor as a tacit rejection of their political legitimacy as rights-bearing subjects of the state. By consigning women to a temporal moment prior to modernity – to 'primitivism' or 'atavism' – they are in practice being placed in a position of permanent antagonism with the modern logics of political rationality, social order and progress. An antagonism to which the state (and society) invariably responds with violence. This space of friction, however, need not necessarily be viewed as benign, as it births possibilities for the active redefinition and reconstitution of ideas of justice from below – that is, from the vantage point of the colonized and the oppressed. The dialectical churning of history remains impossible without such spaces of tension and contradiction, against which modern power arrays itself. Throughout the course of modernity, Captive Maternals have been central to such endeavours of reconstituting the modern from without. That in order to function, capitalist society *needs* their labour, yet routinely violates, negates, undervalues and subordinates its captives, suggests a fundamental relationality to this gendered labour that can be assured only through coercion and violence.

Gendered labour and the state stabilization project

> Plainly put, subjection was anchored in black women's reproductive capacities. The captive female body . . . locates precisely a moment of converging political and social vectors that mark the flesh as a prime commodity of exchange.[69]

The idea of labour appears deceptively to conform narrowly to class structure, which constitutes a very specific relation in society. But any population is, in reality, an aggregate of numerous 'determinations and relations',[70] such that the simple conception of labour might become the starting point for an analysis also of the state, international exchange, markets and so on.[71] Concretely therefore, labour should be understood as 'a combination of many determinations [or] a unity of diverse elements', that is 'as much a modern category as the *conditions* which have given rise' to it.[72] In this sense, both labour and capital are the product of historical conditions that cannot be generalized across time, such that for instance, in modern bourgeois society and under capitalism, the labour-capital relation is primarily enforced through exploitation of 'free labour',[73] different from feudal relations which tied peasant labour and identity to the land.

The *gendered* form of labour may likewise be constituted through relations of exploitation, but such an analysis would need to show concretely how it is that gender actually aids the extraction of surplus value. Demonstrating an exploitative relation between gendered labour and capitalist accumulation remains a challenge in much feminist inquiry in political economy, although there have been some influential attempts to theorize it. For instance, Federici's *Caliban and the Witch* reveals the mechanisms by which production was separated from reproduction in the transition from feudalism to capitalism, and how the resulting sexual division of labour had to be created and enforced through extreme violence.[74] One of the most devastating insights in that work is the recognition of everything that women lost in terms of social power in the transition to capitalism. Witches embodied everything that capitalism had to destroy: 'the heretic, the healer, the disobedient wife, the woman who dared to live alone, the . . . woman who poisoned the master's food and inspired the slaves to revolt'.[75] Again, deviance. Federici issues a detailed account of changes in European women's social status and their social degradation as a result of witch-hunting, whose backdrop was the transition to capitalism.[76]

The objective of this violence in Europe had been the development of a modern capitalist state. In the colonies – on the other side of modernity – the primary objective of violence against women, similarly applied, would have been to subsidize and thus stabilize capitalist accumulation.[77] In *Accumulation,*

Luxemburg illustrates the close ties between the non-capitalist strata (of the colonies) and the material elements necessary for the accumulation of capital. To her, it is precisely the 'primitive' conditions in the non-capitalist realm of production that allow for accumulation to a far more ruthless extent than could be tolerated under purely capitalist conditions. This non-capitalist stratum is dominated by forms of labour that are unwaged, and the recognition of its articulation to capitalist accumulation compels an acknowledgement of the (gendered) forms of labour that enables reproduction outside of the wage labour relation, as critical to capitalism.[78]

Gendered labour thus stood at the intersection of two developments: in the service of imperialist expansion on the one hand, and on the other, towards the stabilization of empire in the colonies. An 'intention of permanence' is written into empire's accumulation path, evidenced by the persistence of this gendered (reproductive) labour regime even in the context of modern democracy. On the question of permanence, Bakare-Yusuf (1997) observes in her brief but important piece on the economies of violence against enslaved people that

> unlike the Nazi atrocities where the aim was the total extermination of a so-called inferior race, the slave system needed the slaves to work. Although a labour system characterized the Jewish Holocaust, destruction was the ultimate aim. Slavery, on the other hand, was *first and foremost a system of labour*. The slavers did not intend the slaves to die; they were concerned to ensure the survival of the black body – albeit in a demoralized form. The black female body is a *useful body because it is both a labouring, sexual and reproducing body* and therefore it was necessary to preserve the health of the enslaved woman. The use of violence was therefore necessary to break them in, to fragment them, to destabilize them and to make them cease to be subjects, to transform them into 'docile bodies' … that become bodies that labour.[79]

While colonies were similarly known for using coercive force in order to procure from women 'bodies that labour,' the compliance of women as labouring subjects has to be understood through the lens of the *social relations* that facilitate such coercion, rather than as a direct response to the state itself, since colonized women had not been the primary subjects of the state. Stated differently, gendered labour is rendered exploitable because of the social obligations that women bear within the social and cultural (kinship) groups to which they belong. In those groups, reciprocal and affective bonds are nurtured such that the co-optation of women's labour time by colonists was indirectly mediated through the disciplinary and coercive structures of the kinship and patriarchal units.[80]

This point regarding colonial governance and the coercive force congealed within its social and cultural edifice becomes even more apparent when contrasted with Europe's transition to peripheral capitalism in the colonies, which followed a different pattern than it did from the agricultural revolution to the Industrial revolution in the metropoles. In this regard, Samir Amin too, emphasizes the insufficiency of economic coercion and argues that for the colonies, the transformation of a natural subsistence economy into a commodity economy was never a spontaneous consequence of the introduction of new manufactured goods that would have caused the peasants to produce agricultural products for exports in order to satisfy new wants. Rather, because the traditional social structures hindered the spread of commodity exchange, '*strictly economic mechanisms [would not] suffice*'.[81] This is why the *political authority* – in this case, a colonial authority – concerns itself with 'stimulating monetization of the primitive economy [. . .]. What is [being justified] here is the *use of methods that are purely and simply methods of violence*, and therefore methods of primitive accumulation'.[82] The process of primitive accumulation in the colonies is in this regard, violent not because the economic transition and accumulation process requires violence per se, but rather '*because it is dependent on social conditions which are not yet realised in the colonies*'.[83]

From the purview of indirect rule, these social conditions ought to be understood in relation to the realm of social reproduction that was mediating the incorporation of natives into the capitalist economy as more and more male labour was forced into the wage economy. Women did not simply make way for this crude incorporation. For instance, on the long resistance waged by South African women against the apartheid regimes imposition of pass laws, Wells (1982) observed that historically, the use of passes as a form of labour control had applied only to men, and whenever attempts were made to extend the system to black women, mass protest quickly resulted. There was a spontaneity to these protests that highlighted both a willingness to challenge formidable political structures as well as the catalytic nature of the social economy:

> [w]hen unfavorable social conditions reached the breaking point, whole communities of women responded as if with one mind [. . .]. The "steam" which empowered the women's struggle came more directly from the social context and was intimately related to the women's own definitions of themselves and their rightful place in society.[84]

This apparent social question gradually compelled the shift among historians to a greater focus on 'the 'cultural specificity' involved in class formation by looking at not only economic determinants, but also at political consciousness and social and cultural ideologies'.[85] Through and through, women's contradictory encounters with the colonial state pushed the boundaries of modernity towards a redefinition of society. On the one hand, resistance brought women into direct and often violent confrontation with the state, and on the other, it signalled women's implicit recognition of state authority as they forcefully inserted their social subjectivities into the domain of 'politics proper'. Both lay bare the material driving force that constituted women's relationship to the state.

Furthermore, the colonial appropriation of labour, both productive and reproductive, was also fundamentally a redrawing of the cultural boundaries of native consciousness: those who *embodied* culture – as givers of life, as markers of the nation, as reproducers of kinship, and as mediators of difference in society – necessarily took on the burden of defending it. In this evolving structure, the real antagonism then would not have been between colonists and their direct captives (e.g. men, migrant labourers), but rather between the modern state and its *indirect* subjects – those women (and men) who marked the internal boundaries of native populations and therefore also, the boundaries of resistance to indirect rule.

While the imperialist extension of political and economic dominion over the colonies is within reason of modern statecraft, the colonial state also arrogated to itself the additional right to intervene into the domain of social life, thus locating itself between the public and private; between social life and political life; and between law and custom. To the extent that such bifurcation had been foundational to the process of colonial state making, the elimination of political difference while maintaining social difference – that primary aspiration of the postcolonial democratizing state – would invariably be a process fraught with anxiety and prone to violence.

Yet beyond the purpose of political stabilization, the process of 'define and rule' bears within it a further structural question regarding what it would take to reconcile a traditional societal realm – which had primarily been defined by reproductive labour as central to the colonial accumulation project – with 'a civil realm that colonists had defined politically by rights'.[86] Stated differently, what would it take to bring into postcolonial society, those working people whose legibility to the state had been primarily mediated by capital that was divorced from the political context? Such a process portends the sustained denial of political power to reproductive labour. The fact that much reproductive labour still goes unpaid, unrecognized and undervalued certainly suggests such a removal from the realm of 'politics proper', but also raises the question then, regarding the substantive nature of the political relationship between women and the modern state. This question is core to the argument I began to make in Chapter 1 regarding the necessity of understanding colonized women as the quintessential modern subjects of the state.

To be clear, this in itself is not a novel argument. Oyěwùmí (1997) too, alludes to this peculiarity of colonized women as being a modern invention (of the colonial state) in her argument that the 'creation of "women" as a category was one of the very first accomplishments of the colonial state'.[87] Yet she stops short of elaborating the necessity of this invention[88] – which I attribute to the social reproductive needs of the colonial state. Oyěwùmí does recognize that 'the starvation wages that men were paid by the colonial government were insufficient to reproduce the family, and women's labor remained as necessary as ever for the survival of the community' (150–51). However, her fundamental argument regarding the devaluation of women and the 'invisibility' of their work renders it impossible to bring her thesis on women into a more central functionality in relation to the colonial state. Analytically, the question haunting the margins of Oyěwùmí's otherwise brilliant work is this: how do we explain the need for the extreme disciplining of a group (women) that putatively had been so marginal to the colonial project? What was at stake, both with the invention of women and with their resocialization as 'second-class citizens'?[89]

In my considered reading, the answer partially lies in the colonial transition which ushers in the need for the stabilization of this gendered division of labour, a process that could not proceed on its own merit. What colonialism did was draw on existing gender, regional, class and ethnic cleavages, through the institutionalization of a (migrant) labour regime that cemented a class-based, gendered and ethnicized society as the condition for the stabilization of colonial rule. The migration of male labour is necessitated by capitalist accumulation, as is the rural-urban bifurcation of the state. Gendered labour thus suggests a much more expansive process of domination that enjoined the state and its legislative apparatus, the family/household as a social, cultural and economic site of production. Hortense Spillers' characterization of female slaves during the 'Middle Passage' also suggests such an economy in the historical course of captivity:

> Because it was the rule, however – not the exception – that the African female, in both indigenous African cultures and in what becomes her "home," performed tasks of hard physical labour – *so much so that the quintessential "slave"* is *not* a male, but a female – we wonder at the seeming docility of the subject, granting her a "feminization" that enslavement kept at bay.[90]

Spillers is here too, highlighting the essential modernity of women. She goes further to elaborate how it becomes possible to conceal or altogether erase this central function of gender in the making of the New World. Erasure is possible because in captivity, reproduction transfers ownership of the offspring (a metaphor for the product), to the slave/colonial master. Spillers formulates this possibility as such: 'under conditions of captivity, the offspring does not "belong" to the mother, nor is s/he "related" to the "owner", though the latter possess it' Here, she is making reference to a 'cultural formation where "kinship" loses meaning, since it can be invaded at any given and arbitrary moment by the property relations'.[91] Indeed, the colonial idea of women as 'passive' subjects allowed colonists to deny women as proper subjects of politics, even as the colonial regime to which women were being subjected made it clear that women were central to the social organization of native labour and colonial capitalist accumulation.[92]

The ushering of captive women into modernity thus takes place via economies that commoditize them and alienate them from the progeny of their labours. That 'product' includes, of course, the democracy that is birthed through the oppression and subjugation of Europe's 'Others'. The outcome (of democracy's inherently predatory tendency in relation to the Black captive subject) is a contradictory relationship between democracy and its putative modern subject: any substantive acknowledgement[93] of the gendered labour and the captivity of those who perform this labour is invariably an indictment of democracy.

The 'womb' – from the period of enslavement, to colonization, to democratization – is held captive for the purpose of conveying the labour that constructs and maintains these societies. But an acknowledgement of the violence through which such captivity is enacted and reproductive labour coerced, is an impossibility. For to do so would be to grant *subjecthood* to these labouring bodies, and doing so causes all sorts of problems for capitalism which it has historically just ignored. The violence of slavery, colonialism and (their inheritances through) liberal democracy, therefore, remains largely a matter of conjecture and speculation. The rape of women is attributed to their waywardness and violation of the strictures of modern society; on the other hand, the men who violate find themselves simply discarded through narratives of excess ('bestial', 'uncivilized', 'dangerous'). On both sides, modernity grounds its generative force within its ability to name its captive subjects in the language of *abjection*.

The two primary questions that arise in this regard both relate to process. First, if as I have already argued, gendered labour had been central to the social and political stabilization of colonial rule, through what labouring processes might we understand this social structuring of colonized society? Second, the fact that the supply of gendered labour was ensured through relations of coercion and violence means that – in lieu of a complete dismantling of the existing structure – the maintenance of this structure of gendered labour in the postcolonial state would necessarily *replicate* the colonial violence that stabilized it in order to function. In what ways, then, does the postcolonial democratizing state reconstitute or mimic the relationship of captivity between colonizer and colonized, if at all? And where do emancipatory possibilities lie for the subject of gendered labour, who remains captive due to their centrality to the political economy of neoliberal capitalist accumulation in the postcolony? I attempt a response to these questions in subsequent chapters of the book.

Captivity, fugitivity and territory as body

The idea of the captive maternal as emerges out of James's invocation is an ungendered figure whom she locates within a range of structural contexts whose survival must be understood in relation to the reproductive processes that stabilize them. The Captive Maternal is in this regard both implicated in the world(s) that they recreate, and victimized by its carceral logics. There is no escape for Captive Maternals as long as their labour, love and 'superpowers' remain interpellated as such.[94] Still, James observes, there are stages which the Captive Maternal can explore or transgress, from conflicted caretaker to protester and movement maker, to maroonage and war resistor.[95] In one of the quoted texts at the beginning of this chapter, James – who distinguishes abolition from revolution and writes increasingly about the latter[96] – speaks of this shift (i.e. from exploitation to the ability to engage in stable living and reproduction of communities that are healthy), as being dependent on 'the ability to control violence.'[97]

James's notion of the ability to control violence is by no means to be understood in the same register as the Weberian notion of monopoly over the means of violence, although the two mirror in quaintly similar fashion, the fundamental problem of modern society: its mode of claiming power through violence. Rather, James is concerned with the possibility of *empowerment* – that is, 'a restorative process that makes way for an authoritative claiming of democratic dividends – rights, freedom, equality, dignity, and life itself'.[98] The absence of these possibilities condemns captives to a life of fugitivity, a concept which conjures up an image of those (for instance, black people in America) who Lisa Marie Cacho (2012) argues, are 'imagined as being the reason why a punitive (in)justice system exists',[99] are criminalized (because 'criminal activity [is] unrecognizable without a black body'),[100] and thus are 'prevented from being law-abiding'.[101] The present period of neoliberal capitalism, for whom liberal democracy is a handmaiden, is similarly one in which reproductive labour is unthinkable without a gendered, racialized and ethnicized body. In the absence of the possibility of abolition (or revolution), such captivity condemns its victims to permanent fugitivity.

The condemnation to fugitivity is similar in nature to a life spent wondering about aimlessly, with neither a fixed abode, nor the possibility to assert claim over one. At the onset of the Euromodern world, fugitivity is preceded by territoriality, variously enforced through the 'doctrine of discovery' and conquest as in the Americas from the fifteenth century, or by colonial occupation as took place in Africa, Asia and the Pacific from the late seventeenth century onwards. Territoriality begets fugitivity, which inevitably leads to captivity. The capturing of labouring bodies differs from the capture of land in as far as we can distinguish between 'territoriality of land' versus 'territoriality of body', although the two are interconnected.

Land as the basis of capitalist accumulation presents significant challenges to late industrializing societies that remain committed to the same extractivist model of development and progress that was followed by their colonial predecessors.[102] The replication in the peripheries of such exploitative capitalist relations that developed countries followed would not surrender its gendered model of accumulation as women (and their gendered labour) come to constitute the 'last colony'.[103] As Utsa Patnaik argues: 'unlike the European colonizing migrant of yesteryear, today's displaced peasants and displaced workers of the South *simply have nowhere to go*'.[104] In the absence of 'new' lands, the remaining frontier of accumulation is now an internal one in the postcolony itself[105] – territorialized through an economic, social and political war that is waged against the bodies, labours and time of gendered subjects: today's Captive Maternals. The 'democracy' that takes root under such conditions and does nothing to challenge the violability of the gendered bodies which modern society holds in captivity on behalf of capital, *surrenders* its political emancipatory possibility: it demonstrates its complicity in the structural violence which capitalism has historically required in order to stabilize its (primitive) accumulation project.

Those seeking to understand the postcolonial subject of gendered violence thus do well to follow the journey, not of colonial modernity in itself, but of those identitarian mechanisms of governance through which the colonial state historically constituted its rule. These mechanisms included ethnicity, caste, gender, class and race and thus were fundamentally social and cultural. The (liberal) democratic refusal to acknowledge these legacies and its tendency of treating them as aberrations rather than as concrete forms of political and social organization has direct consequences, especially for those interpellated through such identitarian logics. As I argue in the chapter that follows, the nature of the problem which the neglect of this structural relationship poses to democratization is this: where they can no longer be enacted by the state as instruments of control, deeply entrenched ethnic, racial and caste-based institutions have tended to function *in statist form* against their own gendered subjects.

5

Democracy's Identitarian Problem: A Consideration of South Africa

It was permissible to allow the destruction of a tribal system that impeded the growth of the country. It was permissible to believe that its destruction was inevitable. But it is not permissible to watch its destruction, and to replace it by nothing, or by so little, that a whole people deteriorate, physically and morally[1]

Politics does not reflect majorities, it constructs them.[2]

At the heart of every democratic struggle in the postcolonial world lies an incipient class struggle, classically defined as a struggle between the productive forces and the social relations of production. Colonial domination had fragmented societies for the sake of its own stabilization through interventions that reconstituted these social relations, such that the organization of working people proceeded along the lines of class as well as ethnicity, caste, race, gender and sexuality – categories that also constitute the social relations of reproduction. In the postcolonial moment, any concrete analysis of the social relations of production has therefore to grapple with the question of *difference*. The argument of this chapter is that where difference can no longer be enacted by the state as an instrument of control, structures and institutions of capitalist accumulation have tended to function in statist form against their own gendered subjects.

The humanity of colonized people is always a mediated one, conditioned upon assimilation into a class, ethnic, gender, racial or caste structure through which they become legible to the state *as a group*, as I have already argued in the preceding chapter. Yet as a group, colonized women had not been the primary subjects of the state, and therefore in the postcolonial period would not have been the primary subjects of redress and rights. Black women's significance in the colonial structure, however, is not in doubt. As labouring and reproductive bodies, black women had constituted the condition of possibility for the stabilization of colonial white minority rule and its accumulation project.[3] But the relationship of colonists to women had been such that colonial officials on the one hand *needed* to incorporate women into the colonial edifice due mainly to the (reproductive) labour question that faced all colonies, while at the same time could render women secondary or marginal to the colonial project through the denial of women's political authority and their characterization as 'passive' and subdued to the control of their male native counterparts.[4]

This latter impulse took the form of numerous and often gratuitous acts of violence against black women, as well as the disavowal of their humanity. The question that this attitude towards women would raise in the postcolonial state therefore was this: to what extent could those whose very humanity had been decentred and disavowed constitute stable subjects of democracy and of rights? A partial response to this question appears in Chatterjee's (2007) critique of bourgeois civil society in postcolonial India, in which he examines the ways in which governments try to produce citizens best suited to fulfil their politics. Drawing on the notion of 'political society'[5] – a community that is constituted through methods that make it difficult for the state to recognize it as legitimate[6] – he shows the claims of political society as being irreducibly *political.* Meaning that they can only be made on a political terrain where rules may be bent or stretched, and not on the terrain of established law and administrative procedure.[7] Refugees, landless people, day labourers, homestead, below the poverty line – are all demographic categories of such governmentally. That is the ground on which they define their claims. These are communities that could only ever make political claims on a political terrain (not on the terrain of administrative law or procedure). Chatterjee then asks how it is that the particular claims of such marginal population groups, often grounded in violations of the law, could be made consistent with the pursuit of equal citizenship and civic virtue. In other words, where does the democratic possibility lie – the possibility of producing a viable and persuasive politics of the governed?[8]

His response is that when there is successful mobilization of political society to secure the benefits of governmental programs for poor/underprivileged population groups, one could claim that there is an actual expansion of the freedoms of people, enabled by political society that would not have been ordinarily possible within civil society. Chatterjee nonetheless does not fully vindicate political society, recognizing the likelihood that: such mobilization will reflect dominant interests and values; that it could ignore or suppress demands of locally marginalized interests; and that it may be socially conservative and insensitive to gender and minority interests. Political society will also inevitably bring into the hallways of power some of the squalor, ugliness and violence of popular life given the strategic use of criminality and violence on the terrain of political society. In other words, that the political form (of political society) does not guarantee the democratization of its social form, suggesting that the reliance of popular politics in postcolonial democracies on identitarian claims can generate new forms of violence, including sexual violence. This fact reflects the '*historical constitution of modernity*' – it reflects a *structure* of inclusion/exclusion/silencing/violence – and is not pathological.[9]

This is a formulation through which we might argue that rights claims have also to take adequate measure of the colonial margins from which black women had been compelled to 'speak' and act – where their speech and actions were routinely delegitimized and the validity of their claims invariably questioned.[10] Implicating a structural edifice in the production of harm means that one is necessarily also tasked with the work of historical excavation, since history allows us to pose the question regarding how and when it is that various identities become injurious, and when it is that such injury becomes *gendered* – and therefore visible to the 'human rights' lexicon that is the basis of redress in liberal dogmatism.

In contexts of oppression and in the absence of the freedom and liberty to claim an identity or to *name oneself*, identities invariably become political and are politicized. In such contexts, it is not enough simply to highlight discrimination, but rather to also ask what it is that different forms of discrimination *do* at particular historical conjunctures. This could also be posed as a question as such: *when* does identity normatively defined – as Black, female, queer, etc., become political (identity), shaped by race, class, ethnicity, gender, sexuality and so on? A concrete response to this question requires illustration of the historical trajectory of this shift from a normative identitarian basis to a *political* one. Colonial modernity is peculiar in constituting such historical-legal-political subjectivity since its territorial demands and accumulation project could be effected only through the forceful incorporation of native society (including migrants) into its economies of production and reproduction.

In mainstream definitions of 'productive labour', a bifurcation is established between the sphere of production and that of social reproduction[11] – between the 'domestic' and the 'public' sphere. The story goes that it is in the private reproductive sphere where the worker most 'belongs to himself' and where 'he performs his *necessary vital* functions outside of production.'[12] It follows then that in this reproductive sphere the worker would be least alienated from their cultural self – the sphere in which identification with one's ethnic, religious, caste, sexuality or gender group is at its most benign and therefore, least *political*. This argument would suggest that the conditions which foment the politicization of identities exceed the confines of the domestic sphere, or conversely, that identities acquire political *relevance* when the structures, conditions and institutions of production subsume the domestic, reproductive sphere. One of the ways this is achieved is through the representation of women as 'reproducers of the nation', 'biological reproducers', 'bearers of the collective' and 'boundaries of the nation'[13] and so on. The appeal to nationalism apparent in such rhetoric constitutes a primary site of *political constitution* of certain subjects that are claimed in possessive form by those who define them (the state, the patriarchs and so on) and who therefore, may discipline them or violate them in order to preserve the collective nationalist project.[14]

The other point worth noting is that while one experiences oppression as an individual, their oppressive identity as 'Black', or 'working class' or 'Xhosa' is always experienced within the respective (racial/class/ethnic) group. Second, because the colonial state did not recognize the individuality of colonized natives,[15] the latter never were the subject of rights, but rather of custom, which again was identified with whole communities and not individuals. The recognition of individuality is furthermore, impossible where complete domination is both the means and the end, because dominion can only be achieved (as well as resisted) *en masse*. In South Africa, for instance, bantustans – designated areas reserved for specific ethnic groups were designed by the National Party government during the latter half of the 1950s to achieve various socio-political objectives that were necessitated by contradictions arising from Apartheid's ideology of racial separation. The Tomlinson Commission[16] concluded that '[t]here is no midway between the two poles of ultimate total integration and ultimate separate development of the two [racial] groups' hence 'sustained development of the Bantu Areas on a large scale' was to be 'the germinal point'. The envisioned apex of a bantustan framework was 'independence' for black ethnic groups within a designated 'homeland'.[17]

As a mode of governance, the political and spatial logics of the bantustans also constituted a basis for the accumulation of difference – ethnic, racial, gender and class – that was crucial for the stabilization of apartheid, and which today constitutes a basis of contradictions internal to the native populations.[18] This combination of the systematic abandonment of black communities in South Africa, and their own internal incoherence as an oppressed group marks an important ideological fault line in the postcolonial course of democracy there. In the postcolony, the liberal individualism which democracy constitutionally enshrines is challenged at every turn by the difference around which native political, social and economic lives had historically been reconstituted. But by far, it is native women that had most threatened the stabilization project because of their social reproductive roles that positioned them between the settler colonial accumulation machine and the large black labour reserve which the 'machine' required in order to function.

Flowing from the foregoing, my argument in this chapter is that in the post-apartheid context of democratization and liberal constitutionalism, *difference* can no longer be *legally* deployed by the state as an instrument of control. As such, deeply gendered, racialized and ethnicized '*social* structures of accumulation'[19] become activated and have tended to function *in statist form*[20] against their own gendered subjects. I elaborate these claims through a reflection on the feminist questions raised by two seemingly disparate political events in post-apartheid South Africa (that nonetheless share a historical genealogy). The first is narrated through the lens of the xenophobic violence that erupted there in 2010 and the second rupture is narrated through the lens of the Marikana massacre that occurred in 2012. The social reproduction question congealed within each of these moments unites gendered subjectivity with identitarian politics in a critique of the post-apartheid liberal democratic state – that is, against liberal democracy as model political community.

Xenophobia and the social reproduction imperative

The term xenophobia is derived from the ancient Greek words *xenos* (stranger) and *phobia* (fear), and in its most original sense refers to the fear or dislike of anything that is perceived as strange or as foreign. Its modern sense denotes 'civic ostracism'[21] and to paraphrase Sundstrom (2013), is sheltered by liberal democracies to which membership is imagined and 'sanctuary [for foreigners] is depreciated as a threat to the rule of law'.[22] Publicly, xenophobia might manifest in acts of violence against those marked as 'foreign', but structurally, xenophobic violence has tended to provide to states an alibi for the postcolonial failure of the redistribution project. In any case, the idea of 'justice' that is reasonably claimed by natives in the postcolony is rendered exclusionary since strangers challenge the presumed boundary between civic/juridical communities (those bounded by the sovereign) and social communities (those bounded by shared cultures/histories).[23] In a country as deeply unequal as South Africa is today, major periodic implosions cannot be understood in isolation from its social basis; that is, cannot neglect the question regarding the survival of the masses of working people amidst extreme immiseration and the necessity for social reproduction which is now seemingly articulated within every political claim.

Xenophobia follows many tributaries and one is that of ethnic nationalities. Any keen observer of politics in post-apartheid South African eventually recognizes the significant manifestation of the colonial trauma there as having congealed as much within its ethnic identities as within its racialized structure. Alongside this is, of course, the plausibility that the same violent manifestations of politicized ethnicity witnessed in other parts of the continent might eventually become a feature of political contestations there too.[24] Some early commentaries (e.g. van den Berghe 1990) noted the likely persistence of ethnic politics amidst democratization, arguing that South Africa 'remains a plural society with a population divided by deep rifts of class, race and ethnicity' and noting the high likelihood that 'race and ethnicity will continue to play a salient role in South African politics for the foreseeable future, with probably a decreasing emphasis on race and an increasing one on ethnicity' (1990 quoted in Szeftel 1994: 186–7).[25]

Interestingly, the logic of ethnic politics in South Africa finds quite early expression in apartheid-era ideology among the white minority population. Studies like Peele and Morse's (1974) were able to predict a person's ethnic background from the party they voted for and vice versa: the white minority 'persistently voted along ethnic-subcultural lines and delineated throughout the country, an Afrikaner population that tended to be less well educated, of lower socioeconomic status, and more heavily concentrated in rural areas than English-speaking South Africans, against whom they were organized in voting blocs, (Peele and Morse 1974: 1521, 1527).[26] It is no surprise then, that the Afrikaner-dominated National Party 'contrived and rewarded politicized ethnicity in order to sustain its own domination'.[27] Beginning from the early sixties, 'the government set out not only to crush its opponents but to reorient African political aspirations towards rural ethnic "homelands" (made up of the traditional labour reserves and some of the dormitory townships of the urban working class) each with a "government" dependent for its budget on funds from Pretoria'.[28] For natives, abeyance to homelands – ethnic subjectivation – served not so much a political posture of resistance as an economic function among native populations: '[f]or millions of Africans, obedience to homeland and traditional authorities became obligatory for access to land and work'.[29]

Most South African studies, however, have tended to minimize the role of ethnicity in explaining the South African situation. Nengwekhulu (1986), for instance, argues that 'white racism and the policies of racial discrimination have not only succeeded in undermining the ideological and political potency of ethnicity and ethnic consciousness but have also succeeded in welding the different ethnic groups into a black nation whose emergence has in turn helped to further submerge ethnicity, giving nation and national consciousness more political saliency than ethnicity and ethnic consciousness' (1986: 34). More ambivalently, Szeftel (1994), while noting the renewed interest in ethnicity in South Africa especially in the wake of ethnic conflict in KwaZulu Natal in the twilight of apartheid, asks whether this interest 'reflects the extent to which ethnic claims in South Africa have widespread support, or represent evidence of the resurgence of ethnicity rather than the assertiveness of heavily-armed political machines'.[30]

The question in relation to which ethnicity interests me, however, is less about its political functionality than the social conditions under which ethno-nationalist identification flourishes. Historical ethnic references have, after all, barely concealed xenophobic intentions: at its core, politicized ethnicity harbours a deep-seated tendency towards expulsion. Liberal 'equality' eliminates any possibility of the procedural determination (via state machinery) of who belongs and who ought not to belong, and invariably shifts such determination on to a social and cultural sphere – the domain proper of captive gendered subjects who mark the boundaries of ethnic nationalities. The distribution of power between native authorities and colonial governments can partly be understood in this regard.

In KwaZulu, the Amazulu leadership seemed to communicate precisely this point in response to violence that was both generalized to the apartheid regime and specific to black populations. For instance, in the early 1980s, Gatsha Buthelezi, Chief Minister of KwaZulu and leader of Inkatha Freedom Party is quoted as having stated the following in a speech to the KwaZulu Legislative Assembly (KLA) on 3 November 1983: 'people from other parts of the country with different ethnic origins… cannot be tolerated, that is, people from other ethnic backgrounds *who do nothing about the terrible circumstances* . . . in the places where they come from'.[31] Inkatha's influence over a mass movement that extended way beyond the rural homelands to establish roots in urban areas certainly also lent itself to white supremacist logics, as it was unclear whether Inkatha's brand of Zulu nationalism 'undermined or underpinned the white state' and whether Buthelezi 'challenge[d] or collaborate[d] with Pretoria'.[32]

Yet in an anticolonial sense,[33] that Zulu nationalism had been buffered by the racist apartheid state cannot explain its *nationalist* form: it neither tells us how the Zulu nation politically reproduced itself nor how it ensured its own internal coherence against apartheid-era divisive politics and resistance within its own ranks. In this singular regard, Southall's (1981) question regarding 'the *social forces* [which] Inkatha represents' ought to be taken into consideration.[34] Among those forces, Southall points to women's power as having been central to a generational reproduction of a political party (Inkatha) that was otherwise widely viewed as being 'primarily a vehicle for an older and more conservative generation'.[35] Women's labours within or on behalf of the party seem to have been majorly demanded for fairly routine, gendered tasks, not unlike those carved out for women in many other African nationalist political formations and liberation movements, although they were also engaged in direct political mobilization:

> Because of the concentration of Zulus in Natal, Inkatha can be further characterized as a regionally-based organization, whilst it is also *considerably dependent upon women*. Over half the membership of 150,000 in 1978 was female, and it is 'woman-power' that reportedly runs Inkatha on a day to day basis. Women played a major role in organizing the Inkatha campaign for the 1978 elections to the KLA; and they also run various communal projects such as vegetable clubs, creches and play centres whilst allegedly being used by the leadership to maintain a *close surveillance* over the Youth Brigade.[36]

The invitation of women into Zulu nationalist politics had been overt, conveyed through messaging which did not conceal the reproductive roles intended for them. Hassim (1988) highlights the political importance of the Women's Brigade for Inkatha, citing Chief Buthelezi's opening address at the Inaugural Congress of the Women's Brigade in 1977: '[t]he people cannot be mobilised and organised and put to work building a better South Africa if the women do not rally their menfolk and their children, *if they do not organise themselves into a disciplined work force for justice*'.[37] Furthermore, during the late 1970s–early 1980s period that was marked by youth restiveness, the Women's Brigade was also held 'responsible for keeping the youth in check . . .[a function that was] to occur at both the ideological and the political level. Inkatha [saw] women (especially mothers) as the bearers of culture and as the medium through which "correct" attitudes (political or otherwise) [would] be transmitted to the youth'.[38]

Women's capacity for surveillance as well as socially reproducing the party's constituency placed them in a special position in the ideological as well as generational reproduction of the (Zulu) nation. In relation to Inkatha, Hassim (1991) argues that these particular constructions of 'gender subjects' were shaped by 'the broader constitution of ethnic or national identity'[39] [and] tradition was 'a key mobilization strategy of Inkatha [through which] women were accorded a special place in the "reinvented" Zulu tradition'.[40] She writes furthermore, that the role ascribed to women in Inkatha 'was not to make, or even shape, policy in any direct way, but rather to "*sustain the forces of change*." Inkatha women [were] perceived as bystanders in history, even though their actual activities may [have been] more central to creating history'.[41] This statement is significant to the extent that it links women's roles not merely to the reproduction of people but fundamentally to the reproduction of *political communities* – to politics itself. And while those roles may not have rendered women as primary political actors, they did in fact constitute a fundamental condition for the conservative *form* of ethno-nationalist, paternalistic politics that were emerging out of Inkatha and which would be carried into the post-apartheid state. Southall (1981) further suggests that the bifurcated structure of the state gave particular form to the party's social base and offers at least a partial explanation for women's influence:

> Its strength amongst women reflects the fact that, for all its support in selected urban areas, *Inkatha's centre of gravity remains firmly located within the Kwazulu homeland*, from which a high proportion of the male population is absent as a migrant workforce at any one time. As in other bantustans, *those who stay behind are more immediately subject to the rule of the chiefs*, who, as paid functionaries of the state, have wielded coercive powers granted to them under the Bantu Authorities system to entrench Inkatha within their areas of authority. Thus, although there have been a number of dissentients, the tribal chieftaincy would appear to have provided the motor power behind the rapid expansion of Inkatha since its revival in 1975.[42]

The foregoing suggests at least two things: one, that the male exodus from the homelands in response to the migrant labour system had created the very possibility for Inkatha's dominance in rural KwaZulu, and second, that that dominance was largely guaranteed by the power and authority that was exercised *on* those who remained behind, mainly women. Women thus bore the burden of defining traditional authority as well as shaping customary governance. Within the colonial modern boundaries of traditional authority, it is women then that could be said to have embodied the *modern subjecthood* of the colonizing, apartheid state – subjected as they were to its indirect coercive violence and exploitative practices via chiefs, as well as to the state's disciplinary regimes.

It is the Bantu Authorities that oversaw these processes of control of women's labours, and did so as paid functionaries of the state. Their reign in the reserves would therefore, have reflected the constitutive (colonial) source of their authority: a coercive, violent form of the state that oversaw the forceful incorporation of women as reproductive labourers into the social structure of colonial accumulation and as boundaries of ethnic nation(s) – and therefore also, *bounded by the nation's logics of who belonged and who did not*. Two ideas arise from the foregoing: first, that xenophobia has to be concretely thought in relation both to the national boundaries (that defined racial and ethnic communities) as well as the boundaries between productive and reproductive labour (that defined gendered communities), which it threatens. Second, that the racialized, gendered and nationalist *forms* which citizenship takes in South Africa today suggest unresolved contradictions of the colonial social structure of accumulation and political control, which manifest *in xenophobic form*. That is, the contradictions (e.g. race, gender, ethnicity) which the post-apartheid state cannot resolve internally are displaced onto 'foreigners'[43] in violent ways.

The link I have so far tried to draw between ethnic nationalism and xenophobia is not itself original. Mamdani (2020) too observes that in urban South Africa, Africans and other persons of colour that are seen as tribal strangers, and thus intruders, are periodically the target of what is called xenophobic violence, suggesting to me that xenophobic violence conceals a fundamental incompatibility between the ethnic inheritances of the colonial state and the liberal investments of the postcolonial democratizing state. Furthermore, in the context of the flailing post-apartheid developmental project, xenophobia becomes an alibi for laying claim on the state and demanding economic rights which foreigners are seen as usurping. For women – caught in the boundary between the ethnic nation and the state – xenophobia becomes a foil for even greater control and ultimately, violence. In this regard, it is necessary to ask whether it is the case that xenophobia exemplifies a legitimate grievance against the state, or whether it simply legitimizes the delegation of statist forms of violence to citizens.

In the contemporary period, waves of xenophobic violence had been observed in South Africa since 1994, but the most explosive one had broken out on 11 May 2008 in the working-class township of Alexandra in Johannesburg and quicky spread throughout the country. The militants were mainly black citizens who exclusively targeted African foreign nationals,[44] and their targets were 'foreign immigrants from countries like Mozambique, Somalia and Zimbabwe, known collectively as *makwerekwere* – a derogatory term for foreigners and onomatopoeia for someone who speaks unintelligibly, a "babbler"'.[45]

Major commentary attributed xenophobia to the failure of the post-apartheid social contract, a consequence of the partial transition of only 'political power to the Black majority [and failure] to create . . . a complete systematic change that included the transformation of socio-economic racist institutions in South Africa'.[46] Others searched for its reasons from within the discourse of anti-blackness, terming the violence as 'Afrophobic' or 'negrophobic' 'because the identity of the criminals is marked in their pigmentation, [in] being Black'.[47] Others, following Fanon, theorized xenophobia as the violent manifestation of the experience of alienation among colonized people.[48] Yet another strand of the thinking saw xenophobic violence as bearing the 'imprints [of] the history of colonial group relations':[49] the recognition of 'its origins in the racism, nationalism, violence, and isolation of the apartheid era'[50] during which 'policies of race-based urban influx control, racially designated group areas, and ethnic "homelands" divided South Africans and made many of them literally and legally foreigners in their own land'[51] – possibly suggesting a rapture in the logics of decentralized despotism – the manufacturing of difference and hatred of the other as the basis of internal group coherence.

Heterodox political economy perspectives have held that neoliberal policy and structural adjustment undermines livelihoods and spurs violent competition over scarce resources such as jobs and housing.[52] Capitalism after all, is unique in its ability to 'construct and mobilize [difference] in continuously changing yet persistently exploitable ways'.[53] Others argue that in contrast with the colonial period, contemporary labour migrants to South Africa are encountering ongoing deindustrialisation and a post-apartheid regime that foments difference as a basis of governance and labour regimentation',[54] an argument similar to those that show the violent recreation of social boundaries that global migration tends to induce.[55]

Hickel's (2014) study is exceptional in drawing a historical link between xenophobia and South Africa's incipient crisis of social reproduction, finding that 'violence against foreigners is less about fixing flows and ordering anomie than about reestablishing the conditions for social reproduction and demarcating the precincts of moral personhood'.[56] His analysis lends critical space to considering not just the political economy of xenophobic violence but also its cultural and gendered basis, arguing that the universalizing bent of the political economy analysis 'tends to miss the culturally particular ways people in South Africa understand economic deprivation. The experience of neoliberalism is shot through with deeply gendered implications informed by the history of the past half-century'.[57] I am entirely persuaded by this argument.

During the postwar period, apartheid planners, concerned about the possibility of black uprising, had sought to generate consent among urban Africans through Fordist-style 'embedded liberalism' as a kind of class compromise that centred on the construction of the modern 'Industrial man', the figure of the married male breadwinner living in a formal township house and working a stable job in manufacturing, mining, or the civil service.[58] This notion of 'industrial man' is itself steeped in neoclassical economic thinking,[59] which does not hold space for the reality that people experience class not simply as individuals, but as members of household units containing unequal gender relations.[60] Furthermore, it is necessary to account for specific historical conditions which may encourage the dominance of ethnicity and class over gender as the basis of action (e.g. as witnessed through nationalist movements), thus the need to avoid stabilizing one category of analysis such as has been the case with gender in neoclassical thinking.

This neoclassical man, so central to South Africans' expectations of modernity in the second half of the twentieth century, rapidly crumbled as new strategies of capital accumulation undermined the conditions for such aspirations and cast most South Africans into a state of abjection – a shift that gave rise to a 'crisis of social reproduction'.[61] One of the most glaring indications of this crisis is the decline in marriage rates, down to less than half of 1960 levels, so that today only 3 of 10 South African adults are married. With unemployment rates as high as they are, most young men find it impossible to raise the resources they need to pay *lobola* (bride wealth) and to establish their own legitimate, respectable homes. This partially explains the complaint most frequently on the lips of vigilantes – mostly young males – 'that foreigners are *taking away their jobs, houses, and women*'.[62] Foreigners stand accused by locals of 'stealing their women by wooing them with cash, outdoing the local competition because [foreigners] have fewer financial responsibilities to kin'.[63] The point of the complaint, Hickel argues, 'is that they feel they are losing their grip on the most basic means of social reproduction'.[64] In Durban, foreigners are accused of 'impregnating local women without paying bridewealth or cleansing fines . . . *the ultimate sign of illegitimate reproduction*'.[65]

This narrative collapses the material and the corporeal: it is not just an abstract complaint against loss of livelihoods – not just the articulation of a right in the post-apartheid democracy to decent jobs and livelihoods – but also a protest against the loss of a presumed *right* to the reproductive capabilities of 'our' women; a measure of the control and power which can be exercised over women, often with violence or with the threat of it. That complaint does not merely protest the captivity of women in abstraction, but *reconstitutes as criminal* the arrogation by foreigners of the control over (South African) women's labours, women's wombs, women's reproductive capacities and their caring labour. The perception of criminality that everywhere invariably precedes punishment for such 'crime' is, in the context of xenophobic violence, conveyed through the 'Captive Maternal' figures of *both* local women and foreign men, enjoined through a narrative of material dispossession. Such interpellation of women as violable subjects that is structured around narratives of gendered labour, dramatizes the material and embodied constitution of democracy's postcolonial gendered subjects. The violation of women as gendered labourers is not reducible to their violation on the basis of gender. Yet the bare liberal political relationship that is established between women and the post-apartheid state is one that denies legibility to women as working people – as survivors too, of apartheid's general dispossession of black people. As labouring subjects, women are rendered invincible.

Women are in other words, stripped of the possibilities of liberation from the conditions of deprivation that fuel exploitation of their sexual and reproductive labours – conditions which in turn subjectivate them in embodied form as targets of sexual violence under capitalism. The discourse of xenophobia which the liberal state authorises instead subjectivates women as members (possessions) of ethnic communities whose codes they are presumed to be violating in concert with 'foreigners'. Those who need the protection of rights but are denied a legitimate basis for claiming rights (through the narrative of violating social and cultural norms) are compelled to reconstitute themselves as *victims* of violence. Emptied of the material significance that embeds the claims of economically oppressed groups, rights assume the alibi of a cultural signifier. The villain in this narrative is no longer the neoliberal capitalist state that in reality is complicit in the indiscriminate immiseration of black people and in the destruction of the conditions necessary for their social reproduction – denied access to land, decent jobs, decent housing, water, healthcare, social welfare and education. Rather, it is a political possibility that is conveyed to women through narratives that caricature them as violators of national boundaries – as the primary subjects of an embodied type of citizenship that constructs a short bridge between gendered nationalisms and embodied violence.[66]

Gendered labour and the soul of Marikana

On 16 August 2012, 34 mine workers were killed by South African police in the town of Marikana in South Africa's platinum belt. The Marikana Massacre, or simply 'Marikana' as it has by now been canonized in its singularity, was an *event*.[67] An event not because it lacked colonial-apartheid era antecedents: its singularity relates to the shock of its staging precisely in the post-apartheid context of democratization – in the course of South African history therefore, unconditioned by prior conditions.

Subsequent commentaries similarly signalling it as event likened Marikana to Sharpeville (1960),[68] to Soweto (1976)[69] and to the 1973 Durban strikes.[70] Some rightly saw the massacre as signalling 'the quasi-official end of post-apartheid South Africa's revolutionary era',[71] a searing indictment of the incipient democracy. These analyses were almost in totality sympathetic to labour (albeit quite narrowly focused on the *productive* labour force), and from that vantage point, grounded the state's brutal response to striking miners in a history of labour dissent, viewing the strikes leading up to the massacre as 'a continuation of the extensive labor militancy [that had] rendered the broader trade union movement a formidable opponent to the [apartheid] regime from the early 1970s'.[72]

Yet, from the early 1970s when labour began to actively resist apartheid, three distinct political traditions had emerged in the labour movement with different perspectives on broader political issues. Among them was a national democratic tradition which argued that labour had an obligation to address socio-economic issues as workers' struggles in factories and townships were *indivisible* and majority of the unions in this category were affiliated with political organizations.[73] They in essence, expressed the necessity to account for the social conditions that provide a political link between labour militancy and the violence of the democratizing state. That is, while demands for better wages and working conditions articulate a contractual obligation between labour and capital, it is the necessity of social reproduction articulated within these demands – and which exceeds capital, being the guarantor of wages, not of rights – that enjoins the state in such demands (in its capacity to guarantee wages *as rights*). In other words, it is the problem of social reproduction that concretely places labour struggles in the domain of the *political*, given the social rights claims that black workers can legitimately place on the postcolonial state.

Labour in its colonial, capitalist and industrial form is constituted both by the social relations of production as well as the *social relations of its reproduction*. This reality invariably raises the spectre of a gendered subject as being central to the postcolonial labour struggle for the soul of the state: that is, reproductive labour – predominantly although not exclusively women – as a subject of the political state. To the extent that claims for better wages and working conditions harbour a deep-seated critique of the state's failure to guarantee the basic conditions of reproducing not just the (male) worker, but also his family, his lineage, as well as his right to participate in the 'male pact' that everywhere the patriarchal state[74] promises to men,[75] then social reproduction and the gendered labour that it requires must logically constitute a fundamental domain of control for both the state and capital.

The event of Marikana ought in this regard also to be understood in relation to the new subjects that it ushered into the broader political consciousness of the black masses: the gendered reproductive structure that constituted a primary condition for the rapture. The reproductive crisis that had been latent in the mining community has largely escaped analysis, with only few exceptions. Chetty (2016) highlighted the history of mining worker recruitment predominantly from South Africa's Eastern Cape as well as from Mozambique and Lesotho. These migrant workers at the time lived mainly in single-sex hostels. The anti-apartheid struggle of the 1980s put pressure on the mining companies to replace the hostel system, and in order to escape the costs of providing housing for the workers, companies offered miners a 'living out allowance' of about $120 a month, many of whom accepted this opportunity to supplement their wages with the equivalent of about one third of their salary.

The unintended consequence, Chetty writes, was that in the 1980s, thousands moved into informal settlements surrounding the mines, settlements that were without basic amenities. In contrast, housing for white mineworkers at London Mining (Lonmin) Platinum Mines were provided in Mooinooi and Brits, areas that are serviced with road networks, sanitation, schools and health facilities.[76] A reproductive crisis was germane to this racialized distribution of facilities among mineworkers. Alexander (2013) similarly raises a social reproduction question central to contemporary labour migrancy, although does not belabour its gendered subject beyond rationalizing workers' demands for higher wages in relation to the family as such: 'labour migrancy should not be confused with the migrant labour system. The latter was institutionalised from the late nineteenth century as a means of supplying labour regarded as "cheap", because, at least in theory, it was subsidised by rural production. Today the reverse happens. Migrant workers' budgets must include support for impoverished rural families'.[77] Both accounts suggest that the basic contradiction between labour and capital,[78] congealed within relations of social reproduction, had to have constituted a core basis for the demand for higher wages through pay disputes that had begun in May 2011.

Furthermore, Pillay's (2013) observation that the violence at Marikana 'interrupts the desire in much of [the labour studies scholarship in South Africa] for a revolutionary worker subject that is fully universal *without the particularities of race and ethnicity*' is also significant in this regard.[79] Pillay directs attention towards the breakdown in the post-apartheid social contract between the state, labour and capital and, here again, raises a social reproduction question that strides the distinction between political unionism and shopfloor unionism that emerged with the formation of a new independent union movement of African workers in the wake of the 1973 Durban strikes. This distinction, Pillay argues,

> took the form of a debate on strategy and tactics but . . . had a larger ideological import. It was animated by the question of whether unions should take up issues that affect their members at the place of production, in the factory, the mine, the issues of wages and working conditions and safety – or whether workers *should also take up issues that affect them not only at the point of production but also in the spaces of their reproduction*, i.e. housing and living conditions, issues of transport, of rents, of passes and influx control.[80]

Marikana marked the recession of political unionism, the return of shop floor unionism and setting aside of 'the ethnic, racial and political divisions of apartheid',[81] so feared by workerist movements as a threat to worker solidarity. Pillay is rightly critical of the strand of scholarship and activism that regarded the return to shop floor activism as marking a new revolutionary politics, broadly defined as 'a way of unmooring the abstract worker *from the fetish of nationalism*', arguing that 'in their minds, the spirit of world history can proceed with shop floor unionism that allows the South African working class to continue the uninterrupted journey of becoming itself, a journey that had been truncated by the victory of political unionism over shop floor unionism, *of nationalism over socialism*'.[82] Pillay thus contests the sufficiency of the capital-versus-labour narrative, rather placing the violence of the strike within the historical context of settler colonialism, and in particular, the identitarian logics through which working people are constituted and eventually violated.

Naicker (2015) likewise critiques the social basis of the violence, citing the fact that the mining company (Lonmin) had long been engaging with traditional leaders from the Congress of Traditional Leaders of South Africa (contralesa) for years prior to the massacre and nearly three years after, as 'a public acknowledgement of the bifurcation that still exists in the South African state today.'[83] Ethnicity comes to stand in for social citizenship in the wake of such acknowledgements: '[i]t is clear that Lonmin and the State still view the workers, most of whom come from the rural Eastern Cape, as belonging to a different sphere of politics compared to urbanized South Africa, *a sphere in which ethnicity plays a large role*.'[84] This ethnic exclusionary language that is regularly mobilized against mineworkers in effect 'de-politic[izes] their attempts to access citizenship rights in the first place'.[85] In these ways, ethnic identity can be mobilized against its bearers by placing them in a sphere that is putatively prior to that of modern politics *proper*, a rural sphere that is 'premodern, backward, archaic'[86] – a sphere out of which male workers migrate and from which women never really escape the burden of social reproduction. In the eyes of the postcolonial democratizing state, the narrative of a primitive sphere effectively delinks social reproduction from politics: the very structure on which the migrant economy is rendered possible is rendered invisible, and its normative violence placed outside of the purview of democratic politics.

Marikana was a post-apartheid event – one expression of the failure of the democratic promise. Its mainstream discourse announced a decisive break between labour, capital and the state as the alliance between state and capital was cemented. Its obscured feminist discourse, however, told the story of a more complex and historically situated struggle: an anticolonial struggle that held maternal modes of organizing in captivity. And while captivity reveals its subject, its object as well as its intentions are often invariably concealed by the prevailing structure, as feminist analyses of Marikana demonstrate. Indirect colonial rule had subjectivated men as tax paying waged labourers, at the same time as women were being constituted as the 'juridical juniors of male chiefs, headmen, fathers, husbands and sons',[87] thereby enforcing a 'gendered separation between male waged work in the urban areas and women's social reproductive labour in the rural areas',[88] as well as in urban settings, maintaining and reproducing miners' capacity to labour.[89] In this regard, the labours of both women and men stood captive to the state and to capital. Why then, as I have tentatively asked in Chapter 4, do women and men survive colonial captivity so differently? One explanation may be found in the nature of the work into which women and men are differentially drawn.

Along this grain, Benya (2015) has examined the reproductive labour question in Marikana through a typology of women's labour at the mines, drawing a distinction between 'town women' and 'country wives': between 'wives who renew the mine labour force within the areas from which migrants originate, - the Eastern Cape, Lesotho, Mozambique – and mistresses who maintain and reproduce their capacity to labour on a daily basis, within easy access of the mines of Marikana'.[90] The line being drawn between wives and mistresses here is not so much a moral one as it is a juridical one, to the extent that while it is the mistresses or town women who carry out the substantive daily obligations of care, they remain unentitled to any legal recognition despite this burden of care:

> The position of most women in Marikana is that of mistresses to mineworkers. It is they who look after the migrant workers day in and day out, as opposed to their legally recognised wives, who remain behind. While most of them have lived together with their mineworker partners for years, some as long as 25 years, servicing them, fetching water, preparing meals and washing dirty, ore ridden work-suits and reproducing their labour, having children and raising them, and

> acting as caregivers to mineworkers when they are sick, they *remain mistresses.* Their precarious position as mistresses and dependence on men's wages mean that they are at the beck and call of their male partners, their lives dictated by men and the mines.[91]

Their status as mistresses might deny women formal recognition in law, devalue their work and render them more violable, but this range of possibilities does not necessarily place the two categories of women, mistresses and wives, on an unequal footing as far as reproductive labour is concerned, precisely because social inequality is concretely (re)produced through *structural* differentiation, not normative difference. Elsewhere, I have argued that sex/gender divisions of labour do not necessarily produce gender inequality. Consider the following example: a working woman who performs certain tasks in her own home for her family is said to be doing unpaid non-market domestic labour that contributes to the reproduction of labour power on a daily and generational basis. If the same woman undertakes identical tasks in someone else's home for pay, she is considered as a being paid employee or a wage labourer. The point here is to understand women's oppression in relation to specific forms of social organization within which our labours are expended, such that the distinction between the two *lies in the social relations of the work*, not in the tasks themselves or the affective characterizations of the worker.[92] In this singular regard, perceived social differences in the status of mistresses, wives and even that of prostitutes, whose labours similarly feature prominently in the social organization of the mines at Marikana, becomes irrelevant.

In a long opinion piece titled 'Marikana: 20 years in the making', Frankel (2012) wants us to understand the massacre as a representation of the democratic failure in South Africa, and relates the labour dynamics to the structural demands of capital, describing a rogue economy in which nothing is sacred. Both prostitution and sex trafficking have been noted in Marikana. According to Frankel (2012), among the most lucrative trades that have emerged in the mining town is a highly profitable business in commercial sex trafficking of young girls and even children to service the needs of both contract and more permanent members of the Marikana mining workforce. He describes an underground world in which local agents of the sex trade are connected to bigger Johannesburg-based syndicates involved 'not only in loan-sharking to miners and other urban people, but also racketeering, drugs and illegal trade in small armaments.' In short, an extensive shadow economy in which the trade in women's reproductive labours (not merely bodies) is as profitable as drugs and guns. The sex-workers, whom Frankel also terms as 'sex slaves' arrive from across the borders 'or in profusion from our rural areas'[93] and 'work out of locked shacks under close supervision of their minder'.[94] That is, *in captivity*. Many women in Marikana or their offspring are similarly reported to have 'turned to sex work as a survival strategy because there are few other jobs for women in the area'.[95]

The extent to which commercial sex work, as well as other care labour performed by 'mistresses' acquires such visibility in the mining 'economy proper' mirrors the historical migrant political economies that emerged across the colonies.[96] It suggests the inadequacy of wages for the sustenance of mining households and dependence of this capitalist economy on the ability to control other labours and sources of income. The trade in sex work, sex trafficking and the informalization of intimate living arrangements through mistresses rather than marriage achieves this aim. But such social relations of production and reproduction are also invariably sustained through violence. To this extent then, the massacre of August 18, 2023, understood only as a response to striking mine workers lends itself to a narrow view. It is not only the labours of miners that the state and capital sought to discipline, but also the lives, livelihoods and gendered economies that constitute Marikana in its entirety. Hart (2007) explains this as 'the depoliticizing thrust of discourses of a Second Economy and the disciplinary practices that accompany them'.[97]

The broader point I seek to make in relation to the foregoing is that the proximity of women to sexual violation in the post-apartheid democracy is fundamentally structured by the social conditions and political economies of place and time. This is similar to a point I have argued elsewhere, that '[t]here is nothing we can particularly understand about "rape culture" or misogyny or violence outside of a concrete understanding of the lived circumstances that produce the subject of the violence as subjugated – that is, subject to a particular set of negative conditions. Subjugation cannot in itself gain legibility when abstracted from a broader social context that constructs popular claims by working people as violations of the liberal codification of a regime of rights'.[98] The guns that silenced 34 lives in Marikana that summer may have been trained by the apartheid regime, but now belonged to the post-apartheid democratizing state. Furthermore, the violence of the apartheid regime could be read in straightforward terms as that which coercively upholds a state that seeks to govern illegitimately. But how are we to make sense of the violence of a (post-apartheid) state that had been granted a popular mandate through a landslide electoral victory? Marikana is in this sense, metaphor for a state that had surrendered its authority as a democracy – including even the power to exert force in defence of its sovereignty – to capital, and in so doing announced the market as the new domain of rights.

Bourgeois rights can be defined only in very narrow terms as the legal and political rights of the capitalist class, and it is easy to understand that the democracy that protects such rights is invariably going to shield them from the claims of the masses. Marx bemoaned this fact in the *Communist Manifesto*, arguing that the bourgeoisie has, 'in place of the numberless indefeasible chartered freedoms, set up that single unconscionable freedom – Free Trade';[99] and that the only equality it knows is commercial equality, based on brutal and shameless exploitation, on a fundamental inequality in relations between the service 'providers' of work and the 'clients' who buy their labour power. In the classical sense the service providers at Marikana were mineworkers, but so were the mistresses and sex workers who emerged in specific response to the demands of that economy.

Yet the working masses are not without blemish: workers are ever increasingly held captive in an endless cycle of consumption, where even the most political of rights are being rearticulated as the right to consume. Contemporary sociological texts, Rancière (2006) points out, replace the 'bourgeoisie' with another subject, 'democratic man', from which point it becomes possible, he argues, to transform the reign of exploitation into the reign of equality, and to make democratic equality identical to the 'equal exchange' of market services.[100] The bourgeois classes, concerned only with profitability, create a 'rights economy' that may be deemed as the commodification of rights. Within the liberal democratic state, rights enter into the realm of market services, alongside commodities, and the 'democratic man' expresses the 'equality' of the relations of exchange as the 'equality' of human rights.[101]

The suggestion here, as I have argued elsewhere, is that it is as consumers that individuals now participate and find meaning in democracy, as identities once defined by the labours of sustaining oppressed communities, a shared anticolonial spirit and social responsibility to the group, come to be structured under the organizing principle of individualized consumerism. Others, like migrant labourers, non-unionized workers, ethnic minorities and women who gain legibility only via subjectivation as 'mistresses' and 'sex workers' in relation to the male workers they daily reproduce, become disenfranchized by an increasingly consumer-driven society, in which they can no longer participate.[102] As a result, the gap between their subjectivities and democracy's services continues to grow (Nielsen 2007). The stories of mass protest and wildcat strikes in South Africa are also stories of the state's irresponsiveness to the basic demands of individuals driven ever further away from the state by the punishing demands of consumerism. The state's response has, not unexpectedly, been antagonistic, as these individuals are recognized less as deserving citizens and more as intrusive/disruptive elements in the liberal democratic pact. In South Africa the 'slow death' of the democratic citizen has been years in the making, as intensified economic competition entrenched through the explicit alignment of capital with state interests narrows the scope for the radicalization of the democracy.[103]

In the rural domains where the wives of migrant mine workers remain captive to custom, there is no reasonable expectation that women will receive justice from the state for the violations that traditional authorities commit against them.[104] In the post-apartheid context of Marikana, women gain legibility as *direct* subjects of the democratizing state but, paradoxically too, of its violence. The native question – the question regarding the stabilization of minority rule over a majority native population – re-emerges as a fundamental contradiction in the post-apartheid state when examined against the question of rights. This is because the native question is a pre-democratic question to the extent that is not burdened by question of rights, liberties or equality in relation to native, colonized peoples. In the colonial situation, rights 'proper' belong only to colonialists—*those who govern are its primary subjects.* In the putative democracies of the postcolony, the subjects of rights are as diverse as the groups that are enjoined within the nation state: gender, race, caste, class, ethnic, migrant, etc. As such, the native question congeals within it a fundamental contradiction of *difference*, which the postcolonial/post-apartheid state inherits.

The postcolonial democratizing state is burdened by ethnic, racial, religious, caste, class and gender inequalities, which harbour a crisis of social reproduction whenever the state's capacity for redistribution is diminished, and, therefore, intensify dependence on gendered labour to undertake the reproductive burden. This captive labour of social reproduction that is performed predominantly (although not exclusively) by women thus stands implicated in the reactionary nationalisms that the state occasionally authorises through xenophobic violence, or through its violent realignments with capital as in the event of Marikana. In both instances, women do not emerge as legitimate subjects of rights in their own right but rather *embody* the question of redistribution that confronts every postcolonial state. That reproductive labour remains so invisible and impermeable to the language of rights ought to be understood in relation to such embodiment: again, *captivity always reveals its object, not its subject.* Ultimately, where democracy cannot resolve the hereditary contradictions of colonization that demand resolution through redistribution, rights claims have tended to threaten state stability. Such claims pit the state against its own labouring subjects (both productive and reproductive) in the service of capital and imperialism, and invariably provoke the state's disciplinary power.

Lisa Marie Cacho (2012) has written about the antiblackness that marked the aftermath of hurricane Katrina in 2005 on the U.S. Gulf Coast, in an important book that examines how human value is made intelligible through racialized, sexualized, spatialized and state-sanctioned violences, as well as the ways in which social value is contested and condoned through legally inflected notions of morality. In it, she argues that 'racial stereotypes are not degrading because race is devalued. Stereotypes are degrading because they link race to other categories of devaluation, just as race is redeemed when linked to other properties of personhood universalized as socially valuable, such as heteronormativity or U.S. citizenship'.[105] This argument finds some relevance in the contexts described above. To the extent which I have argued that the subject of xenophobic violence in South Africa defies any easy identification outside of the structures of accumulation and social reproduction that necessitate(d) his or her presence in the colony and now republic, the substantive emphasis of our analysis must be placed on the structures, conditions and institutions that devalue labour.

Those conditions include the political communities that are reconstituted through democracy, which in its relation to capitalism, assigns value not on the basis of political equality but rather, economic equality as I argue via Rancière above. In this regard, the categorization of men as purely productive (labour) places them in a domain of class analysis in which surplus value – value 'proper' – can simply be understood in conformity with Marxian theories of value in which the notion of exploitation is central. But what to make of reproductive labour, which constitutes the actual domain within which the devaluation of both productive and reproductive labour takes place? These are the cultural realms into which every identity 'other than class' – gender, ethnic, caste, sexual and racial stereotypes – are condemned. In those realms, value is made intelligible not through the logics of profit-making, but through relationality:[106] the demand that a subject be valuable often produces violence, in part because what is made visible as valuable often requires a negative 'other'. To paraphrase Cacho, calling workers 'foreigners' is both 'criminalizing and alienating'. It also erases the relationality (between productive labour and reproductive labour) that constitutes working people everywhere.

The acts of violence unleashed by the South African public against foreign nationals/migrants in 2010 and the violence unleashed by the South African state against its own public in Marikana share a common identitarian problem: the former seeking to expel national minorities from the republic and the latter seeking to expel national majorities from the democracy. Also revealed by both is a structure of social reproduction that is fundamentally weakened by the failure of the post-apartheid state to reconcile the imperative for redistribution with the ideal of social and political equality that democracy ultimately promises.

In this regard, the social and political stabilization of that society cannot be concretely understood in neglect of the crisis of social reproduction that the redistributive failures of the state portend. Gendered labourers, especially women, embody this labour and are therefore caught between the state's disciplining violence and the subjective violence of the communities that need them but marginalize them as 'sex worker', 'mistresses', 'wives', 'our women'. These are sub-gender identities with no equivalents in law and therefore impossible as subjects of rights. To quote Spillers (1987), the nomenclature through which black women are claimed for the tasks of reproduction 'describe a locus of confounded identities, a meeting ground of *investments and privations* in the national treasury of rhetorical wealth. My country needs me, and if I were not here, I would have to be invented.'[107] The misnaming of women conceals a deep desire to negate their humanity in the hope that they might altogether renounce their 'right to rights.'

In the quote that opens this chapter, Paton (1948) bemoans the colonial compulsion to destroy the native structure and psyche, and warns that what was destroyed had been much more than the tribal system: colonialism fundamentally undermined the social, physic, material and cultural fabric that constituted the humanity of native populations. Struggles for democracy in the postcolonial state are in this regard, obliged to reckon with the nature and legacies of that destruction. Attempts towards justice often encounter a juridical challenge because rights claims are invariably constrained by the liberal state's residual tendency towards difference as a mode of social and political control. The identitarian politics here function in a manner similar to any other political ideology, with the tendency, as Soper (1986) finds, to '*universalize violence* whenever there is need for liberation of the "principles and ideologies" from which individuals claim for rights and progress'.[108]

It is Schmitt's argument that while claims of equality are inherent in democracy, bourgeois democracy cannot resolve these claims because it 'rests on compromise: hence all of its solutions are in the end temporary, occasional, never decisive'.[109] What is suggested here is that bourgeois democracy cannot guarantee the stability of its subject. Furthermore, universalism is implicit in democracy's claims for equality, a factor which altogether flattens out difference. But perhaps most significantly, Schmitt finds that 'liberalism will tend to undermine the possibility of the political in that it wishes to *substitute procedure for struggle*. Thus . . . legitimacy and legality cannot be the same: indeed, they stand in contradiction to each other'.[110] For the postcolonial modern state, this then is the fundamental tension: an invariably violent struggle for liberation between the *political* form of the state (sovereign, constitutional, juridical) and its *social* form (constituted through its various groups – ethnic, caste, gender, race, sexuality etc.). Those historically tasked with reproducing its social form, as 'boundaries of the nation', 'reproducers of the nation', 'biological reproducers', and as 'bearers of the collective', most threaten its political form and therefore are most subjected by its disciplinary regime.

It is a singular indictment of democracy that it has managed to ignore the anticolonial premise of the clamour for it in the postcolonial world – that it continues to benefit from the same historical structures and institutions of social reproduction *in their original form*, as those that upheld colonial capitalist accumulation and slavery prior to that. For any liberatory potential it might hold beyond this colonial character, democracy must acknowledge its indebtedness to working people everywhere, to Captive Maternals, to the populations of surplus labour that from below continue to demand the labours and time of working people for their own survival. Democracy in the postcolony is, in other words, illegible outside of its relationship to this structure of social reproduction that ironically, is most vociferous in renewing calls for the 'deepening of democracy', and is at the same time subjugated by it.

6

'The Art of the Unspeakable':[1] An Anatomy of Gendered Violence in Postcolonial South Africa and India[2]

In the deep heart, the unsayable is said, and silence does not become an absence of speech, but the presence and saying of the unsayable.[3]

The subjects of this chapter are one survivor and one victim of rape, enjoined through an analysis that strings together a critique of postcolonial gendered violence through two artistic interventions: the award-winning South African play titled *Tshepang: The Third Testament* (2003), which deals with the unspeakable trauma and violence of rape, and the documentary *India's Daughter* (2015) based on the 2012 Delhi gang rape and murder of twenty-three-year-old 'Nirbhaya'. Each of these interventions enjoin us to consider the ways in which certain bodies enter into the public sphere. Their presumed availability as well as fragility, the fact that they are infantilized and therefore stripped of the right to say no. They raise historical questions regarding a major tension inherent in the idea of 'consent': that is, what is entailed when our lived bodies are fundamentally contradictory to our juridical being. They show how difference both marks the terrain of violable bodies and is flattened out by liberal juridical redress of rape. The chapter also considers the limitations of liberal politics of recognition when those for whom redress against sexual violence is sought are unable to 'speak', let alone appeal to the courts for justice – that is, are illegible in their subjective constitution – but rather have to appeal to the public as the only viable channel through which to gain visibility to the state's organs of justice. In this regard, a core questions which emerges is this: how is the anticolonial meaning of justice modified by the private appeal of the liberal juridical subject to the public – this liberal subject itself a relic of colonial jurisprudence?

Lara Foot Newton's award-winning play titled *Tshephang: The Third Testament* – eponymously named after its main subject – tells the tragic story of the rape of a tiny female human.[4] As prefaced by Newton (2005) in the text of the play,

> [i]n 2001 South Africa was devastated by the news of the brutal rape of a nine-month-old child by the name of baby Tshepang. It was thought that she had been gang raped by a group of six men. Later it was discovered that the men had been wrongly accused and that the infant had, in fact, been raped and sodomised by her mother's boyfriend. Once the story of baby Tshepang hit the headlines, the scab was torn off a festering wound and hundreds of similar stories followed. Each story was equally horrific. 'A five-month-old baby', 'A two-year-old girl' . . . and so the list grew.[5]

When Lara Foot's[6] searing play, *Tshepang: The Third Testament* returned to the stage in 2018, one critic aptly observed of its success that 'it needs that excellence to survive, because otherwise it would be easy to ignore and forget about the play – just like we try to do with the issue [of rape] itself'.[7] That the banality of rape in our present times is such that a mere telling of the act would not suffice in bringing its subject to our attention demands pause. Initial reports of the rape had indicated that baby Tshepang had been gang raped by six men and not surprisingly, had lost traction with the press when it was eventually established that it had been done by 'only' one man. It seemed to be that it was the *collective* criminality of men that was considered newsworthy, not so much the *act* of violence that may have criminalized them. The narrative of one rapist and one victim does not conform as neatly to the stereotype of 'problem people'.[8] I watched the play at the Joburg Theatre in 2018 and was struck by two things then. The first was the complexity of humanity that it had conveyed through the bare narration of this brutal act of violence, and the second was its surprising ability to evoke something other than revulsion for those that had failed baby Tshepang. I wept at the end of the play, uncertain whether my devastation stemmed from the sheer brutality of the act or from its tender portrayal. It all felt too familiar.

In the years afterwards I have sat with two seemingly irreconcilable sentiments regarding the portrayals in the play: on the one hand and quite predictably, an unassailable grief for baby Tshepang and the millions of others that have shared her fate elsewhere, unseen. On the other, a deeply sympathetic attitude towards those that had been led to brutalize her: her mother; her mother's boyfriend; the female 'aunt' that witnesses the rape and does nothing; the *shebeen* queen that numbs her charges and numbs society; the young man that himself had been brutalized as a child and who in adulthood becomes the mother's lover and rapist of her child; the white policeman who required evidence through baby Tshepang's broken lifeless body in order finally to confirm the brutality of the society his ancestors had birthed; the hopelessness that marks those forgotten strips of inhumane abodes that still dot South Africa's urban landscape despite the formal ending of apartheid in 1994. I read *Tshepang* as a searing indictment of the post-apartheid democratizing state – a representation of the imminent implosion of the social contradictions that were festering and trying to find political expression under the current arrangement. It reflected 'the historical reality of [the] people, [which could only be] carried to success by the overcoming or correct solution of the internal contradictions between the various categories characterizing this reality'.[9] In its artistic rendering on stage, *Tshepang* exposes many of these contradictions from the vantage point of a gendered subject.

The play is narrated in its entirety by only two characters – Simon (Ruth's friend) and Ruth (Tshepang's mother). 'Simon tells the entire story and acts out all the characters. Ruth is silent. The only props on the stage are a loaf of bread which 'represents the baby, and the broom which represents Alfred Sorrows [Tshepang's rapist]'.[10] On stage, 'a woman with a small bed tied to her back with a blanket sits on a heap of rock-like salt, which covers a pile of animal skins'.[11] Throughout the play we hear the sound of salt being rubbed onto an animal hide – a 'manic and obsessive rubbing of the salt' [the proverbial salt on the wound; the curse of 'Lot's wife'] only interrupted on occasion when Ruth stops to listen to Simon. Throughout the play, Ruth remains mute: 'she doesn't say a word, not any more'.[12] The mother's silence had been an artistic decision on the part of the director:

> silence is sometimes far more powerful than words. That is not to say you have silenced the character . . . It wasn't just silence. She was rubbing the salt and was very present. It came back to being a mother . . . what do you say? What do you say? Should she have spoken? I think the silence allowed us to look at her and really be with her because she was doing something. She had salt and was grinding it . . . a metaphor for in the wound.[13]

Simon's soliloquy is repeatedly punctuated with the observation that 'here nothing ever happens. Nothing at all'. The state has long forgotten this remote, impoverished community. The utter mundanity of daily life there is apparent in the idling of young unemployed men, young women whose main resort for survival is prostitution, and sex and alcohol are the daily drugs that numb this reality: 'wake, wipe, eat, drink, naai,[14] sleep'.[15] In that community, farm owners still compensate labour with third-grade alcohol: 'The dop system[16] . . . All the wine that is too kak to sell, De Villiers gives to the workers as payment. It's been happening for years. My father's father was paid like that, and so was my father'.[17] Three generations of men trapped by a vicious structure that condemns them to a life of repetition – lives in which humanity acquires the quality of mere objects – a fungibility that equates female genitalia with any penetrable object: 'a man, given half the chance, will put it in anything'.[18] This is violence that has long lost the potency of *instrumentality* that might lend to it the gaze of criminality or punishability. It is violence that appears meaningless, its ultimate banality executed under conditions of such extreme desolation that describe not the monstrosity of the people but rather their capacity to commit extreme forms of violence under the guise of 'the ordinary'. The lack of discontinuity between the routine and the event:

> [for] people who commit infant rape, different to pedophilia where there is grooming, [it] is *often a one-off act of extreme violence, and often comes from people that have experienced extreme violence in their lives.* I am not for a moment excusing the act, but trying to [make] sense of the cycle of violence and this worthlessness that has come out of apartheid, and specifically in these small communities where there is just absolutely no hope.[19]

Against the dominant narrative in studies of sexual violence that pits survivors of violence against those who perpetrate violence, one might in the context of this community, consider a more historical/structural narrative that implicates both the *conditions* that produce those who are violable as well as those who violate them. Yet still, the viability of implicating the structures and conditions of violence seems to depend on the possibility of linking such violence to something else:

> what struck me at the time was the *psychotic nature* of the violence. That it wasn't only associated with poverty; obviously it is associated with substance abuse. But there is a psychosis that comes from trauma.[20]

The problem, however, with the pathologization of violence is that it negates the possibility of approaching violence as a historical and therefore *political* problem: that is, as a problem that allows us to see both those who commit violence and those who survive it as gendered *subjects* of violence,[21] albeit produced at different stages on the continuum of violence. The pathologization of sexual violence also renders agency virtually impossible as modern law has not yet found the language to criminalize madness. If making sense of violence constitutes the fundamental condition for addressing it, then the nature of violence that is 'unspeakable' places into question both the law that does not have a language for it and its meaning in the context of democracy.

The meaning (and genealogies) of violence

From Benjamin's (2007) treatise on violence emerges the argument that 'given the conditions under which humans live, they need to resort to violence to attempt to achieve justice. Only through power can justice be achieved. But precisely insofar as it is achieved through power, it is unjust. For Benjamin, the concepts of power and justice are mutually exclusive insofar as power is equivalent to force and violence'.[22] His endeavour to illuminate the relationship between violence and the law in *Critique of Violence* denies violence any form and meaning prior to entering the sphere of moral relations that are defined by law and justice. For Benjamin, the law is rotten because it is based on an instrumental use of violence that functions only as a means to (both founding and preserving) power and never as a just end. The law in other words, is linked basically to power, not justice. This suggests that violence in the hands of individuals threatens the legal system (power) and so the law condemns not violence per se, but rather seeks to preserve the law itself: 'violence, when not in the hands of the law, threatens it not by the ends that it may pursue but by its mere *existence outside the law*'.[23] Any violence that exceeds the state's boundaries of reason signals the limits of the law – that is, demarcates those for whom the law can no longer provide protection and for whom justice is in this reading, impossible.

I have already mentioned the unanticipated sympathies that the play arouses: our compassion extends beyond baby Tshepang to also embrace Alfred Sorrows, the perpetrator, as well as those who were supposed to protect her: Ruth, her mother and Alfred's mistress, and Sarah, 'the one who [witnessed the act but] did nothing when it happened. Just lit a match and walked out of the room'.[24] We come to understand from Simon's narration of their lives, their own desperate childhoods, fated trajectories and the implosions they would no doubt encounter in some near future. 'Sarah wears a visible scar on her neck where her boyfriend stabbed her, her mother owned a shebeen, and she had been pimped off way too young. Alfred's father had a very young houvrou (mistress) called Margaret'. Margaret, we are told, 'was angry all the time. Especially when Alfred wet his pants, because it was she who had to do the washing' – the care labour.[25] Margaret's own implosion, Simon narrates, arrived on an ordinary day:

> One day when Alfred was about three we were play playing in the yard with Jaintjies Jacobs . . . Alfred loved laughing at Jaintjies's funny faces. That day, Jaintjies was in good form, and Alfred was laughing and laughing and laughing. Then suddenly, Alfred was standing in a pool of liquid, which happened to be pee. When Alfred realized what had happened he started to shake. He was

> terrified. And then it happened, Margaret, the houvrou, came around the corner and saw Alfred standing in his pee. From nowhere she grabbed a broom and started to beat Alfred...At first I thought it was a joke, and then I saw her face. She had become the devil. I . . . watched as she pummeled Alfred until his small body lay quietly in a pool of piss. Then she stopped and, for a moment, reflected on what she had done and then . . . then . . . AYEEEEEE! She began to beat him again. It was my mother who took him to the hospital, and was my mother who nursed his broken body for many months.[26]

In that moment, little Alfred's broken body is identical to baby Tshepang's broken eviscerated body,[27] both rendered visible only by the brutal acts of violence to which we the public bears witness. What is the source of this violence, and what ought to be the target of our rage? The moral imperative of the law would want us to vilify the perpetrator of violence – in this case, Margaret, Alfred's caregiver and then Alfred. It would want us to affirm its ultimate power over violence. But the moral arc of *justice* would redirect our gaze towards the structures and conditions that produce violence as a norm. Alfred's injury drew no moral outrage: the black male body is constituted *as* violent and violence towards it only confirms its presumed violent nature that in turn warrants disciplinary violence (the power to wield violence that preserves the law).

The initial public outrage that met the news of baby Tshepang's rape when it was thought to have been done by six men waned when eventually only one man, Alfred, was implicated: 'They all arrived. The press, the newspapers, television, film, cameras, USA, Britain, Johannesburg, Amsterdam. They all came here. What a story – six men raped a nine-month-old baby. You see! You see how shit you are? You see how shit you all are?'[28] It was not the extreme act of violence against baby Tshepang that had directed attention to the case, but rather the imperative to expose the 'historical criminality' of Black men, which could then *confirm* the law (the norm) and therefore preserve it. It is this same logic that renders Alfred's broken little body illegible as a violated body, for such recognition would undermine the law-preserving function to which the colonial state put violence: the deniability of black men's trauma is here equivalent to the law's preserving force.[29] Here again, Benjamin is instructive in suggesting that we might understand something about the effectiveness of violence by examining the public's reaction towards it;

> for one reflects how often the figure of the "great" criminal, however repellent his ends may have been, has aroused the secret admiration of the public. This can result *not from his deed* but only from the violence to which it [the public] bears witness. In this case, therefore, the violence that present-day law is seeking

> in all areas of activity to deny the individual appears really threatening, and *arouses even in defeat the sympathy of the masses against the law.*[30]

The social context of Benjamin's analysis is class struggle and more broadly the fascism of the 1930s, specifically the right that is guaranteed to workers to strike, what he terms as violence that is still 'permissible' within the legal system and therefore so feared by the law. The media spectacle and public attention that brings this small community into the public domain in the wake of the rape similarly suggests an authorized gaze. We must consider in this instance again a question I already posed in Chapter 4: what it is that violence *does* for democracy. Simon's outrage at outsiders' attempts to villainize Ruth in this narrative provides a partial response to this question:

> Shame on you! Shame on all of you! Who do you think you are? Coming here with your cameras and your accusations. Pointing your painted ugly fingers at us. Where were you, where were you? What are you doing here? Get out of here! Take you cameras and get out! *This town was raped long ago*. This town was fucking gang-raped a long, long, long, long time ago! Shame on us? Shame on you, shame on all of us![31]

His indignation lays bare the sense of abandonment that this community has mostly known in the wake of apartheid. His anger mirrors Ruth's own sense of abandonment, which expresses itself through a violent act of self-mutilation to which Simon bears witness:

> When I got to her house, the four-room, before I even walked through the front door I knew something was wrong. The door was standing open and there was a terrible silence and a terrible stink. Ruth was lying on the single bed, the one with the pink bedspread. The one where Siesie [baby Tshepang] had been raped. Next to the bed was an empty Star Pilchard tin. The lid had been three quarters opened and its sharp round edge was covered with a reddish brown gooey stuff. It was Ruth's blood. Her chest was covered in the same gooey stuff, her hands, her face. She had cut out her one breast, and tried to do the same to the other.[32]

On its own terms, it is not possible to make sense of the meaning of the violence that is meted out on the body of a nine-month-old child. The rape of Tshepang cannot be classified as incest (against which the law militates, but ultimately seeks to protect the family); she was raped by her mother's lover, by a 'stranger'. Modern law has shown itself woefully incapable of criminalizing the violation of 'strangers', of those not yet under its control. There is no evidence in speech that could be elicited from baby Tshepang regarding the extent of her pain and injury other than her broken mangled body itself. But the law *requires* not just evidence of pain but also its articulation by those who can bear punishment: through whom the law can preserve itself. In a world in which women exist in captivity to their roles as caregivers, and where their primary subjectivity emerges through the social reproductive labours that mediate their relationship to the state and to capital, the only vocabulary that could communicate the pain of this perceived failure of care – the only possibility of speech 'that allows its indictment'[33] in the lexicon of the liberal canon – is the *body*. Ruth's muteness and self-mutilation *is* speech in Tshepang's name.[34] It is a form of punishment that is required in order to confirm the familial bonds which women reproduce, the gendered labour which in extreme form expresses itself as *violence*.

Parallels exist elsewhere, as V. Geetha (2016) shows in the historical context of the Partition of India and Pakistan. The violence of the Partition, she writes, was marked by 'Hindu and Sikh women "choosing" suicide over dishonour as they fled marauding mobs of violent Muslim men . . . as families and homes were ripped apart and men saw their paternal authority challenged in unexpectedly cruel ways, they sought to retain whatever sense of honour they could by calling on their women to kill themselves – *in effect choose real death to the symbolic death that ensues when a woman is raped and her honour, and by implication familial honour, is lost*'.[35] In the play, Ruth has no apparent familial obligations to a husband or male relatives, save for a lover who is also the villain in this story. How then might we make sense of the source of the force that compels her towards the 'symbolic death' that she commits by severing her breast, that most intimate cradle of life for her child? Through the lens of her *captivity*: a claim that what liberal democracy requires (of violence) is not to recreate violent societies as such, but rather to delegate to those it holds captive the resolution of excess harms for which it cannot account. This is one of the fundamental ways in which gendered (reproductive) labour circulates in the realm of the political.

V. Geetha writes of an 'intense anxiety about sexual dishonouring [which translates] into self-destructive violence',[36] a suggestion that the preservation of conjugal, familial, communal ties – the very basis of the nation-state – invariably elicits gendered violence as a disciplinary mechanism. At its most extreme, the stabilization of the nation-state *requires control over the bodies that perform reproductive labour* and therefore authorizes wilful violation of those gendered subjects that constitute (and therefore, threaten) its boundaries. These reproductive bodies cannot escape violence. But the mere fact that these histories of gendered regulation have found expression in discussions around the 'rights of women' does not necessarily signal permission to speak about the relationship between sexual violence and the nation-state, for as V. Geetha notes in the context of the Partition, '[t]o speak of these relationships was, in effect, *to compromise nationhood itself*.'[37] Nationalism's requirement of "blood sacrifice," in Ambedkar's terms, remains buried, and within it '[t]he part played by women . . . has not been sufficiently noticed'.[38]

Though Ruth spoke no words, everything she said in relation to her child was heard. Of the silences that are 'uttered', Motsemme (2004) tells us that 'women's silence . . . should be viewed as part of a range of "languages of pain and grief" to narrate often hidden but troubled elements of their recent past'.[39] In seeking to extend the interpretative field of 'speech' that becomes legible to the juridical order, Motsemme ultimately argues that 'it is when the language of silence, which forms part of the "economy of the invisible," is also uncovered that we have a better view of those *privatized experiences of living daily in violent contexts*'.[40] It allows us to move beyond pathologies of violence with no real signifiers in the law, towards a concreteness that connects (both the violence that is committed and that which is experienced) to something that *has been lived.*

Reflecting on the meaning of such violence, Lara Foot shared with me her sense that '*a psychotic breakdown is not the same as a traumatic response to the perpetration of violence*'.[41] It is a significant distinction being conveyed here that delineates on the one hand, the type of violence that is unimpeachable because its root (psychosis, *madness*) is better ascribed to the gods in a transcendental sense – and on the other, the kind of violence whose root can concretely be located within the structures, conditions and institutions (of democracy) that *fail to apprehend the very violence* which they provoke in those whom they disappoint. Democracy's visible structures (citizenship, identity, family, society); its conditions (free association, sovereignty, jobs, security, speech); and its institutions (schools, hospitals, housing, infrastructure, media, religion) all stand accused on this count of failing the people at their margins, and therefore, of provoking their anger. Why the wrath against the failures of democratic institutions targets gendered, labouring bodies is not always apparent, but must remain central to our inquiries.

We cannot make sense of this kind of (gendered) violence in the language that is handed to us by democracy, precisely because such violence militates against democracy at every turn, indicts it and rejects all of its symbols (free media, police, visibility itself). What then gives meanings to this violence, and what does this violence mean? At a deeper level, what tools (in humanist terms) do we have of making sense of violence at this level? The violence committed on baby Tshepang, and that which Ruth visits on herself certainly extends beyond the realm of liberalism's comprehension: 'words is rubbish', declares Simon in a final reconciliation with Ruth's three-year silence.[42] Is the meaning of this violence merely that this is how structural violence *expresses* itself? What are the terms under which such violence might be understood when we acknowledge the reality that the human vocabulary with which to articulate it is in fact so limited in the face of sustained oppression, that it becomes not simply a problem of democracy but of the entire spectrum of our histories of captivity?

That problem, we might conclude, is ultimately expressed through violence, which is what gives *meaning* to violence, such that the expression (acts) of violence becomes critique itself, of societal violence. In Benjamin's framework, such violence remains within the confines of 'violence as means' but also exceeds it to the extent that it also provides a possibility of pointing us towards justice:[43] that is, to a violence that is not reducible to means only but also to just ends. The use of violence may in other words be read as an attempt by the colonized to exit their conscription. Artistic expressions or creative fabulations, such as is achieved through the play *Tshepang*, provide one avenue through which we might then *extend* our critique of violence. One avenue through which we might transcend the strict definitions, norms and laws within which modern liberal jurisprudence defines for itself what meets the juridical thresholds of violence. For those that 'speak' their trauma from the margins of modernity, creative (or Hartman's 'critical') fabulations, constitute a space of subjectivation which democracy might recognize through its norms of 'freedom of expression', 'freedom of speech', but not yet, as *human rights*. In the final act of the play, Ruth stands and looks out into the distance and (finally), quietly utters the name of her child: 'Tshepang'. Simon joins her 'as they look out into *nothingness*', and the lights fade on stage.[44] Every fear we carry regarding the inevitable subjection of yet another child to the unspeakable violence that baby Tshepang bore is embodied in that moment.

Unspeakable violence

> Serial killers are model prisoners because their victims are not in the prison.[45]

What does it mean to have the *power* to kill, maim, mutilate and rape, but not the *right* to kill, maim, mutilate and rape? This is a question that exposes a fundamental antagonism between the power which the state wields through its sovereign and juridical form, and the claims which it is required to settle on behalf of its subjects. We are presented with a modern state that authorizes violence at the same time as it denies, through punishment, the legitimacy of this violence. The violence which the colonial state mobilized against the colonized was always excessive – that is, its justification could not be found in the nature of relationship between the colonizer and the colonized due to the disproportionate power which the former wielded over the latter. *There is no moral possibility of colonial violence since it is illegitimate.* This moral question, however, cannot be sidestepped in the context of democratization, since it is expected that those who commit rape *do* know the difference between right and wrong. To borrow from elsewhere, this knowledge can be established 'by asking whether they would do the same if they were next to the police. If the answer is *no*, it means they know the difference between right and wrong. *They just do not care*'.[46] They do not care, not because they have lost the capacity to tell the difference between right and wrong, but because they no longer perceive of any real difference between the punishment of the law and the deathly sentence which they already live through their daily lives. What then, does it portend for democracy when the *threat* of punishment is no longer sufficient to deter violence?

Those questions haunt the narrative of the gang rape and murder of a young woman that occurred in Delhi on a cold night on 16 December 2012. Jyoti Singh, a twenty-three-year-old medical student from Delhi, was brutally raped and killed on a moving bus by a gang of six men. That attack in India's capital led to a national outpouring of rage and alarmed a global audience, with protesters demanding a long-awaited change in attitudes towards women. An important cinematic rendition of this event by Leslee Udwin titled *India's Daughter: The Story of Jyoti Singh* (2013) poignantly retold a story that elicited two major responses – one an official state response and the other a citizen response. The state response predictably sought the banning of the film on the grounds that it was 'highly derogatory' and an 'affront to women', while the citizen response constituted a public courtroom, variously characterizing the rapists' documented statements as 'constituting hate speech', as being 'self-incriminatory' and as 'violating the accuseds' right to a fair trial'.[47] The film also opened up space for feminist debates: around hate speech and freedom of expression; around the proliferation of sexualities and violence against women; around the meaning and impact of images and words, and the different levels at which representation works; and around media representations of the non-Western Other from a neocolonial location (the film had been produced by the BBC and made by a British filmmaker).[48]

Udwin's (2014) documentary is a raw depiction of society along its historical cleavages where gender, caste and class intersect to produce violence. It deals convincingly with a number of significant themes, but also leaves much to our speculative sense. In the opening sequence of the film, the defence lawyer for the rapists makes the following statement:

> The moment she came out from her house with a boy who was neither her husband nor her brother, she left her morality and reputation as a doctor, as well as a girl's morality also in the house and she came out *just like a "woman."*[49]

This assessment is striking in what it reveals about the layers of protection which a woman must achieve in order to escape violation – the extreme vulnerability of simply being woman/human. By such reasoning, Jyoti's decision to go on an outing with a male friend on the night she was raped would be construed as foresaking the institutional cover which marriage, the professions, or family might have accorded her. The absence of all three is established first at the scene of crime as a *moral* issue (i.e. availing her for judgement by society at large on the basis of her gender), and then in the criminal justice space as a *juridical* matter (i.e. interrogating her relationship with these institutions). Neither of the crimes against her (rape and attempted murder) enter into the juridical consciousness of the defence as being material. Jyoti's fundamental subjectivity as a violated woman is set aside as the defence machinery rather trains its eyes on her audacity to violate the conditions of her safety – suggesting her captivity to these social institutions:

> A female is just like a flower. It gives a good looking, very softness performance [sic], pleasant. But on the other hand, a man is just like a thorn. Strong, tough enough. That flower *always* needs protection. If you put that flower in a gutter, it is spoilt. If you put that flower in a temple, it will be worshipped.[50]

> The idea of the gang rape is to send a message – you are not to breach this boundary. This is a boundary between us and you to do with power.[51]

Jyoti's family was impoverished and had had to sell ancestral land in order to afford her medical school fees. She herself worked night shifts, from 8 pm to 4 am at an international call centre to cover her hostel fees, and slept no more than four hours a night. The night she was raped and murdered was the interlude between her last day as a medical student and her first as a medical intern. Like had been done to baby Tshepang, the violence of her rapists left her disembowelled: '[s]omeone put his hand inside her and pulled out something long . . . It was her intestines'.[52] Commentators in the juridical sphere who tried to make sense of its meaning set the tone for displacing its brutality onto a realm beyond humanity:

> The rape was extremely brutal. And it [is] something very unusual to find that you not only rape the girl, but you put an iron rod and take out her entrails . . . this is something I can't understand. What kind of human beings are those who do something like that?[53]

A patrolman called attention to Jyoti and her male companion who had been dumped from the moving bus, still alive: 'about 30–35 men gathered, but no one helped . . . no one stepped forward. After some time, a PCR [police control room] van arrived and they were taken to the hospital. *She looked like a cow looks after giving birth to a calf*.[54] Doctors conveyed the scale of her injuries to her parents as such: '[t]he system by which the human body functions is all gone. We do not know which parts to join. She will not survive more than 2 to 3 days . . . We do not understand how she is alive'.[55] Not the *fact* of the rape, but a *functionality* related to the brutality of the injury, became the story that mobilized the criminal justice system:

> [t]he whole idea was, the case was so brutal, the conviction, if it is earlier...is much better, it gives a good message to the society . . . Almost all the resources of this district, I'll say a strength of more than 2,000 persons . . . were commanded by this special investigation team, and everything was put into this case. As per the Criminal Procedure Code of India, in such cases like murder, rape and all these heinous cases, we normally get the time permitted for us to file a charge sheet as 90 days . . . but in this case, we had filed the charge sheet in 17 days.[56]

An act so ordinary within the everyday confines of 'India's rape capital' was reconstituted as the *exception*. That even the brutalised body does not escape its captivity to/within the nation – that its most pronounced political subjectivity and juridical legibility *requires* injury in order to suffice for mere redress before the law – is the reality which we must confront through these narratives. This is the crucible upon which democracy must account for itself and against which it must clear its name. In the commentaries, modernity itself stood implicated in the subjectivation of a particular kind of womanhood and the shock of its violation:

> a young woman who represented a symbol of new aspiration sent shock waves through the society. In the last 15–20 years the economy has changed a lot in India and its created opportunities for young women and single women to come and work, and it's raised expectations across a range of classes of young, single women of how they should be *allowed* to live their lives.[57]

But *where* does the space exist for young, single women to live their lives when that space is equally shorn by young men that have nowhere to go? Young men that are chronically unemployed? The mother of the seventeen-year-old Juvenile that had been convicted alongside the others although tried separately in the Juvenile Justice Board had this to say about the news: 'We woke up in the morning. The police came here. They said "your son has been caught, he has done such and such." He'd been gone for three years. I thought he had died somewhere. When the police came, I found out that he's still alive'. Where does the space for justice reside when young men too, only finally encounter their legibility for punishment (and therefore, confirmation of their humanity), through *crime*?

The outraged response of India's public received wide media coverage and eventually pressured the government into constituting a formal review process through The Verma Committee, a judicial committee charged by the government of India with canvassing all opinion about how the problem of rape could be addressed. Specifically, the committee was mandated to: 'look into possible amendments in the Criminal Law to provide for quicker trial and enhanced punishment for criminals committing sexual assault of extreme nature against women'.[58] In the film, Maria Misra describes the report as a '. . . landmark [one that was] *striking in its extreme liberalism*'.[59] The report 'made a number of very important recommendations. For instance, that things must happen much faster in the Indian judicial system . . . that the definition of sexual assault needed to be broadened, that the language of modesty and shame needed to be removed from the Indian Penal Code'.[60] In other words, its recommendations targeted the legal/institutional framework of sexual violence: it reimagined rape as an archaic problem of modern society and sought to bring it into the purview of modern law and regulation. It was a procedural reaction to a structural problem, a response to an equally liberal question emerging from civil society demanding accountability for the failure of rights in modern India:

> this was not just about a rape and an amendment to a criminal law. We were very determined that we were not going to let down society. *Offences against women was a part of the story*. The full story needed to be told. We felt that we would fail that fantastic civil society which gathered around India Gate with candles, if we did not tell them the true story.[61]

That 'true story' which the law apparently could tell from its vantage point was that '[t]he constitution provides for equality [which] hasn't happened because the men don't allow it to happen. And they feel that that's their hold on women and also its because of the historical tradition of patriarchy which has been over the years embedded into men and into women'.[62] The demands for accountability 'threatened the establishment' and the unabating protests of the public breached the boundaries of its monopoly over violence. It morphed into a standoff between 'protesters and police', and all the while, Jyoti lay broken in hospital, fighting for her life, deprived of speech: '[h]er condition deteriorated. She was very troubled. She was in great pain. *We could not talk*'.[63] Jyoti lost her battle on 29 December 2012. Of the period after, her father too, reflected on the unspeakable:

> For a father who once upon a time let his baby girl sleep over him, who had held her in his arms and played with her, who held her finger and taught her to walk, to have to set fire to that daughter during cremation by his very hands, this is very difficult. The most difficult. When I remember this moment, *I am unable to speak*. Words just don't come out.[64]

The Verma Committee was in essence tasked with concealing the utter ineptitude of the existing law in the face of violence that is considered 'excess'. But the 'shame' which the Verma Report sought to erase from the law does not belong to the perpetrators of violence alone. It is the shame of the entire society – of the families and communities and most certainly, of the legal regime itself that denies legitimate expression to the structures that produce those who violate and those who are violated on a daily basis. The shame of homelessness, unemployment and the utter immiseration produced by capitalist society belongs also with the postcolonial democratizing state. A striking observation was made of the only Juvenile implicated in case, that 'this boy was like millions of Indian children who are street children, toiling to survive. Sometimes working in a "dhaba" [small tea shop], sometimes working on a bus. And then whatever happened after that in their company this gang rape took place and he was party to it. This boy, in my opinion, *did not have any serious aberrations*. This boy had suffered endless misery in life. He was a child in need of care and protection . . . he was a typical profile of a child who *had* to be like this'.[65] This child is also young Alfred in baby Tshepang's story.

My point here is not to draw any crude link between poverty and violence, but rather to ask what happens when the exception which the state establishes through rape, as shown in Chapter 3, encounters societies in which violence is so normalized as to escape the moral indignation of society. Society in which '[b]eating and violence has become the story of every house'.[66] All of the accused are shown in the film as having come from backgrounds of devastating poverty,

> where their surroundings are not very good and there is overcrowding. That is a very common scene, that women have been tortured and beaten, or sexually

> abused by their male partners or husbands. And they have seen prostitution also running in their area and neighbourhood area . . . so it is not a very new thing to them. *And that's what actually makes [the rapists] again and again surprised that "why we"?*[67]

Why them indeed, out of a million other young men who they imagined had been 'allowed' to commit similar violence every day, were they being differentiated: '[t]hey've made this such a big issue. People have committed bigger crimes and nothing has happened to them. In Barabanki after the rape, her eyes were taken out. Sometimes they put acid on girls. There was another rape where they burnt her alive. Wasn't that wrong? If ours is wrong, then that was wrong too'.[68] The inability to confirm an act of violence on its own merit suggests a society that is inclined to keep producing violence in order to recognize itself, as well as a state and justice system that has continually to reach for exceptional forms of violence in order to *deny* the normalization of violence. The Juvenile in the case received the maximum sentence of three years for his age; one of the accused died by suicide in his jail cell; and the remaining four co-accused, Mukesh Singh, Akshay Thakur, Vinay Sharma and Pawan Gupta were sentenced to death. The court declared this to be 'the *rarest of rare cases* that warranted the death penalty'.[69] One of the most remarkable statements made in the wake of the death sentence came from the wife of one of the accused:

> Am I not a daughter of this country? Don't I have the right to live? Will there be no more rapes in Delhi? Will you hang all rapists? *A woman is protected by her husband.* If he's dead, who will protect her *and for whom will she live*? I don't want to live. Priyanshu, my son, is a child. He understands nothing. I will strangle him to death. What else can I do?[70]

The unspeakable finally and concretely proclaims itself as that burden which people bear of their caste abandonment and class abandonment, as well as the consciousness which the wretched of the earth must surely sow alongside other sources of personhood in the face of the state's abandonment. This *is* the real source of the 'hatred of democracy' – that which the law, rights, democracy itself, dare not say out loud. That gendered violence comes to substitute all of these other subjections – that rape takes on the concrete and accumulated form of all of that which can finally elicit a response from the state – ought to tell us something about the absolute necessity of the gendered nature of democracy's subjections. The law is not just a battleground for redress, but also an arena that mediates the re-subjectivation of the very targets of its redress: '[t]he death penalty will make things even more dangerous for girls. Now when they rape, they won't leave the girl like we did. They will kill her. Before they would rape and say, "Leave her alone, she won't tell anyone." Now when they rape, especially the criminal types, they will just kill the girl. *Death*'.[71]

In a society that has gagged its political minorities and rendered them as passive subjects of rights, *speech becomes a dangerous thing* and exposes a paradox that is deeply embedded in the juridical interpellation of women and that is enacted as a reaction to the violence they experience in violent society: that 'rights have no inherent political semiotic, no innate capacity either to advance or impede radical democratic ideals', and this is precisely because 'their liberatory and egalitarian force is always historically and culturally circumscribed'.[72] Part of the liberation that rights promise is that it must, in any society that has lost its capacity to see the humanity of the other, at least invoke a sense of shame in the accused, or promise that evidence of the pain of victims will assuage the wounds of the violated. But the face of banality haunts any system whose members hold the recognition that they too, have been failed by it: 'when I saw them, *they had no fear in their eyes, no shame*. No remorse at all for what they had done'.[73] It is impossible for liberal democracy's juridical artillery that is steeped in a vacuous morality to humiliate in any worse sense, those who modern society has all but abandoned.

That modern society resets itself at its margins – through the bodies of women, backward castes, immiserated people – might be suggested by the fact those populations never seem to escape their positions at the margins of 'society proper': that an absolute imperative exists to maintain those boundaries. It is those at those margins which liberal democracy, through its artillery of law, rights and entitlements, has sought to regulate and sustain in place, both through the (gendered) violence it enacts on the one hand through the bodies of some, and which it punishes through the bodies of others on the other. Around this fulcrum of gendered violence, those that have been rendered violable and those that are punishable bear a similar burden in the eyes of democracy. Both groups are ultimately subjugated by a democracy that is sustained, in the words of Langston Hughes, only 'through compromise and fear' and therefore might have a cynical investment in its demise – a fact which threatens both the (liberal) state and its allies in civil society and capital. On the kind of democracy that guarantees only to some, rights, recognition, freedoms and justice which it cannot guarantee to others, Hughes writes,

I have as much right
As the other fellow has
To stand
On my two feet

And own the land.

I tire so of hearing people say,
Let things take their course.
Tomorrow is another day.
I do not need my freedom when I'm dead.
I cannot live on tomorrow's bread.[74]

The devastating effects of modern society and the liberal variant of democracy which it has ushered in this late period and that has been birthed through colonial violence, is that its indifference to social and political inequality has rendered violence so banal as to make it impossible to recognize its destructive force without prior validation as such by the law. It denies speech and subjectivity both to those who violate and those that are violated and imposes the language of rights as the mode of its articulation, which in turn requires power – 'the powers against which it arrays itself as well as the power it must claim to enact itself'.[75] But where is power to be sought when violence is illegible beyond that of the law?

Jyoti final words to her mother before she breathed her last are striking in the layers of meaning that they convey: 'Sorry, mummy. *I gave you so much trouble. I am sorry*'.[76] They speak of an 'unpayable debt' – 'a debt someone owes but that is not hers to pay'.[77] They convey the symbolic order which structures the psyche of girls very early on – that they will neither be heard, nor be believed, unless someone else (an assigned caregiver) *embodies* their violation. This expectation is concealed within even the most advanced of antirape legislation in the postcolonial world.[78] It is evidenced by the histories of racist medicalization of black female bodies that are routinely denied correct treatment because the pain of a racialized gendered body[79] is not recognizable as injury without physical evidence.[80] Jyoti's apology *to* her mother conveys her *recognition* of the violence of the subjugative order into which girls are born. Violence only *confirms* the normative order. It is wielded not merely as a 'weapon' (instrumentalized), but also serves a material function in the reproduction of the juridical order itself – in validating the law's unique purpose of mediating 'justice' – for whom gendered bodies have historically been proxies through which those who violate can convey their own disenchantment with democracy.

In the colonies, modern law has established its absolute exception through sexual violence which it conveys every so often, not through the violence of rape itself, but through the *spectacular telling* of such violence. Juridical recourse becomes the only possibility of speech. The rapes of Baby Tshepang and Jyoti violate the boundaries of captivity of gendered labour on which the modern state is founded. They expose the reproductive/care economies that draw a direct line between the household and the state: 'those who are charged with your care have abdicated their responsibility of care and in so doing, compel the state to assume responsibility for your care'. Not through material provisions, as the postcolonial imperative for redistribution demands, but through *rights* – the liberal interpretation of freedom. While Jyoti conveys her apology directly, Baby Tshepang's is indirectly conveyed through the void created by her mother's muteness. Silence is the refuge of those who understand the *condition* of their claims in relation to a state that has long abandoned them. That condition is a duty of care that reproduces a deeply gendered relationship between Captive Maternals and the capitalist state, and which pegs rights claims to this duty of care.

None more than the rape of a child communicates the threat which any attempt to abdicate that duty of care poses to the stabilization of the liberal state. The elaboration in Chapter 4, of Joy James's illustration of democracy's balancing act through the analogy she draws between the seesaw and the 'fulcrum' on which it rests, and the balance of forces that reproduce democracy as such, is worth restating here. As James shows, any attempt by the oppressed to approach the 'intersection' (i.e. any attempt to be free) poses a threat to the 'balance' on which the captor/oppressor constructs their notion of democracy: to reach the intersection (the 'fulcrum') is to topple the seesaw – acts that are read as sabotage and always met with 'retaliatory violence to punish that disturbance'.[81] Those who dare to expose the fragility of modern democracy and to impose on it a demand for care rarely escape the brutal reminders of their own state of captivity.

'*I am sorry*'. Even in death, Jyoti conveys an understanding of the meaning of the breach of this 'care boundary' and does so into a void. That void is haunted by an understanding of the meaning of her life and of the boundaries within which her gendered body is authorized to exist. The apology is also an act of care, an act of compassion towards her mother, as if to say: 'because you reproduced a woman you are liable to suffer even more violence'. Were Baby Tshepang able to speak, she too might have uttered words of regret for the burden she understands her mother, the person conscripted as her caregiver, would no doubt have to bear indefinitely. Her apology would, like Jyoti's, convey a counterintuitive understanding of the reality that the real subject of the law's vilification would *not* be her rapist, but rather those like her mother, who breach the boundaries which liberal democracy (through its language of rights) establishes at its very foundation, between those who are likely to rape (modernity's product *per excellence*) and those who stand defenceless against modernity's violence.

The muteness of Tshepang's mother and her self-mutilation is the only evidence we have that she would have fought to save her child. The grief of Jyoti's parents is the only certainty we can have that the blame is not hers to bear, that culpability for this brutality belongs somewhere else. It is that 'elsewhere' that must again constitute the concrete terrain of our struggles over the meaning and promise of democracy if there is to be a reversal of democracy's tendency to accumulate subjects against whom it also retains the ultimate power to silence through its constitutive juridical order.

Epilogue: Democracy's Subjections

> *the laws and institutions of formal democracy are appearances under which, and instruments by which, the power of the bourgeois class is exercised.* The struggle against appearances *thus becomes the path leading to 'real' democracy, where liberty and equality would no longer be represented in the institutions of law and State but* embodied in the very forms of concrete life *and sensible experience.*[1]

The modern idea of democracy is distinctly burdened by modernity's subjugating orders,[2] against which liberalism has so far presented only a weak defence on behalf of formerly colonized people.[3] Yet especially for peoples of the Third World, democracy remains a mode of political organizing that is worth struggling over precisely because by its very logic, it is constituted as a battleground of ideas that are also articulated from concrete experiences borne out of popular struggles. From the margins of history, it remains necessary to define for ourselves an idea of democracy which reflects our realities and the various articulations of freedoms and rights which the people express from different social positions. Such is not pursued with the mere intention of bringing colonized people into a universal fold of humanity, but rather of establishing new parameters that reflect the relevant social questions of our own context and times. There is both an anticolonial and a decolonial imperative that constitutes such an articulation of democracy in the Third World. Historically, the anticolonial imperative 'affirmed the right of peoples to be free of colonialism, the right of peoples to develop economically, and the right of peoples to exercise their national culture'.[4] Those rights were not realizable in a socially unequal world. The anticolonial tendency as such 'acknowledges that equal rights can be realized *only in a world that has transcended the great social inequalities* that define the neocolonial world system'.[5]

The idea then, that struggles for democracy ought to be preceded by another set of struggles that are directed against social inequality, is fundamental to reconciling democracy and its *subjects* in the Third World. A critique of democracy and its proclaimed values is central to this endeavour of reconciliation. And so, against the 'liberalism, including petty bourgeois radicalism [that] tends to absolutise the question of human rights as a central question and the rights struggle as the backbone of democratic struggles . . . as an end in themselves', Shivji (2023) elaborates a more concrete aim of such critique as being 'to reconstruct the human rights ideology to *legitimise* and *mobilise* people's struggles'.[6]

An unsettled question that emerges from this formulation is this: how are popular struggles to be legitimated by the very structures whose violence have necessitated such struggles in the first place? Why would colonized people continue to contest the negation of their humanity using the same language (of democracy, of rights) into which their exclusion has been written? How are we to think of democracy when even its revolutionary tendencies (via the anticolonial project) have yet to articulate a clear position with regard to the question of its gendered/marginal subjects? Stated differently, the object of the critique of democracy is not the idea of democracy itself, but rather a critique of those structures, institutions and processes that are enacted in its name – a critique of the concrete domains of total social and political life. Such a formulation raises the question regarding who, then, is the *subject* of democracy.

A partial response is provided in Chapter 1, in which I argue through Spivak that 'both as object of colonial historiography and as subject of insurgency, the ideological construction of gender *keeps the male dominant*', such that to speak of a 'female subject' of violence becomes an oxymoron that retains this erasure, as it represents an essentialized reading of violence – the idea that women face violation on the basis only of their biological sex/gender. To speak, however, of a 'gendered subject' of violence is to foreground a *structural process* in the colonial production of violence against women. The idea of 'democracy's subjections' is therefore an attempt both to implicate democracy in this structure that subjugates gendered bodies and to charge it with the task of liberating those subjects.

The decolonial tendency does something more. I have argued elsewhere that the clarification of the method and the subject of theory is necessary because what the colonial canon does is deny the existence of (or presume the absence of) certain subjects of history. The implication is that colonial theory often does not reflect the social and material realities of those 'Others' it claims to theorize and represent. This erasure also means that a key task of decolonial theory and praxis becomes that of writing those marginalized subjects back into history, culture and political society.[7] Such a process raises a number of significant questions: who is the subject of feminist history in general, and who is the gendered subject of Third World feminist history? Both are questions that decolonial feminism inescapably encounters in seeking to define its meaning, relevance and location in the tradition of anticolonial and decolonial theorization. Gendered subjects are historical subjects to the extent that they appear *both as an invention of colonialism* and occupying the unique position of *not being translatable outside of (or being specific to) the political, cultural and economic structures and contexts* in which they operate. In other words, gendered violence in the colonial milieu has to be understood distinctly from the gendered violence that is perpetuated in the context and name of democracy, although a structural legacy certainly binds the two contexts.

What I set out to examine in this book was the association between colonialism, democracy and gendered violence, framed within three major arguments. The first is that the gendered labour/reproductive labour question is a necessary condition for women's legibility as subjects of both the colonial and postcolonial state. Second is that this mode of subjectivation renders colonized women as quintessentially modern subjects of the state because of the articulation between their labour and their political subjectivity. The third major argument of the book has been to show that this mode of subjectivation produces a structure of governmentality that places women/gendered subjects at the centre of any decolonial/democratic possibility in the postcolonial world.

The question of violence cuts through each of these arguments and is presented throughout the preceding chapters as being the primary structure of legibility for gendered subjects (concretely theorized as *labouring* subjects) in both the colonial and the postcolonial democratizing state. In other words, a fundamental lens for judging the strength of a democracy lies in its ability to minimize the modern state's attachment to violence as a mode of governance. This is a formulation which suggests that postcolonial democracy is haunted by both a history and a presence of feminist anticolonial and postcolonial struggles against exploitation, erasure and violence – 'struggles against [liberal democracy's] appearances' – to which the state and capital characteristically respond with violence. At the same time, postcolonial democracy is confronted by the ethical responsibility against violence which the colonized place upon it. The apparent contradiction between these two positions highlights a core tension that runs throughout the book: that is, that the very possibility of democratic life is circumscribed for those that are subjectivated through modern democracy's violent histories, yet who are compelled to respond to this violence *within* the logics of democracy.

The book's central conceptual idea regarding 'democracy's subjections' as such relates to the injuries that result from colonial logics and practices of accumulation and control, and which left unattended, have a tendency to manifest as so many contradictions in the postcolonial democratizing state. The regime of gendered labour which colonial/historical capitalism requires is the primary contradiction with which the book grapples. My critique foregrounds the gendered and feminist subject of violence, inquiring into the nature of democracy when its subject is not the universal rational man envisioned by Euromodernity, but rather is one who emerges in relation to the colonizing structures of gender, race, class, ethnicity and caste – on the 'Other' side of that modernity. What does democracy demand of/from such a subject, and what, if at all, does it concede to them? Though a critique primarily directed towards the state with the aim of exposing some problems which colonized people encounter in their clamour for freedom, there is an unstated attempt to reconcile the book's major arguments regarding the gendered subject of violence with an anticolonial feminist theory of democracy.

Again, we might pose this question: what does it mean to be a *subject* of democracy? To both be subjectivated by democracy and be subjected to it? The gendered subject at the heart of this book – specifically, woman – occupies all three coordinates in relation to democracy: they are its quintessential modern subject; are subjectivated/brought into political consciousness by it; and are subjected/held in captivity by it. On its own, the idea regarding the quintessential modernity of women is an uncontroversial statement and has found expression in the broader literature concerning other oppressed groups. Patrick Wolfe (2010), for instance, has articulated one version of this claim, arguing that 'colonialism's centrality to the global industrial order . . . means that the expropriated Aboriginal, enslaved African American, or indentured Asian is as thoroughly modern as the factory worker, bureaucrat, or flaneur of the metropolitan center'.[8] In his evaluation of Wolfe's claim, Chakrabarty (2011) writes that '[i]f these disparate figures are all equally modern, and thoroughly so, then clearly their "modernity" has little to do with differences in their levels of education, urbanity, or any other forms of cultural capital. In what sense could they then be equally modern? Is "modern," then, simply a synonym for the "global industrial order," and is anybody caught up in it modern by definition?'[9] What significance, in other words, should we (the colonized) attach to *who* it is that is considered as being modern? What does it mean for feminists invested in historicizing a modern gendered subject (of labour, of violence, of the state) to 'make a simultaneous claim to being heirs to the Enlightenment while critiquing it?'[10] Why does modernity *matter* as the scene of our critique?

In the colonial modern context, it matters fundamentally first, because modernity also constitutes the *scene of our subjection*. That is, our suffering, subjugation – violence itself – is rendered visible only through the modern language of 'freedom', 'rights', 'equality' and so on, that establishes the boundaries between everything else that is prior to modernity. The reproductive work that is performed daily and generationally towards the social reproduction of workers and society only encounters the possibility of exploitation and devaluation when it enters into market relations proper and constitutes a 'gendered labourer'. Likewise, rape becomes legible as injury only in the presence of law, where it constitutes the exception, and establishes a 'gendered subject of violence' that henceforth is held up for regulation as evidence of democracy's promise.

Second, because the violence that is committed in the name of modernity implicates the colonizer, the discourse of 'civilization' (and for that matter, the proclaimed 'primitivism' of the colonized) is not verifiable on the terms of the colonizer alone: only the violent responses of the colonized (the anticolonial struggle) confirm our understanding of the nature of the oppression to which we are subjected. In Césaire's words, our criticism derives from the understanding

> that no one colonizes innocently, that *no one colonizes with impunity either*; that a nation which colonizes, that a civilization which justifies colonization – and therefore force – is already a sick civilization, a civilization that is morally diseased, that irresistibly, progressing from one consequence to another, one reputation to another, calls for its Hitler . . .[calls for] its punishment.[11]

In other words, it is not possible to 'civilize barbarism' without fundamentally negating civilization. That the wounds inflicted by colonization cannot simply be bandaged over by an invented democracy: each wound that the colonizer inflicts on the one hand 'decivilizes and brutalizes' him, and on the other, awakens in the colonized an indignation that is not so much a clamour for the past, but rather a sense that we have *known* freedom, have known societies that were cooperative and democratic and humane. In this sense colonial violence does not show the colonized what modernity is, nor does it particularly succeed in making the colonized forget their desire for liberation. Colonial violence is not irrational in relation to the logics of domination, to the extent that it is a necessity for the control of native populations. But in a Fanonian sense, neither is the violence of the colonized, which demonstrates our knowledge of the values that define us, and as such the categorical imperative to struggle, which the desire for liberation raises for the dispossessed:

> For my part, I make a systematic defense of the non-European civilizations. Every day that passes, every denial of justice, every beating by the police, every demand of the workers that is drowned in blood, every scandal that is hushed tip, every punitive expedition, every police van, every gendarme and every militiaman, brings home to us the value of our old societies.

> They were communal societies, never societies of the many for the few.
>
> They were societies that were not only ante-capitalist, as has been said, but also *anti-capitalist*.
>
> They were democratic societies, always.
>
> They were cooperative societies, fraternal societies.
>
> I make a systematic defense of the societies destroyed by imperialism.
>
> They were the fact, they did not pretend to be the idea; despite their faults, they were neither to be hated nor condemned. They were content to be. In them, neither the word *failure* nor the word *avatar* had any meaning. They kept hope intact.[12]

Despite this defence of the colonized in general and their relationship to democracy, the question that will no doubt still linger in the mind of the reader would be, *why the focus on* women? In a humanist sense there is nothing inherently unique about colonized women: the trauma of violence in general which we have experienced belongs to every person that modernity had the audacity to cast as an 'Other'. But the *gendered* nature of this violence denies to certain subjects of modernity the possibility of closure – the long historical thread that connects the womb that is birthed in the slave ship --> to the 'womb of Western' theory --> to that of the Enlightenment --> to the womb of colonization and finally in the present --> to the womb of liberal democracy, would be *illegible* if not through the lens of these gendered subject(s) of modernity. That seemingly invisible thread of continuity that incorporates women/gendered labour into every facet of capitalist development – their subjugation and trauma interspersed with resistance and numerous small victories – ultimately defines women's quintessential modernity.

Only the possibility of averting shame causes one to blush. Only the necessity of (social) reproduction that confronts humanity at every turn, and the impossibility of complete elimination of the source of that reproduction – the fundamental contradiction that gendered labour poses to modernity – guarantees to those so subjected, that the state and capital *will* endeavour to find ways to sustain it in order to sustain themselves. That 'shame' and that sustenance has come in the form of a whole body of jurisprudence, state policy and traditional authority targeted towards the regulation of gendered violence (but really, the regulation of gendered, labouring bodies) that today shows up as a set of rules recognizable in liberal language as the 'rules of the game' – of democracy. Democracy in the modern world has brought into political consciousness (subjectivated) gendered subjects whose struggles ought to be taken as evidence both of democracy's failures and its endless promise. Liberation does not guarantee one without the other, but demands that we recognize the contradictions in order to 'heighten them' – for it is only at that furthest point that the possibility of revolutionary transformation is to be found.

In her philosophical memoir *The Alchemy of Race and Rights*, Patricia J. Williams (1991) proposes a powerful justification for the rights claims presented by marginalized individuals and communities. In it she argues that where one's experience is rooted not just in a sense of illegitimacy, but in *being* illegitimate, in being raped and in the fear of being murdered, then the black adherence to a scheme of both positive and negative rights – to the self, to the sanctity of one's own personal boundaries – makes sense. Relatedly she insists that the best way to give voice to those whose voice had been suppressed was to argue that *they had no voice*.

I understand this argument as meaning that in the aftermath of a subjugated existence, the idea of justice – of legibility to a *just* state – only becomes a possibility through the political reconstitution of those whose voices and ways of self-identification had been appropriated *for* and subsumed under the dominating force (the colonizing power). But what does it mean to argue that one has no voice? This question is complicated by the ambivalence which colonial domination ascribes onto the colonized: that is, the ways in which gender silences its subjects functions within a structure of domination that also draws on ethnic, class, caste, racial and sexual differences to violate and deny legitimacy to the anticolonial project.

Social antagonisms are in this sense both instruments of subjectivation and domination, and the basis of action. Where the anticolonial impulse was to unite the colonized by suppressing difference, the decolonial imperative lies in the necessity of making room for difference to play out in the contested space of democratic politics while denying it the subjugating power it otherwise possesses in the absence of a liberation ethic. In its extreme sense, democracy ought not to impose any limits on what we can demand or what we can get. But in a modern world that has so far not learnt to exercise any restraint in relation to what it can demand of those (gendered bodies) that reproduce it on a daily and generational basis, any notion of 'democracy without limits' cannot but accumulate ever more violable subjects. Yet, that violence (in Marx's terms, the violent reorganization of society) remains a feature of democratic society in the postcolony is not itself the calamity: the real calamity of modernity is that the bourgeoisie democracy to which we are clinging remains fundamentally unable to recognize the *multiplicity* of terrains that today are determining the social order.

Democracy is bound to invite multiple competing claims and visions of government, and its success ultimately 'lies in the possibility of organizing resistance [to tyranny] around *difference*, not as something that need necessarily be reconciled', but as a practice that might allow for the expression of as many notions of liberation as there are oppressed groups in the world.[13] It is said, after all, that '[a] man who calls his kinsmen to a feast does not do so to save them from starving. They all have food in their own homes. When we gather together in the moonlit village ground it is not because of the moon. Every man can see it in his own compound. We come together because it is good for kinsmen to do so'.[14] Third World feminists have long gathered evidence of our own marginalization and long perfected our struggles against gendered exploitation and oppression. It should not be too difficult to imagine then that our contemporary invitation to a broader community to consider the question of democracy from the vantage point of its gendered subjects comes from concrete knowledge regarding the cost of such neglect and, in the simplest expression of democracy's promise, comes from a fundamental belief that it is good to do so.

Endnotes

Preface

1 Robert Fatton Jr (1990), 'Liberal Democracy in Africa', *Political Science Quarterly*, 105(3): 455–473, 457.

2 In this work I predominantly draw on the notion of the 'anticolonial' rather than 'decolonial' because of the conceptual and methodological clarity that I consider to be possible with the former. While I see this work as broadly addressing the contemporary question of decolonization, the exact meaning and framing of what it means to decolonize remain a subject of intense debate and disagreements. The choice of this concept is thus an attempt at demarcating clearer conceptual and analytical boundaries. For me, anticolonialism as an organizing concept is also useful in signaling a critique and movement *against* colonialism, as well as the moral and ethical expectation that its *narration* belongs to the colonized. Decolonization as a method has assumed wide incorporation and appropriation precisely because its narration enjoins both the colonized and the colonizer. Finally, recuperating the anticolonial for an analysis of the present also opens up the anticolonial archive in practical and material ways to which the 'decolonial' archive does not easily lend itself.

3 See Touraine, Alain (2005), 'The Subject Is Coming Back', *International Journal of Politics, Culture, and Society*, 18(3/4): 199–209.

Introduction

1 Issa Shivji (1983), 'Seven Theses on Reform and Revolution', *Journal of African Marxists*, 4: 45–53, 50.

2 Frantz Fanon (1963), *The Wretched of the Earth*, New York: Grove Press, 36 (added emphasis).

3 Ayed Arafah, personal communication.

4 Ibid., emphasis my own.

5 Ibid.

6 The meaning of *Sumud* (steadfastness) has varied across different periods and contexts. For example, during the first Intifada (1987–1988), *Sumud* meant resistance by staying on the land, general strikes, acts of civil disobedience,

symbols, etc. In the second Intifada (2000s), *Sumud* was reduced to continuing with daily life and movement despite the occupation restrictions; PA replaced PLO. As Dana (2020) explains, 'during the 1970s and 1980s, Palestinians in the Occupied Palestinian Territories (OPTs) adopted the politics of *Sumud* in response to the Israeli policies and practices. *Sumud* was a localized strategy of resistance that stressed the centrality of the Palestinian national identity for political and social empowerment and achieving a collective sense of belonging and presence in the land' (Dana 2014, cited in Dana 2020: 195). Dana (2020) further explains *Sumud* strategy as having advanced a wide range of resistance tactics and practices in almost every societal sphere, distinguishing two main types of *Sumud*: 'i) the static *Sumud* during the 1970s that was characterized by passive resistance to support the peoples' steadfastness and adherence to the land; and ii) the resistance *Sumud* during the 1980s, which was defined by active popular resistance to Israeli soldiers and settlers, as well as extensive grassroots participation in political and economic initiatives. With the creation of institutional infrastructure and the expansion of grassroots-based organizations, resistance *Sumud* was instituted in the structures and functions of trade unions, women's and students' movements; and professional and voluntary committees specializing in agriculture, health, education, and art. The grassroots organizations played a vital role in enhancing the mass-based socio-economic struggle and introduced innovative methods to achieve self-reliance and self-sufficiency through local production and boycott of Israeli products. *Sumud* politics, particularly in its active form, culminated in the first Palestinian intifada (1987–1993)' (Dana 2020: 195).

7 Amber Noelle Merucci (2021), '"We Don't Need the Key, We'll Break In": Learning about the Occupation through Aesthetic Encounters with Three Artists', unpublished doctoral thesis, York University, 133 (original emphasis).

8 Ibid., 134.

9 Ibid.

10 Ibid.

11 Ibid., 135.

12 Ayed Arafah, cited in Merucci, 136 (added emphasis).

13 Merucci, 137, original emphasis.

14 In statist discourse, democracy appears as a mentality of government and a technology of rule – the people, mere objects of governance. In liberal democratic discourse, 'liberalism (understood as constitutional and limited government, the rule of law, and the protection of individual rights) … is invariably coupled with democracy (understood as the selection of government officials by universal suffrage)', in an equation that imagines that the means of selection justifies the end, whatever those may be (Plattner 1999: 121). In the Marxist tradition, democracy is implied in the possibility 'for collective intervention to mould society' (Patnaik 2012: 32). Here we might agree with Patnaik (2012) that a focus on the 'forces

and relations of production' is too narrow and often conceals 'the fact that people, even as they have acted out the historical process, *have yet been objects of it'*. Liberation as such demands 'the transcendence of capitalism, the creation of property relations where people own the means of production in common, [which] then becomes the basis for the liberation of people from the 'trap of history', their transformation from being 'objects' to being 'subjects' of history' (ibid., original emphasis). In the Marxian argument, the historical process has to render visible its subject as a precondition for their liberation.

15 Khanyile (2020), cited in Leuscher et al. (2022: 4).

16 For instance, in *Seeing Like a Feminist,* Nivedita Menon (2012) asks us to carefully consider 'the term 'rape' and its implications', asking whether anybody would ever say that rape is acceptable. Her response to this question exposes the contradiction I seek to highlight above: 'From the most complacent patriarch to the angriest feminist, all would declare rape to be a terrible crime. But the apparent consensus is mythical, for the reasons behind arriving at this opinion are diametrically opposite. For patriarchal forces, rape is evil because it is a crime against the honour of the family, whereas feminists denounce rape because it is a crime against the autonomy and bodily integrity of a woman. This difference in understanding rape naturally leads to diametrically opposite proposals for fighting rape' (2012: 113).

17 It is a struggle that ultimately is deathly for both that it deathly for both vis-à-vis other forces.

18 My use of this terminology recognizes trans-womanhood as well as biologically-assigned and queer womanhood.

19 I borrow here from Peter Stallybrass' (1998) important piece titled 'Marx's Coat', in which he traces 'the 'economic cell-form' that occupies the first chapter of Capital [that] takes the form of a coat. The coat makes its appearance not as the object that is made and worn but as the commodity that is exchanged. And what defines the coat as a commodity, for Marx, is that you cannot wear it and it cannot keep you warm. But while the commodity is a cold abstraction, it feeds, vampire-like, on human labour.' In *Capital,* Stallybrass argues, 'Marx's coat appears only immediately to disappear again, because the nature of capitalism is to produce a coat not as a material particularity but as a "supra-sensible" value (Marx 1976 [1867]: 165, cited in Stallybrass, 183). The work of Marx's *Capital* is to trace that value back through all its detours to the human labor whose appropriation produces capital. This leads Marx theoretically to the labor theory of value and to an analysis of surplus-value. It leads him politically to the factories, the working conditions, the living spaces, the food, and the clothing of those who produce a wealth that is expropriated from them' (Stallybrass 1998: 183).

20 For instance, Durba Mitra's (2020) *Indian Sex Life: Sexuality and the Colonial Origins of Modern Social Thought*; Jessica Hinchy's (2019) *Governing Gender and Sexuality in Colonial India: The Hijra, c.1850–1900*; Elsbeth Locher-Scholten's

(2000) *Women and the Colonial State*; Holden and Ruppel's (2003) *Imperial Desire*; and Anjali Arondekar's (2009) *For the Record: On Sexuality and the Colonial Archive in India,* are among an important body of scholarship that take the colonial state as a historical basis for a critique of sexuality and the production of gender as an organizing concept in modern society.

21 For instance, Jacques Rancière's *Hatred of Democracy* (2005), Issa Shivji's *The Concept of Human Rights in Africa* (1989), Nikita Dhawan's *Decolonizing Enlightenment* (2014), Mahmood Mamdani's *Citizen and Subject* (1996), Chantal Mouffe's *Democratic Paradox* (2000), Partha Chatterjee's *The Politics of the Governed* (2007) and *The Black Hole of Empire* (2012) and my own earlier work *States of Violence* (2018) are all studies concerned in some way with the limits of liberal democracy and which explore the historical articulation between colonial and postcolonial violence, and identitarian struggles for justice and liberation.

22 Contrast this with the *exclusion* of enslaved Black people in the United States as the very basis and structure of that democracy (see Michelle Alexander (2010), *The New Jim Crow: Mass Incarceration in the Age of Colorblindness,* New York: The New Press, 26).

23 Mamdani (1996) sees the failure of post-independence states to de-ethnicize their native populations as constituting a primary question for postcolonial democracy and decolonization.

24 See Chatterjee (1993, 1986).

25 That is, as Oyèwùmí (1997) argues of precolonial Yoruba society, the relation between the human body and social roles, positions and hierarchies was not gendered.

26 Here I draw on Nancy Fraser's (1997) argument that regarding bivalent collectivities – those she sees as differentiated by virtue of *both* the political-economic structure *and* the cultural-valuational structure of society. When oppressed or subordinated, therefore, they suffer injustices that are traceable to both political economy and culture simultaneously. Bivalent collectivities, in sum, may suffer both socio-economic maldistribution and cultural misrecognition in forms where neither of these injustices is an indirect effect of the other, but where both are primary and co-original. In that case, neither redistributive remedies alone nor recognition remedies alone will suffice. Bivalent collectivities need both. Fraser, however, considers these injustices as constituted within two distinct realms that are not necessarily reconcilable – an argument with which I am not convinced. I consider it necessary when thinking within contexts of colonization where the native question raises a fundamentally political question to also give due consideration to the political sphere (political identities), since under colonial logics of accumulation and dispossession, political economy and culture are approached primarily as *political problems* of the state.

27 Nikita Dhawan (2013), 'The Empire Prays Back: Religion, Secularity, and Queer Critique', *Boundary* 2, 40(1): 191–222, 196.

28 Ibid.
29 Audre Lorde (1984), 'The Master's Tools Will Never Dismantle the Master's House', in *Sister Outsider: Essays and Speeches*, Audre Lorde (ed.), New York: Crossing Press, 110.
30 Scott, *Conscripts*, 119.
31 Dhawan, 'Affirmative Sabotage', 67.
32 Dhawan (ibid.); Michel Foucault (1984), 'What Is Enlightenment?' in *The Foucault Reader*, Paul Rabinow (ed.), New York: Penguin, 45.
33 Dhawan, 'Affirmative Sabotage', 68 (emphasis added).
34 My formulation here is indebted to Mamdani's ongoing theorizations of the idea of political violence (1996; 2001; and 2020).
35 Cited in Scott, *Conscripts*, 171.
36 See, for instance, Jacob Levy and Iris Marion Young (2011), *Colonialism and Its Legacies*, Plymouth: Lexington Books; and Sankar Muthu (2003), *Enlightenment Against Empire*, Princeton: Princeton University Press.
37 Dhawan, 'Affirmative Sabotage', 69.
38 The major target of my critique throughout the book is the 'actually existing' liberal form of democracy, which is the form that much of the Third World has inherited in the late neocolonial period. This inheritance is exclusionary, based upon the denial of 'Other' histories and the negation of subjectivities that do not conform to the white, male liberal individual idea, and therefore marks the inherent violence of liberal democracy in the Third World.
39 Gayatri Chakravorty Spivak (1994), 'Bonding in Difference', in *An Other Tongue: Nation and Ethnicity in the Linguistic Borderlands*, Alfred Arteaga (ed.), Durham: Duke University Press, 279.
40 Gayatri Chakravorty Spivak (2007), 'Feminism and Human Rights', in *The Present as History: Critical Perspectives on Global Power*, Nermeen Shaikh (ed.), New York: Columbia University Press, 259.
41 Dhawan, 'Affirmative Sabotage', 70.

Chapter 1

1 See Hadeel Assali, 'The Paraguay Transfer Scheme, Documentary'. Others have spoken about a 'counter-archive' (e.g. see Ozban 2014) and 'anti-archive' – that is, how to record events which resist documentation or to archive in ways that subvert usual practices of archiving?
2 This is a general claim that is, however, alive to important nuances that have been brought to the understanding of native subjectivity. For instance, Fanon's *Year V of the Algerian Revolution* begins with the argument that 'native' is structurally

gendered as a violated female and even anticipates Spivak's argument about rape (see 'Algeria Unveiled'). In his argument, when articulated as *active*, the 'native' is invariably male, even though there is countless footage and documentation of Indigenous women liberation fighters.

3 Joy James (2016), 'The Womb of Western Theory: Trauma, Time Theft, and the Captive Maternal', *Carceral Notebooks.*

4 Karl Marx (1934), *The Eighteenth Brumaire of Louis Bonaparte*, Moscow: Progress, 18.

5 Karl Marx (1971), *Writings on the Paris Commune*, ed. H. Draper, New York: International Publishers, 198.

6 Although I use the term democracy throughout the text, my critique is of its 'actually existing form', liberal democracy. The formulation of democracy by scholars such as Rancière tends to apply it in Eurocentric ways, which presume either Greco-antiquated versions or Euromodern exemplars locked in *liberal* democratic models. Those models, in my view, do not account for subjects specific to colonial modernity.

7 See Larry Diamond (2008), *The Spirit of Democracy: The Struggle to Build Free Societies throughout the World*, New York: Henry Holt & Company; Larry Diamond and Marc F. Plattner (2010), *Democratization in Africa: Progress and Retreat*, Baltimore, MD: Johns Hopkins University Press.

8 Mahmood Mamdani (1996), *Citizen and Subject: Contemporary Africa and the Legacy of Late Colonialism*, Princeton, NJ: Princeton University Press.

9 Partha Chatterjee (2012), *The Black Hole of Empire: History of a Global Practice of Power*, Princeton: Princeton University Press.

10 See Durba Mitra (2020), *Indian Sex Life: Sexuality and the Colonial Origins of Modern Social Thought*, Princeton: Princeton University Press; Jessica Hinchy (2019), *Governing Gender and Sexuality in Colonial India: The Hijra, c.1850–1900*, Cambridge: Cambridge University Press; Elsbeth Locher-Scholten (2000), *Women and the Colonial State: Essays on Gender and Modernity in the Netherlands Indies, 1900–1942*, Amsterdam: Amsterdam University Press; and Anjali Arondekar (2009), *For the Record: On Sexuality and the Colonial Archive in India*, Durham and London: Duke University Press.

11 See Nancy Fraser (2017), 'Crisis of Care? On the Social Reproductive Contradictions of Contemporary Capitalism', in *Social Reproduction Theory: Remapping Class, Recentering Oppression*, Tithi Bhattacharya (ed.), London: Pluto Press, 25.

12 Chatterjee, *Black Hole of Empire*, xi.

13 Ibid.

14 Lata Mani (1998), *Contentious Traditions: The Debate on Sati in Colonial India*, California: University of California Press.

15 Ann Laura Stoler (2002), *Carnal Knowledge and Imperial Power: Race and the Intimate in Colonial Rule*, Berkeley: University of California Press, 6, emphasis added.

16 Ibid.

17 Ibid., 1, emphasis added.

18 Ibid., 6. Stoler deals in this regard with 'connections between parenting and colonial power, between nursing mothers and cultural boundaries, between servants and sentiments, and between illicit sex, orphans, and race [which] emerge as central concerns of state and at the heart of colonial politics, [and which were] at once so pertinent and consequential and so invisible and effaced in how colonies were ruled and in the historiographies of them' (6).

19 Ibid., 8.

20 Mahmood Mamdani (1996), *Citizen and Subject: Contemporary Africa and the Legacy of Late Colonialism*, Princeton, NJ: Princeton University Press, 4.

21 I use these two terminologies interchangeably to highlight their co-constitution and the structural nature of gender. Much of the literature makes reference to a 'woman question'; however, while pointing to the gendered nature of the colonial state, asserting a woman question has tended to treat women as a separate problem of the colonial state, rather than as fundamental to its structural form and dynamics of rule.

22 Cited in Elizabeth Schmidt (1990), 'Negotiated Spaces and Contested Terrain: Men, Women and the Law in Colonial Zimbabwe, 1890–1939', *Journal of Southern African Studies*, 16(4): 622–648, 627.

23 Ibid.

24 Ibid.

25 Ibid.

26 Ibid.

27 Ibid., emphasis added.

28 Ibid., 646. See also George Chauncey (1981), 'Locus of Reproduction: Women's Labour in the Zambian Copperbelt, 1927–1953', 7(2): 135–164; Marjorie Mbilinyi (1989), 'Women's Resistance in "Customary" Marriage: Tanzania's Runaway Wives', *African Discourse Series*, 1: 211–254; Margaret Strobel (1979), *Muslim Women in Mombasa, 1890–1975*, New Haven: Yale University Press; Sharon Stichter (1977), *Women and the Labour Force in Kenya, 1895–1964*, Nairobi: IDS.

29 Ibid.

30 Ibid., 647.

31 I developed a brief introduction to this claim in my earlier work titled *Gender, Ethnicity and Violence in Kenya's Transitions to Democracy: States of Violence*, but did not explore it beyond the introductory chapter. This claim, far beyond its application in the previous work, forms the basis of the theoretical argument developed in the present work.

32 Mamdani, *Citizen and Subject*, 6, emphasis added.

33 Ibid., emphasis added.

34 Ibid.

35 Ibid., 7.

36 Ibid., 8.
37 Ibid.
38 Ibid., 16.
39 K.M. Sheeba (2002), 'Modernity in Social Reform Discourse: The Women Question in Colonial Kerala', *Proceedings of the Indian History Congress*, 63: 931–938, 935.
40 That which apparently women were *not*, rather than what they were.
41 Partha Chatterjee (1993), *The Nation and Its Fragments: Colonial and Postcolonial Histories*, Princeton, NJ: Princeton University Press, 117, emphasis added.
42 Here I note a departure (that nonetheless exceeds my present concern) that there is also a form of patriarchy premised on the idea of legitimate versus illegitimate males. The illegitimate ones endanger women and thus produce the 'woman question' as requiring the intervention of the colonizing males and females (as exemplars of their males' legitimacy).
43 Sheeba, 'Modernity in Social Reform', 936.
44 Anne McClintock (1995), *Imperial Leather: Race, Gender and Sexuality in the Colonial Context*, London: Routledge, 219.
45 Ibid., 223.
46 Ibid., 225, emphasis original.
47 Ibid., 226.
48 Patricia M.E. Lorcin (2012), *Historicizing Colonial Nostalgia: European Women's Narratives of Algeria and Kenya 1900-Present*, New York: Palgrave Macmillan, 8.
49 Ibid., 12, emphasis added.
50 Ibid., 34.
51 Ibid., 197.
52 Who in any case have found ample biographical and autobiographical representation in the literature. See for instance, Lorcin, *Colonial Nostalgia*; Gillian Whitlock (2000), *The Intimate Empire: Reading Women's Autobiography*, New York: Cassell; Lora Wildenthal (2002), *German Women for Empire, 1884–1945*, Durham: Duke University Press; Errol Trzebinski (1977), *Silence Will Speak: A Study of the Life of Denys Finch Hatton and His Relationship with Karen Blixen*, Chicago: University of Chicago Press; Margaret Strobel (1991), *European Women and the Second British Empire*, Bloomington: Indiana University Press; Kumari Jayawardena (1995), *The White Woman's Other Burden: Western Women and South Asia During British Colonial Rule*, New York: Routledge; Elspeth Huxley (1974), *The Flame Trees of Thika*, London: Cox & Wyman; Karen Blixen (1986), *Letters from Africa 1914–1931*, Trans. Anne Born, ed. Frans Lasson. London: Picador.
53 See Chanock (1985), Hussin (2016), Mamdani (1996).
54 I develop this argument more concretely in Chapter 2 through a reading of repugnancy clauses as they functioned in the colonies and show their core as mediating a gendered relationship between colonized women and men, and a political relationship between women and the colonial state.

55 Kanchana Mahadevan (2002), 'Colonial Modernity: A Critique', *Indian Literature*, 46(3): 193–211, 198.
56 Mamdani, *Citizen and Subject* [2017], xx.
57 Ibid [1996]., 109, emphasis added.
58 Ibid., 110.
59 Leigh Brownhill (2009), *Land, Food, Freedom: Struggles for the Gendered Commons in Kenya, 1870 to 2007*, Trenton: Africa World Press Inc; Silvia Federici (2004), *Caliban and the Witch: Women, The Body and Primitive Accumulation*, Brooklyn, New York: Autonomedia; C. D., Deere (1990), *Household and Class Relations: Peasants and Landlords in Northern Peru*, Berkeley: University of California Press.
60 Tithi Bhattacharya (2020), 'Liberating Women from "Political Economy": Margaret Benston's Marxism and a Social-Reproduction Approach to Gender Oppression', *Monthly Review*, https://monthlyreview.org/2020/01/01/liberating-women-from-political-economy/ (accessed online on 5 January 2020).
61 Milan Kundera (1985), *The Unbearable Lightness of Being*, New York: Harper & Row, 135.
62 The idea of a more radical democracy has found critical expression in the literature over the past twenty years (see Rancière (2009); Brown (1995, 2006); Little &; Lloyd (2012)). It is a proposition which often departs from a critique of actually existing forms of democracy and extends its analysis to questions of difference, the particularities of political place and time, and to questions of power and resources on a global scale. My own elaboration intervenes in the debate by placing the idea of democracy's radical possibilities more narrowly in the colonial historical purview of its disavowed gendered subject: that is, apprehending one proposition out of the myriad that have or could be posed in generality.
63 The Aba Women's War in Nigeria is an enduring illustration of this powerful marginality of women. A historical event variously referred to as the 'Aba Women's Riot of 1929' and 'the Women's Revolt of 1929', scholars have also pointed out the attempts at subversion: that terming this event a 'riot' by the British was a deliberate attempt to downplay its impact on future history, and by extension, a denial of women's agency. The British refused to acknowledge that the war was, in fact, a systematically organized socio-economic protest movement (that cut across six ethnic groups – Ibibio, Andoni, Ogoni, Bonny, Opobo and Igbo women) of southeastern Nigeria comprising women motivated by specific grievances, directed at achieving certain clear-cut social, economic and political goals. The women's demands were radical: that the government exclude women from taxation; to stop [government] counting personal property and arresting of prostitutes; cancellation of rent payments for women's market sheds; abolish fees for licenses to stage women's dances; dismissal of the warrant chief; and that men too, should no longer taxed (see U.E. Umoren (1995), 'The Symbolism of the Nigerian Women's War

of 1929: An Anthropological Study of an Anticolonial Struggle', *African Study Monographs* 16(2): 66–7).

64 Leigh Brownhill (2009), *Land, Food, Freedom: Struggles for the Gendered Commons in Kenya, 1870–2007*, Trenton, NJ: Africa World Press, writes of Kenya that 'women's political actions . . . were new insofar as (a) the unifying forces of colonial taxation, forced labour and land alienation had organized men to join women in a coordinated rejection of colonialism; and (b) the indigenous resistance was focused against both European occupiers and the local African men who collaborated with them'. This resistance was organized in two ways – through gendered class alliances among women activists and men, and actions targeting the male deal (47–8).

65 Among the conceptualizations explaining this process is the notion of 'male deals' which 'facilitated corporate access to…subsistence resources' (ibid., 2009: 28). Women's location in the colonial political economy rendered them choiceless in the matter of circumventing this access: 'Chiefs in particular took on the task of compelling commoners to make themselves available for compulsory unwaged public service, such as road building, and both waged and unwaged labour on the European settler plantations located near the "native reserves"'. The prevailing migrant wage labour regime meant that 'the chiefs mainly forced peasant women to work . . .' resulting in grievances that also shaped their resistance against the chiefs and settlers (ibid., 29).

66 A state of emergency (the Emergency) was officially declared in Kenya on 20 October 1952 and began with the arrest of Jomo Kenyatta and 145 other African political figures, most of them Kikuyu. For a good elaboration of the circumstances that culminated in the Emergency, see Bruce J. Berman (1976), 'Bureaucracy and Incumbent Violence: Colonial Administration and the Origins of the "Mau Mau" Emergency in Kenya', *British Journal of Political Science*, 6(2): 143–175.

67 Marina Santoru (1996), 'The Colonial Idea of Women and Direct Intervention: The Mau Mau Case', *African Affairs*, 95 (379): 253–67.

68 Lisa Marie Cacho (2012) draws an important distinction between criminalization and stereotyping that puts this question into perspective: to be stereotyped as a criminal, she argues, is to be misrecognized as someone who committed a crime, but to be *criminalized* is to be prevented from being law-abiding – that is, the impossibility for the criminalized to access rights and to lose moral ground/moral credibility to question the laws that exclude them.

69 Chatterjee, *Black Hole*, xii.

70 Mahadevan (2002), for instance, highlights gendering of caste in point to the insufficient attention paid to 'the codification of Hindu Law that established a system of brahminical Sanskrit studies alongside the British system, [t]he latter [of which] has contributed to the production of a homogenous colonial subject in a gendered context by excluding peasants, tribals and so forth – an exclusion that has persisted to this day in a very violent form' ('Colonial Modernity', 197).

71 Mahadevan (2002), citing Yuval-Davis and Anthias (1994) show these invocations to include: as biological producers of ethnic collectivities; reproducers of the boundaries of ethnic/national groups; reproducers of ideology and transmitters of culture; as symbolic representatives for the construction or reproduction of ethnic boundaries; and as participants in national, economic and military struggles.
72 Ossome, *States of Violence,* 283.
73 Nikita Dhawan (2014), 'Affirmative Sabotage of the Master's Tools: The Paradox of Postcolonial Enlightenment', in *Decolonizing Enlightenment: Transnational Justice, Human Rights and Democracy in a Postcolonial World*, Nikita Dhawan (ed.), Berlin: Barbara Budrich Press, 40 (emphasis added).
74 This is a formulation of democracy that transcends liberal democracy.

Chapter 2

1 Gendered subjectivity might be understood in broad terms as those injuries, exclusions, erasure and forms of subjecthood/being or 'non-being' that are historically constituted on the basis of gendered positionality within the social and political milieu. For analytical ease, I focus throughout this work only on the interpellation of women into this milieu; that is, on the historical subjectivation of women as 'gendered' and 'violable.'
2 Gayatri Chakravorti Spivak (1993), 'Can the Subaltern Speak?' in *Colonial Discourse and Post-Colonial Theory*, Patrick Williams and Laura Chrisman (eds.), London: Harvester Wheatsheaf, 102.
3 Ibid., xi.
4 Nikita Dhawan (2014), 'Affirmative Sabotage of the Master's Tools: The Paradox of Postcolonial Enlightenment', in *Decolonizing Enlightenment: Transitional Justice, Human Rights and Democracy in a Postcolonial World*, Nikita Dhawan (ed.), Frankfurt: Barbara Budrich Publishers, 30.
5 As Dhawan argues, even critical thinkers like Adorno, Horkheimer and Foucault disregard colonialism in their critique of the Enlightenment – for instance, the erasure of the Haitian Revolution, historically one of the most significant appropriations of the Enlightenment principles (ibid., 30).
6 E.g. Muthu (2003; 2012); Festa and Carey (2009); Levy and Young (2011).
7 Dhawan, 'Affirmative Sabotage', 30.
8 Ibid., 37.
9 Jennifer Pitts (2005), *A Turn to Empire: The Rise of Imperial Liberalism in Britain and France*, Princeton: Princeton University Press, 2–3.
10 Ibid.
11 To paraphrase Foucault, being a historian of the present involves self-consciously writing with the present in mind; it means engaging in a project 'that is deliberately

both historical and critical, in that it is concerned – *outside all prescriptive intent* – with determining the conditions of possibility of [in present interest, democratic] experience in modern times', Michel Foucault (1973), *The Birth of the Clinic: An Archaeology of Medical Perception*, transl. A. M. Sheridan Smith, New York, xix (added emphasis).

12 David Scott (2004), *Conscripts of Modernity: The Tragedy of Colonial Enlightenment*, Durham: Duke University Press, 2. Scott's interpretation aside, Foucault's point is that historicizing the present modernizes it since one has to posit a future from which the present is made present. In other words, that we can only apprehend the present through its anticipation. Foucault's insight is that understanding the present as present is to historicize it, but the point, at least at the levels of disciplines, is that this also raises the problem of historical normativity. This normativity brings *legitimacy* to the present, which then requires an interrogation of the legitimating practice of historicizing. This problem offers some explanation regarding Foucault's move from 'history' to 'genealogy'.

13 Nikita Dhawan, 'Affirmative Sabotage', 66.

14 Scott, *Conscripts*, 119.

15 Dhawan, 'Affirmative Sabotage', 67.

16 Michel Foucault (1984), 'What Is Enlightenment?' in *The Foucault Reader*, Paul Rabinow (ed.), New York: Penguin, 45.

17 Dhawan, 'Affirmative Sabotage', 68 (emphasis added).

18 Scott's claim that we cannot not be modern might be read as a forceful interpellation by Euromodernity's self-proclaimed subjects that places them within a particular conversation. So, while acknowledging the modernist roots of colonialism, the ways in which the colonized respond reveal practices shaped in spite of modern subjugations. See also Paget Henry's (2007) critique of Scott's anti-essentialism.

19 Ato Sekyi-Otu (2018), for instance, argues that, '[s]uch is the vicious paradox of some African and Third World critics of "universalism": their obsessive-compulsive Eurocentrism; their wilful captivity to the very discourse they are avowedly sworn to divulge and dethrone; their exclusive preoccupation with the things the West does with words in order to enforce its particulars as universals; their trained habit, in contrast, of being utterly incurious regarding what our grandmothers do with words of evaluative judgment that have universals for their predicates. It is as if purveyors of Eurocentrism *and* their critics drink from the same cup and end up inebriated in separate beds but with kindred distractions. That must be the reason why "universalism" is chief among those ritual anathemas of anti-imperialist or, as they say, "counter-hegemonic", discourse' (Ato Sekyi-Otu, *Left Universalism, Africacentric Essays*, 35).

20 Scott, *Conscripts*, 171. It is, of course, the case that we can (and ought to) relativize the Enlightenment as but one effort among others (such as those throughout the

history of Africa, Asia and the Americas) to deal with questions of domination as well as resistance to domination. But my own interest in the colonial modern structure that issues from 1884 to 1885 (Berlin Conference) onwards, and which offers its justification through Enlightenment discourse which even the anticolonial discourse in Africa does not succeed in evading.

21 Dhawan, 'Affirmative Sabotage', 69.

22 Nayoung Aimee Kwon (2015), *Intimate Empire: Collaboration and Colonial Modernity in Korea and Japan*, Durham: Duke University Press, 9, emphasis added.

23 Ibid., 10.

24 Ibid.

25 Ibid., emphasis added. The problem, however, is not merely one of representation, which retains the hegemonic validity of the center/Western universality by suggesting an aspiration towards inclusion rather than a critique of the (violent) exclusion.

26 This paradox also allows us to critique the liberal basis of democracy that is identified with human rights, and thus a shift away from any formalistic understanding of democracy.

27 Dhawan, 'Affirmative Sabotage', 70, 71.

28 Dhawan, 'Affirmative Sabotage', 41.

29 Ibid.

30 Ibid.

31 Elsbeth Locher-Scholten (2000), writing on the Dutch Indies, poses the question regarding whether white women were participants and perpetrators within the colonial project, its opponents or its victims. She argues that European women were 'not the hapless onlookers of empire, but were ambiguously complicit both as colonisers and as colonised, privileged and restricted, acted upon and acting'. The struggle for women's voting rights for instance, offers a fine example of this situation. When Dutch women crossed the equator, they lost their voting rights, which they had won in in the Netherlands. In their struggle for this right in the Indies they firstly opted for the right to vote for themselves, basing their argument on their contribution to the colonial project (2000: 30).

32 Cited in David Scott (2004), *Conscripts of Modernity: The Tragedy of Colonial Enlightenment,* Durham: Duke University Press, 103, emphasis added.

33 Ibid., 104.

34 Nikita Dhawan (2007), 'Can the Subaltern Speak German? And Other Risky Questions – Migrant Hybridism versus Subalternity', http://translate.eipep.net/strands/03/dhawan-strands01en/ (accessed 20 May 2019).

35 Gayatri Chakravorty Spivak (1995), 'Supplementing Marxism', in *Whither Marxism?*, Steven Cullenberg and Bernd Magnus (eds.), New York: Routledge, 115.

36 Dhawan, 'Can the Subaltern Speak German?'

37 Recall here Gramsci's (1971) recognition that 'subalternity refers to the situation in which one class becomes subjected to the decisions of another. Subalternity cannot be explained in hegemonic terms, because it is achieved through subordination and silencing' (cited in Peyman Vahabzadeh (2007), 'The Conditions of Subalternity: Reflections on Subjectivity, Experience and Hegemony', *Socialist Studies/Études Socialistes*, 3(2): 93–113, 98).

38 Ngugi wa Thiongo (1964), *Weep Not, Child*, Heinemann: Nairobi, 34–35.

39 The British colonial government issued Emergency Orders in October 1952. The orders gave the government martial law powers. The situation was declared to be an emergency because of the massive oathing ceremonies held by the Kikuyu, the spread of the Land and Freedom army (the *Mau Mau*) from the urban areas into the rural districts and rise of violence against Loyalist Kikuyu. In Kiambu district, Senior Chief Waruhiu, a prominent pro-government spokesman, was assassinated. His murder was the event which precipitated the announcement of the state of Emergency and the British declaration of war against the Land and Freedom army (see Cora Ann Presley (2003), *Kikuyu Women, the Mau Mau Rebellion, and Social Change in Kenya*, Baltimore: Inprint Editions, 127).

40 Part of Ngugi's point is also that *mûndû* (person) is here taking on *mundu* (masculine) form through the colonial assertion of 'man' over 'person'. Among the Gikuyu, the wife and the husband are *mûndû*, suggesting much more in the slap, since Ngotho is making a claim less to achieving *mûndû* and instead one of replacing the master in the form of manhood.

41 Lynn Schler (2004), 'Writing African Women's History with Male Sources: Possibilities and Limitations', *History in Africa*, 31: 319–333, 321.

42 Ibid., 326.

43 Ibid., added emphasis.

44 ibid., 328.

45 Ibid., 331.

46 Ibid., added emphasis.

47 Ibid., 332, emphasis added.

48 See for instance, Brownhill (2009), Thomas (2003), MacKenzie (1998), Santoru (1996), Kanogo (1987b), and Mies (1986).

49 Sheba (2002: 935).

50 Ibid., 936.

51 Chowdhry (1996).

52 Hannah Arendt (1968), *The Origins of Totalitarianism*, New York: Harcourt, 275.

53 For a detailed discussion of the relationship between women and the nation, see Yuval-Davis and Anthias (1989), *Women-Nation-State*, London: Palgrave Macmillan.

54 Lyn Ossome (2018a), *Gender, Ethnicity and Violence in Kenya's Transitions to Democracy: States of Violence*, New York: Lexington Books, 4.

55 Kimberlé Crenshaw (1989), 'Demarginalizing the Intersection of Race and Sex: A Black Feminist Critique of Antidiscrimination Doctrine, Feminist Theory and Antiracist Politics', *University of Chicago Legal Forum,* 1(8): 139–167, 142.

56 Ibid., 143.

57 Ibid., 145.

58 Lyn Ossome (2023), 'Intersectionality from the Margins: Historical Subjects/Subjectivation in the Global South', in *The Routledge Handbook on Intersectionality Studies*, Kathy Davis and Helma Lutz (eds.), London: Routledge, 46.

59 Ibid.

60 Ibid. Consider, for instance, Crenshaw's (1989) argument that '[i]n order to include Black women, both [Black liberationist and feminist] movements must distance themselves from earlier approaches in which experiences are relevant only when they are related to certain clearly identifiable causes (e.g., the oppression of Blacks is significant when based on race, of women when based on gender). The praxis of both should be centered on the life chances and life situations of people who should be cared about without regard to the source of their difficulties' (1989: 166).

61 We can, of course, acknowledge the presumption of the group (Black women) in Crenshaw's formulation. My critique relates to the individualistic ways in which the liberal canon of rights interpellates its subjects of rights.

62 Ossome, 'Intersectionality from the Margins', 47.

63 See Maria Mies (2014[1986]), *Patriarchy and Accumulation on a World Scale: Women in the International Division of Labour,* London: Zed Books, for a detailed discussion of the nature of this hierarchization.

64 Barbara Foley (2018), 'Intersectionality: A Marxist Critique', *Monthly Review,* online at: https://mronline.org/2018/10/22/intersectionality-a-marxist-critique/ (accessed on 16 May 2019).

65 Furthermore, while it is possible for women to mobilize themselves out of class oppression, the same cannot be said about class *exploitation.* Oppression can be experienced at a micro level by individuals, but the structural nature of exploitation means that it is *always* experienced collectively by the oppressed as a group.

66 A. Sohn-Rethel (1978), Rosa Luxemburg (1925).

67 Spivak, 'Can the Subaltern Speak?' added emphasis.

68 That which apparently women were *not,* rather than what they were.

69 Partha Chatterjee (1993), *The Nation and its Fragments: Colonial and Postcolonial Histories*, Princeton, NJ: Princeton University Press, 117, emphasis added.

70 Ibid., emphasis added.

71 Ibid., 119, emphasis added.

72 Luise White (1990), *The Comforts of Home: Prostitution in Colonial Nairobi*, Chicago: University of Chicago Press, 226.

73 Ibid., 221.

74 Ibid., 221, emphasis added.

75 Ibid., 224.

76 Ibid.

77 Ibid.

78 Ibid., emphasis added.

79 Ibid., 228.

80 Ibid.

81 Ibid., 227.

82 Ibid., emphasis added. See also Ossome, *States of Violence*, Ch. 2.

83 Chatterjee, *The Nation and Its Fragments*, 121.

84 Ibid.

85 Ibid., emphasis added.

86 See White (1990), Thomas (2003) Robertson (1997).

87 This, for instance, is Chatterjee's (1993) point in his argument that 'if nationalist ideology in late nineteenth century Bengal legitimized the subjection of women under a new patriarchy, its history must be a history of struggle', insisting on an 'autonomous subjectivity of women', which he then reads biographically through the 'inner space of the middle-class home' (p. 137).

88 Saba Mahmood (2005), *Politics of Piety: The Islamic Revival and the Feminist Subject*, Princeton, NJ: Princeton University Press, 23.

89 Ibid. Mahmood has critiqued – albeit in a differing historical context of Muslim women under the Islamic Revivalist Movement in Egypt – the liberal-progressive impulse to reduce the complexity of Islamist movements to the trope of 'resistance', viewing the relationship between Islamism and liberal secularity as one of proximity and coimbrication rather than of simple opposition or accommodation (2005: 24–25).

90 Ibid., 35.

91 Ibid.

92 Ibid., emphasis added.

93 Mahmood Mamdani (1996), *Citizen and Subject: Contemporary Africa and the Legacy of Late Colonialism*, Princeton, NJ: Princeton University Press, *Citizen and Subject*, 137.

94 Ibid., 121.

95 Ibid.

96 Ibid.

97 Ibid.

98 Ibid., 117.

99 See Mamdani, *Citizen and Subject*, Ch. 4; Chanock (1985) for a detailed consideration of the notion of repugnancy in the law.

100 Ibid., 116–117.

101 Mamdani, *Citizen and Subject* [2017], xx (added emphasis).

102 Mamdani, *Citizen and Subject*, 110.

103 Sita Ranchod-Nilsson (1992), 'Educating Eve': The Women's Club Movement and Political Consciousness among Rural African Women in Southern Rhodesia, 1950–1980,' in *African Encounters with Domesticity*, Karen T. Hansen (ed.), New Brunswick: Rutgers University Press, 195.

104 Ibid., 198.

105 Ibid., 198–199.

106 Ibid., 199.

107 Ibid., 199 (added emphasis); see also Ranger 1981.

108 Mamdani [2017], *Citizen and Subject*, xvi.

109 Ranchod-Nilsson, 'Educating Eve', 199.

110 Ibid.

111 Ibid., 205.

112 For an extended discussion of this phenomenon, see Leigh Brownhill (2009), *Land, Food, Freedom: Struggles for the Gendered Commons in Kenya – 1870 to 2007*, Trenton: Africa World Press Inc.

113 Ranchod-Nilsson, 'Educating Eve', 203.

114 Mamdani, *Citizen and Subject,* 122–123.

Chapter 3

1 Mamdani, *Define and Rule*, 46.

2 Various definitions of customary law pertain, but they are generally defined as 'the aggregate of accepted customary practices, usages, mores and norms which are accepted as binding [suggesting that] the acceptance of the customary practices is a crucial factor in any inquiry of a custom's validity. This view of customary law as a system of norms emanating from the common consciousness of traditional African society is . . . the generally accepted understanding of customary law. With the advent of colonialism, these norms no longer derived their validity from the spontaneity and consensuality of traditional society, rather from what the courts declared them to be', cited in Derek Asiedu-Akrofi (1989), 'Judicial Recognition and Adoption of Customary Law in Nigeria', *The American Journal of Comparative Law*, 37(3): 571–593, 573–574. See also Channock (1985), Mamdani (1996).

3 Morgan Jerkins (2023), 'The Outsiders: Why Black Audiences Love Italian American Screen Icons', *Vanity Fair,* https://www.vanityfair.com/hollywood/2023/09/italian-american-film-black-audiences (accessed on 1 October 2023).

4 Asiedu-Akrofi, 'Judicial Recognition', 571.

5 Ibid., added emphasis.

6 Ibid.

7 Ibid., 572.

8 Ibid., 581.

9 Ibid., 580.

10 The literature distinguishes between premodern 'custom' which had historically existed as the 'force of habit' within precolonial social and cultural life, and colonial 'custom' tied to the notion of 'customary law' which was an instrument of indirect rule governmentality. Martin Chanock (1985) ethnographic study offers a particularly good summation. I draw here on Francis Snyder's (1988) review article: 'African customary law is recent in origin: it derives from the specific economic, institutional, and socio-cultural conditions of colonial rule. He situates the development of customary law carefully in its broader context, of which two features, in his view, are especially significant. The first embraces economic changes, in particular the development of commodity production and migratory wage labour. The second is what he calls 'legalization', the development of a *specifically legal mode* of dealing with conflicts. The first is that the colonial period represented a relatively sharp break in social relations, broadly conceived, including legal and economic relations. The second is that the so-called customary law developed and applied in state-sponsored courts was relatively novel, not a direct translation or expression of previously existing or concurrently existing rural norms. Though focusing on the colonial period and state law, Chanock's argument is therefore inevitably concerned with other parts of this temporal and institutional matrix. It is necessarily concerned with the pre-colonial period, especially the extent of continuity (as well as change) with the colonial period. It is also necessarily concerned with non-state law, particularly the nature and extent of its relationship to state, including but not limited to so-called customary law. He distinguishes between customary law and custom. The latter refers to the 'norms and practices existing in the pre-colonial period and . . . those used in dispute-settlement, not involving governmental agencies, under colonial rule' (Chanock, 1985: 240, n. 1).

11 Ibid., 581.

12 Ibid., 587, added emphasis.

13 Hartman, 'The Belly of the World,' 169.

14 Ibid., added emphasis.

15 Ibid., 170.

16 Michel Foucault (1976), *The History of Sexuality*, Vol 1, London: Penguin, 93–94 (added emphasis).

17 Ibid., 96. This formulation exceeds the system of 'Law-and-Sovereignty' predominant in political thought and instead examines power mechanisms on the basis of a strategy that is immanent in force relationships, including sexual relations/sexuality. It asks what the most immediate, most local power relations are in any specific type of discourse on sex or in the politics of sex present in a particular context (ibid.).

18 Willem Bosman (1967) [1705], *A New and Accurate Description of the Coast of Guinea*, London. Cited in Jack Goody, ed. (1973), *The Character of Kinship*, Cambridge: Cambridge University Press, 175.
19 Bosman, *A New and Accurate Description*, 199, cited in Goody, *Kinship*, 175.
20 For a concrete theorization linking the accumulation of life and reproductive labour to the historical accumulation of capital, Maria Mies (2014) and Federici (2004) have been most influential. See also earlier work by Fortunati (1981).
21 Jack Goody (1973), 'Polygyny, Economy and the Role of Women', in *The Character of Kinship*, J. Goody (ed.), Cambridge: Cambridge University Press, 185.
22 Ibid., 188.
23 Ibid.
24 Audrey Richards (1964), 'Authority Patterns in Traditional Buganda', in *The King's Men: Leadership and Status in Buganda on the Eve of Independence*, L.A. Fallers (ed.), London: Oxford University Press, 257.
25 Ibid.
26 Richards, 'Authority Patterns', 258 (added emphasis).
27 Ibid., added emphasis.
28 Ibid., original emphasis.
29 Ibid., 258–259, added emphasis.
30 L.A. Fallers and S.B.K. Musoke (1964), 'Social Mobility, Traditional and Modern', in *The King's Men: Leadership and Status in Buganda on the Eve of Independence*, L.A. Fallers (ed.), London: Oxford University Press, 162.
31 Richards, 'Authority Patterns', 288.
32 Fallers and Musoke (1964), 'Social Mobility', 204.
33 John Tosh (1978), *Clan Leaders and Colonial Chiefs in Lango: The Political History of an East African Stateless Society, c.1800–1939*, Oxford: Clarendon Press, 151–152.
34 In precolonial Nigeria society, for instance, Chuku (2009) writes that 'women exercised political power and influence through their membership in all-female age-grades and title societies in which members acquired power and authority as they advanced in age, thus, while the most junior age-grades performed the most menial jobs, the most senior ones made decisions on important issues that affected the state. They performed some executive functions, and also carried out certain judicial roles. In matrilineal Ohafia society, for example, there was the Ukeabua Ndi-Inyom age-grade (the women's executive arm), which performed both executive and judicial functions in the society. Women's title societies furthermore, conferred political power and influence on their members. Examples of such title societies included the Otu Odu (Ivory society) in Onitsha, Ogbuefi society (cow-killer) in Oguta, Loloanyi, Ogbaidi and Ogbunobodo (one who kills in the town's square) in Nsukka, Iyamba in Arochukwu, Ekwe in Nnobi and the Onwene in Onicha-Ugbo. While Loloanyi was the highest and most important women's title (the equivalent of the male Ozo title among the Nsukka), Ogbuefi was the highest

female title in Oguta. In addition to enhancing their social status and political power, these societies also offered the initiates avenues to exercise religious power in their communities. Goddess-focused religions – as in Igbo society – provided women an opportunity to control certain religious, political, and judicial functions through societies dedicated to the goddesses. The Earth Goddess, the Idemili, Agbala, Onishe, Araba, and Nimo Kwome are a few examples of powerful female deities in Igbo society. Priests and priestesses who served these deities and acted as mediums between the spirit and human worlds exercised enormous power, authority, and respect in society'. In these regards, 'women and their organizations acted as checks and balances in Igbo sociopolitical structures' (Gloria Chuku (2009), 'Igbo Women and Political Participation in Nigeria, 1800s-2005', *The International Journal of African Historical Studies*, 42(1): 81–103, 86–87).

35 Ibid., 89.
36 Ibid.
37 Ibid.
38 Ibid., 89.
39 Ibid., 91.
40 Ibid.
41 Ibid.
42 That is, the incorporation of women as being one of the methods used by the colonial state to monitor and control categories of the population (in this instance, women) that were considered subversive and/or dangerous. Yael Berda (2013), for instance, makes this point by extending the debate beyond the literature that predominantly associates practices of surveillance of population with (Western) modernity and the intensification of practices of security defined by the 'Global War on Terror', arguing that these surveillance and security developments were developed in the colonies to manage civilian populations (Berda 2013: 627). The shift 'from securing territory to monitoring populations' begins in the colonies (ibid., 628).
43 Other examples of such deviations were staged elsewhere on the continent. In Kenya the story is told of Chief Wangu wa Makeri, said to have become 'so intoxicated with conceit and craze for power that she danced naked before a crowd who promptly removed her from power' (Oduol 1993: 167).
44 Saidiya Hartman (2016), 'The Belly of the World: A Note on Black Women's Labors', *Souls*, 18(1): 166–173, 171.
45 Melissa Demian (2014), 'On the Repugnance of Customary Law', *Comparative Studies in Society and History*, 56(2): 508–536, 532.
46 Giorgio Agamben (1998), *Homo Sacer: Sovereign Power and Bare Life*, trans. Daniel Heller-Roazen, Stanford: Stanford University Press, 6.
47 Claire C. Robertson (1997), *Trouble Showed the Way: Women, Men, and Trade in the Nairobi Area, 1890–1990*, Bloomington and Indianapolis: Indiana University Press, 99.

48 Ibid.

49 Ibid.

50 Ibid., added emphasis.

51 Ibid., 99–100, added emphasis.

52 Tabitha Kanogo (2005), *African Womanhood in Colonial Kenya: 1900–50*, Oxford: James Currey, 57.

53 Ibid., 56.

54 Ibid.

55 I borrow this formulation of displacement from W.E.B Dubois, who opens his 1903 text, *The Souls of Black Folk*, with the rhetorical question, 'How does it feel to be a problem'? Dubois informs white America that he isn't 'a problem' nor is there a 'Negro problem' in America. According to Dubois, the only problem that persists is the perception and treatment of the Negro because of the colour of his skin. Dubois likens the colour of Negro skin to a veil because it keeps him and other Negroes 'shut out from the rest of the world' (p. 2). It divides the Negro from white American society because white Americans can't see past the Negro's veil. As a result, the Negro isn't extended the same opportunities nor granted the same liberties as his white counterparts.

56 Susan Brownmiller (2002), 'Foreword', in Tanaka, Y. (2002), *Japan's Comfort Women: Sexual Slavery and Prostitution during World War II and the US Occupation*, Y. Tanaka (ed.), London & New York: Routledge, xv.

57 Ibid.

58 Tanaka (2002) reveals the direct role of top-ranking officers of the Japanese Imperial forces in organizing and controlling the system. It involved collaboration between government ministries – namely, the Ministries of the Army, Navy, and Foreign Affairs – and the military (Yuki Tanaka (2002), *Japan's Comfort Women: Sexual slavery and prostitution during World War II and the US occupation*, London & New York: Routledge, 5).

59 Ibid., 4 (added emphasis).

60 Ibid., 5.

61 Ibid.

62 I approach this formulation from the argument I illustrated in the introduction and Chapter 1, that women had not been the primary political and economic subjects of the colonial state, but that the absolute necessity of their (re)productive labour could be established through an examination of the social and cultural structures of indirect rule. In this sense, the depoliticization that I reference here is an attempt to situate sexual violence in the social governance structure of the state and not a negation of the political salience of sexual violence. As I argue in Chapter 4, the context of democratization moves us to think beyond the gratuitous nature of violence that is established where human rights are completely negated (such as in the context of slavery), towards an interrogation of what it is that violence *does* in a political sense.

63 The language of rape as gendered violence gains recognition only at the limit of colonial customary law – that is, is recognized as a statutory offence precisely because its criminalization is affected under modern law. This suggests too, the challenge of trying to make sense of rape outside of modern (colonial and postcolonial) law – a move that may require a different conceptualization or retroactive thinking.

64 The term *ressentiment* originates in Friedrich Nietzsche's (Leipzig 1969/1887) historical analysis of morals and describes a constraining sociocultural condition that brews a feeling directed against powerful agents (Tzanelli 2012). *Ressentiment* combines an awareness of powerlessness vis-à-vis hierarchical power with the hope of an imaginary vengeance to compensate for this impotence (ibid.). Or as Asma Abbas (2014) explains, '*ressentiment* is the feeling of being wounded repeatedly by an injury: a sufferer internalizes the injury, relies upon it for meaning, and seeks a cause for it outside of herself, keeping the hurt current and valid. The search for a cause, just like the wounding, is enacted repeatedly, always terminating on another entity – an individual or a group – that is both the cause of the wound and the rightful target of hurt feelings. In the longevity of the wound is rooted an identity for the injured, who are called upon to react to the cause of the hurt, even to negate it, in order to seek redress and justice. In this process, new political and moral values are generated. This feeling's potential to mediate, often even encapsulate, moments within an individual's ethical and political experience accounts for its status as a political concept' (ibid.).

65 Hannah Arendt (1951), *The Origins of Totalitarianism*, New York: Schocken Books, 286.

66 Ibid., 294 (added emphasis).

67 To the extent that even the most centralized of political regimes tends towards the fomentation of difference as a weapon against the threat of broad-based solidarity.

68 Katherine Luongo (2010), 'Domestic Dramas and Occult Acts: Witchcraft and Violence in the Arena of the Intimate', in *Domestic Violence and the Law in Colonial and Postcolonial Africa*, E. Burrill, R. Roberts and E. Thornberry (eds.), Athens: Ohio University Press, 180.

69 Ibid.

70 Ibid., 180–181 (added emphasis).

71 This discourse of the occult might be read as one possible answer to the question dilemma posed in above regarding the difficulty of conceptualizing rape outside of the colonial modern lexicon (see note 65 above). The occult might be one of the ways available to retroactively (from the present) conceptualize/understand rape in the premodern/precolonial context. This task, however, exceeds my present objectives.

72 Ibid.

73 Ibid.

74 Ibid., emphasis both original and added.

75 Ibid.

76 Ibid., 184.
77 Ibid., 194, original emphasis.
78 White fear of the black male as sexual predator.
79 Lynette A. Jackson (2002), 'When in the White Man's Town': Zimbabwean Women Remember Chibuera', in *Women in African Colonial Histories*, Jean Allman, Susan Geiger and Nakanyike Musisi (eds.), Bloomington: Indiana University Press, 195.
80 Ibid.
81 Ibid., 194–195.
82 Compulsory medical examinations of African men and women for venereal disease was made official government policy in some of the colonies as a prerequisite for receiving passes to seek work.
83 Jackson, 'When in the White Man's Town', 193.
84 White, *The Comforts of Home*, 221.
85 Jackson, 'When in the White Man's Town', 198.
86 Politicized by linking gendered labour to the racial structure of capitalist accumulation, which pushes the class struggle beyond the domain of capital firmly into an anticolonial domain where struggles are directed towards dismantling the totality of the social structure of colonial domination, not just its class structure.
87 See an elaboration of this argument in Lyn Ossome (2023), 'Intersectionality from the Margins: Historical Subjects/Subjectivation in the Global South,' in *The Routledge Handbook on Intersectionality Studies*, Kathy Davis and Helma Lutz (eds.), London: Routledge, 44–46.
88 See Chatterjee (1993), Mamdani (1996).
89 Paul Vinogradoff (1924), 'The Juridical Nature of the State', *Michigan Law Review*, 23(2): 138–153, 138.

Chapter 4

1 W.E.B. DuBois (1920), 'The Damnation of Women/Children of the Moon', *Darkwater: Voices from within the Veil*, New York: Harcourt, Brace and Company (emphasis added). In the US this characterization may be extended to men, who are often captive to the 13th Amendment and provide prison slave labour.
2 Joy James (2020), 'From Slave Ships to Black Lives Matter – Session 3', https://www.youtube.com/watch?v=k0pwUC3nAJI (accessed on 9 November 2020, emphasis added).
3 Ibid. (emphasis added). I use this in refence not to democracy *writ large*, but in specific relation to Western democracy exported to former colonies or neocolonies.
4 In a similar but historically distinct expression of this claim, Orlando Paterson (1985) writes of the 'association between civilization and slavery', a link he considers as being a '*sociohistorical necessity*'. Highlighting what he considers to

be an historical enigma, Paterson argues that '[i]n the Western world…[s]lavery is associated not only with the development of advanced economies, but also with the emergence of several of the most profoundly cherished ideals and beliefs in the Western tradition. The idea of freedom and the concept of property were both intimately bound up with the rise of slavery, their very antithesis. The great innovators not only took slavery for granted, they insisted on its necessity to their way of life. In doing so, they were guilty not of some unfathomable lapse of logic, but rather of admirable candor. For Plato and Aristotle and the great Roman jurists were not wrong in recognizing the necessary correlation between their love of their own freedom and its denial to others. The joint rise of slavery and cultivation of freedom was no accident. It was…a sociohistorical necessity'. See Orlando Paterson (1985), *Slavery and Social Death: A Comparative Study*, Cambridge, MA: Harvard University Press, viii–ix (added emphasis).

5 Hortense Spillers (1987), 'Mama's Baby, Papa's Maybe: An American Grammar Book', *Diacritics*, 17(2): 64–81, 65.

6 This is also the broader question framing the book.

7 This chapter has benefited from critical and thoughtful comments from Joy James, whose work inspires it, and to whom it is dedicated.

8 Joy James (2016), 'The Womb of Western Theory: Trauma, Time Theft, and the Captive Maternal', *Carceral Notebooks*, https://sites.williams.edu/jjames/files/2019/05/WombofWesternTheory2016.pdf, 255 (emphasis added).

9 Ibid., 255.

10 Ibid., 256 (emphasis added).

11 Colonial modernity does not accord individuality to the colonized in the same way that Euromodernity does to its ('white-Anglo-Saxon, male') Western subject.

12 David Scott (2004), *Conscripts of Modernity: The Tragedy of Colonial Enlightenment*, Durham: Duke University Press, 19.

13 Mamdani, for instance, argues that the only thing peculiar to natives as a group is that they are grouped as such by the civil law: we only understand them as natives *in relation to* the settlers who create them in law [Mahmood Mamdani (2020), *Neither Settler nor Native: The Making and Unmaking of Permanent Minorities*, Cambridge: Harvard University Press, Ch. 3].

14 One of the reasons people are denied personhood relates to the criminalization of their identity. Lisa Marie Cacho (2012), for instance, argues in relation to media representations that presume the innocence of white people and the guilt of black people that the basis of racial stereotyping is essentially that criminality is inconceivable without black bodies. In the American context from which she writes, she shows that there are those racialized people who are criminalized as a group ('illegal aliens', 'gang members', 'terrorist suspects'), who are unable to comply with the 'rule of law' because U.S. law targets their being and their bodies, not their behavior. To be Black/Latinx is to be criminalized in this way – and to

be criminalized is to be prevented from being law-abiding – the impossibility for the criminalized to access rights, to even lose moral ground, because the law presumes their immorality.

15 Lyn Ossome (2018a), *Gender, Ethnicity and Violence in Kenya's Transitions to Democracy: States of Violence,* New York, Lexington Books, xvi.

16 Ibid., xvi–xvii.

17 Mamdani, *Define and Rule,* 2.

18 This right has at least two sides: the claims that states and others make about why they have a right to rule, and the *empirical* fact of whether their populations accept or at least tolerate this claimed right.

19 Mamdani, *Neither settler nor Native,* 160.

20 Mahmood Mamdani (2012), *Define and Rule: Native as Political Identity,* Cambridge, MA: Harvard University Press.

21 Ibid., 2 (emphasis added).

22 On the other side of this, the foundation of colonial civil administration was racism, through which a 'civilized' space was demarcated and access to rights and the state determined on the basis of proximity to whiteness.

23 Jeff Guy (2009), 'Women in Labour: The Birth of Colonial Natal.1 "Inkom' imbiw' etsheni kobelungu"', paper presented at the History and African Studies Seminar University of KwaZulu-Natal on 29 April 2009, 4.

24 Ibid., 4 (emphasis added).

25 Ibid., emphasis added.

26 I am making specific reference here to the Black subject-object, not the white subject.

27 Federici's argument in *Caliban and the Witch* is precisely that gender and femininity are not purely a 'cultural reality, but a specification of class relations', and so the sexual division of labour that controls women's reproductive labour must as such be manipulated by the new ruling classes as a precondition for the production of surplus value as they develop capitalist relations of private property. Federici illustrates in great detail how these controls and changes were enforced through violence (see Silvia Federici (2004), *Caliban and the Witch: Women, The Body and Primitive Accumulation,* Brooklyn, NY: Autonomedia, 14).

28 Federici, *Caliban,* 83.

29 Ibid., 222.

30 Oyěwùmí (1997) makes a similar observation regarding native women's double burden, that African females were colonized by Europeans as Africans and as African women. They were dominated, exploited and inferiorized as Africans together with African men and then separately inferiorized and marginalized as African women (See Oyèrónkẹ́ Oyěwùmí (1997), *The Invention of Women: Making an African sense of Western gender discourses,* Minneapolis: University of Minnesota Press, 122).

31 Here, I am pointing towards the problem of intersectionality that I have explored in some detail elsewhere (Ossome, 2023), where I argue that when directed towards an analysis of the colonial condition, intersectionality is tasked with showing the specific historical trajectories through which women emerge (or that demand women's appearance) at the 'intersection' as either female, or Black, or both. In other words, in contexts of oppression and in the absence of the freedom and liberty to claim an identity or to *name oneself,* identities invariably become political and are politicized. In such contexts, it is not enough simply to highlight discrimination, but rather to also ask what it is that different forms of discrimination *do* at particular historical conjunctures. This could also be posed as a question as such: *when* does identity normatively defined – as Black, female, queer, etc., become political (identity), shaped by race, class, ethnicity, gender, sexuality and so on? Global intersectionality studies have not yet responded adequately to this question, failing as they do to illustrate the shift from a normative identitarian basis to a *political* one. My argument ultimately is that colonial modernity is peculiar in producing this historical-legal-political subjectivity with which intersectionality theory has to grapple. For a longer engagement with this debate, see Lyn Ossome (2023), 'Intersectionality from the Margins: Historical Subjects/Subjectivation in the Global South', in *Routledge Handbook of Intersectionality Studies*, Kathy Davis and Helma Lutz (eds.), London: Routledge.

32 This in part is the point Césaire (1972) is making when he argues that the instruments of colonial power rely on barbaric, brutal violence and intimidation whose end result is the degradation of Europe itself: its mechanisms of asserting colonial power reflect its own 'barbarism' and 'degradation'. Its various modes of violence against the colonized are already hardwired into its approach to the expansion of capitalism beyond Europe.

33 Oyěwùmí (1997), *The Invention of Women*, 122 (emphasis added).

34 Gender is always present, even as nonbinary or ungendered or trans. Its function, however, among the colonizers is a tendency towards a heteronormative identitarianism that functions politically to exclude gendered 'others', and socially to stabilize the notion of a labouring body as female. Such stabilization is both a cultural *and* political endeavour.

35 Mahmood Mamdani, *When Victims Become Killers: Colonialism, Nativism and the Genocide in Rwanda*, Princeton, NJ: Princeton University Press, 23 (emphasis added).

36 Ibid (emphasis added).

37 James, 'The Womb of Western Theory', 256 (emphasis added).

38 Ibid., 257 (emphasis added).

39 Ibid., 258 (emphasis added).

40 Ibid.

41 Ibid.

42 For a more recent critique of conventional intersectionality, see Joy James (2022), 'Maternal (In)Coherence: When Feminism Meets Fascism', *Parapraxis I*, 145–157.

43 James, 'The Womb of Western Theory', 277.

44 Lynn M. Thomas (1997), 'Regulating Reproduction: State Interventions into Fertility and Sexuality in Rural Kenya, c. 1920–70', Ph.D. dissertation, University of Michigan, 218–267.

45 Cited in Brett L. Shadle (2006), *'Girl Cases': Marriage and Colonialism in Gusiiland, Kenya, 1890–1970*, London: Heinemann, 187–188.

46 Ibid.

47 The idea with much currency in Africanist literature that colonial officers 'sought to balance colonial demands for African land and labor against the need to maintain political control and to fulfill the "white man's burden" of civilizing the "barbaric" and improving women's status' [Lynn M. Thomas (2003), *Politics of the Womb: Women, Reproduction and the State in Kenya*, Berkeley: University of California Press, 5]. See also Cooper (1994); Stoler (1991).

48 Mamdani (2020) notes in the South Africa context too, that the Kaffir Commission of 1852–1953 had similarly identified a political risk associated with the unchecked progeny of African men, arguing that if 'the Kaffirs were rapidly becoming rich and independent', this was 'evidence of the increasing means of sensual indulgence available to the males'. There followed the moralizing conclusion [that] '[t]heir prosperity would be welcome if it were the fruit of men's regular and honest industry, but it flowed in fact from polygamy and female slavery'. And so, the commission made its most 'enlightened' recommendations: that polygamy and lobolo (bride wealth, the practice of a groom and his family paying his bride's family) be prohibited by law (as cited in Mamdani 2020: 155).

49 As cited in Shadle (2006): 'Colonial officials' hostility to African women's mobility reached its peak in the 1930s, even as metropolitan critiques of colonial policies toward women did the same. The histories of these countervailing trends overlapped only slightly, but as they came together, they spawned impassioned missives and mass meetings by the critics, condescending memoranda and frustrated reports by officials. Twice in the decade activists in Britain forced the Colonial Office to undertake investigations into the status of African women. The first, in 1930–1932, began as an inquiry into female circumcision and the health of the colonized population, but what emerged was an attempt to determine if African women lived as if enslaved to their menfolk. The second investigation, which stretched from 1935 to 1937, was intended to discover the existence and extent of forced marriage of African women. Only with the outbreak of war were attentions turned elsewhere' (2006: 56). See also Thomas (1997).

50 Ibid., 69.

51 Mamdani, *Neither Settler nor Native*, 34.

52 James, 'The Womb of Western Theory', 277.
53 Saidiya Hartman (2021), *Wayward Lives, Beautiful Experiments: Intimate Histories of Riotous Black Girls, Troublesome Women and Queer Radicals*, London: Serpent's Tail, 224.
54 Ibid., xv (emphasis added).
55 Ibid., xvii (emphasis added).
56 Kimberlé Crenshaw (1989), 'Demarginalizing the Intersection of Race and Sex: A Black Feminist Critique of Antidiscrimination Doctrine, Feminist Theory and Antiracist Politics', *University of Chicago Legal Forum,* 1(8): 139–167, 157.
57 Ibid., 157–158 (emphasis added).
58 As immutable subject, white women must also then be seen a non-labouring subject. The mere fact of their existence confirms the norm (of white supremacy), while the labour involved in perpetuating that norm is parceled out to black women, condemned as they are to a life of constantly proving their humanity.
59 Durba Mitra (2020), *Indian Sex Life: Sexuality and the Colonial Origins of Modern Social Thought*, Princeton & Oxford: Princeton University Press, 6–7.
60 Ibid., 2.
61 Ibid., 175.
62 Nthabiseng Motsemme (2007), 'Loving in a Time of Hopelessness: On Township Women's Subjectivities in a Time of HIV/AIDS', in *Women in South African History*, Nomboniso Gasa (ed.), Cape Town: HSRC Press.
63 Ibid., 370 (emphasis added).
64 Ibid.
65 Here we might also think of the sterilization campaigns that have been targeted at poor, working class and HIV positive women in Third World countries in the name of reproductive health. Where the state abrogates women's autonomy and freedoms in this way, how does one make sense of the rights claims directed at this same state that is holding women in captivity?
66 Anne McClintock (1995), *Imperial Leather: Gender, Race and Sexuality in the Colonial Contest*, New York & London: Routledge, 182.
67 Ibid.
68 Ibid (original emphasis).
69 Saidiya Hartman (2016), 'The Belly of the World: A Note on Black Women's Labors', *Souls*, 18(1): 166–173, 168.
70 Karl Marx (1971), *The Grundrisse*, edited & trans. David McLellan, New York: Harper & Row, 34.
71 Ibid.
72 Ibid., 37 (emphasis added).
73 Ibid.
74 Federici, *Caliban.*
75 Ibid., 11.

76 See also Stacy Schiff (2015), *The Witches: Suspicion, Betrayal, and Hysteria in 1692 Salem*, New York: Black Bay Books.
77 Rosa Luxemburg (1951), *The Accumulation of Capital*, London: Routledge. See also Lyn Ossome and Sirisha Naidu (2021), 'The Agrarian Question of Gendered Labour', in *Labour Questions in the Global South*, Praveen Jha, Walter Chambati and Lyn Ossome (eds.), New Delhi: Springer.
78 Luxemburg, *Accumulation*.
79 Bibi Bakare-Yusuf (1997), 'The Economy of Violence: Black Bodies and the Unspeakable Terror', in *Gender and Catastrophe*, R. Lentin (ed.), London and New York: Zed Books, 318 (emphasis added). This argument, however, may not be correctly applied to the Americas, as both in formal slaver and the post-civil war enslavement of convict prison lease system, the enslaved were worked to death, with the understanding that one could easily purchase another.
80 Enforced through both child-bearing and child-rearing.
81 Samir Amin (1976), *Unequal Development: An Essay on the Social Formations of Peripheral Capitalism*, trans. Brian Pearce, Sussex: Monthly Review Press, 204 (emphasis added).
82 Ibid (emphasis added).
83 Ibid (emphasis added).
84 Julia C. Wells (1982), 'The History of Black Women's Struggle against Pass Laws in South Africa 1900–1960', unpublished PhD thesis, Graduate School of Arts and Social Sciences, Columbia University, 19–22.
85 Shula Marks and Richard Rathbone, Eds. (1982), *Industrialisation and Social Change in South Africa: African Class, Culture and Consciousness, 1870–1930*, London and New York: Longman.
86 Mamdani, *Citizen and Subject*.
87 Oyěwùmí, *The Invention of Women*, 124.
88 Oyěwùmí's concern is significantly with the *effect* which this invention had on African females and the (re)ordering of African society more broadly – effectively defining 'females as "women" and hence second-class colonial subjects unfit to define their own destiny' (127).
89 This question, of course, is somewhat tempered when one thinks of Leopold in the Congo, chopping off hands that are supposed to pick more rubber out of fear of having one's hand severed: the fact that there is irrationality and gratuitous violence.
90 Hortense J. Spillers (1987), 'Mama's Baby, Papa's Maybe: An American Grammar Book', *Diacritics*, 17(2): 64–81, 72–73 (original emphasis).
91 Ibid., 74 (original emphasis).
92 Marina E. Santoru (1996), 'The Colonial Idea of Women and Direct Intervention: The Mau Mau Case', *African Affairs*, 95: 253–267.
93 Here I am referring to acknowledgement in democracy's language of 'inclusion', 'equality', 'representation', 'justice' and so on.

94 Joy James (2020), 'From Slave Ships to Black Lives Matter—Session 3', https://www.youtube.com/watch?v=k0pwUC3nAJI (accessed on 9 November 2020, emphasis added).

95 See Joy James (2021), 'We Remember the Attempts to Be Free', *Millennials are Killing Capitalism,* https://millennialsarekillingcapitalism.libsyn.com/we-remember-the-attempts-to-be-free-joy-james-on-black-august-and-the-captive-maternal; and Joy James, *In Pursuit of Revolutionary Love*, Divided: London, 2022.

96 See Joy James (2021), 'The Captive Maternal and Abolitionism', *Canadian Journal of Cultural Studies*, 43: 9–23.

97 Ibid.

98 Ibid.

99 Lisa Marie Cacho (2012), *Social Death: Racialized Rightlessness and the Criminalization of the Unprotected*, New York: New York University Press, 4.

100 Ibid., 2.

101 Ibid., 4.

102 In the most basic sense, the doctrine of *terra nullius* simply no longer applies. Newly independent states, in other words, have to propose a development path that does not rely on 'free access to cheap raw materials, labour and markets in the colonies' as the reality of that model was one of depletion and finite availability (Mies 2014: 201). The 'progress' which capitalist societies recorded had been based not only on the exploitation of the 'free' wage labourers and unpaid wage labourers (housewives) there, but also on the plunder and exploitation of colonial lands and people – practices that are ongoing in various guises today. Opting for this model means that Third World governments cannot similarly do without such exploitation and plunder – of private land, nature and the commons; of wage labourers; and of women's (gendered) unpaid labour as the basis of accumulation (Mies, 2014).

103 Ibid.

104 Ibid.

105 Utsa Patnaik (2012), 'Some Aspects of the Contemporary Agrarian Question', *Agrarian South: Journal of Political Economy,* 1(3): 233–254, 250–251.

Chapter 5

1 Alan Paton (1948), *Cry, the Beloved Country,* New York: Penguin Books, 126–127.

2 Stuart Hall (1987), *The Hard Road to Renewal: Thatcherism and the Crisis of the Left*, London: Verso, 266.

3 Lyn Ossome (2018a), *Gender, Ethnicity and Violence in Kenya's Transitions to Democracy: States of Violence,* London/New York: Lexington Books, xvi.

4 E. Marina Santoru (1996), 'The Colonial Idea of Women and Direct Intervention: The Mau Mau Case,' *African Affairs*, 95(379): 253–267, 256.
5 Chatterjee proposes the notion of political society as one way of understanding the vast domain of politics in the 'Third World' which falls outside hegemonic Western notions of state and civil society. This domain, often marked by the stamp of illegality, nevertheless contributes to the immense democratic churning that characterizes much of the Third World (in Partha Chatterjee (2007), *The Politics of the Governed: Reflections on Popular Politics in Most of the World*, New York: Columbia University Press), 54.
6 Such methods include organizing through collective violation of property laws and civic regulations; making a claim to a habitation and livelihood as a matter of right and using association to pursues such claims; and other 'imaginative possibilities of a community (e.g. its capacity to invent relations of kinship, produce a new rhetoric of political claims.
7 Chatterjee, *The Politics of the Governed*, 53–78.
8 Ibid.
9 Ibid.
10 L. Ossome (2023), 'Intersectionality from the Margins: Historical Subjects/ Subjectivation in the Global South,' in *The Routledge Handbook on Intersectionality Studies*, K. Davis and H. Lutz (eds.), London: Routledge.
11 I adopt a basic definition of social reproduction related to the daily reproduction of working-class households through the acquisition and provision of such basic needs as food, shelter, clothing and healthcare (Katz 2001). In contemporary capitalist economies, social reproduction hinges on the interplay between three major institutions: households, markets and the state (Antonopolous and Hirway 2010; Dickinson and Russell 1986).
12 Marxist perspectives show certain peculiarities of labour power, one being that it is the only commodity that cannot itself be produced capitalistically (e.g. on the basis of wage labour and the extraction of surplus value. There are no capitalist enterprises, no portion of total social capital devoted to and specializing in the production of living labourer whose capacity to labour is then purchased as an input to the manufacture of other commodities. Labour power is also unique in that of all commodities under developed capitalism, it's production and reproduction is antithetical to capitalist forms of organization and as such remains external to the sphere of surplus value production. This peculiarity establishes the radical separation in modern capitalism of the sphere of production of commodities from the sphere of reproduction of labour power (see James Dickinson and Bob Russell (1986), 'Introduction: The Structure of Reproduction in Capitalist Societies,' in *Family, Economy and the State: Social Reproduction Under Capitalism*, J. Dickinson and B. Russell (eds.), New York: St. Martin's Press, 1–22).

13 Nira Yuval-Davis (1997), 'Women and the Biological Reproduction of the Nation', in *Gender and Nation*, N. Yuval-Davis (ed.), London: Sage, 26.

14 In *A Dying Colonialism*, Fanon (1965) makes a similar observation in relation to the politics of the veil in Algeria: 'Beneath the patrilineal pattern of Algerian society, the specialists described a structure of matrilineal essence. Arab society has often been presented by Westerners as a formal society in which outside appearances are paramount. The Algerian woman, an intermediary between obscure forces and the group, appeared in this perspective to assume a primordial importance. Behind the visible, manifest patriarchy, the more significant existence of basic matriarchy was affirmed. The role of the Algerian mother, that of the grandmother, the aunt and the "old woman", were inventoried and defined' (1965: 37).

15 The exception was a few landed, elite, educated and aspirational natives, mainly male, who were accorded certain civil rights, although even these were never identical to the full range of rights and liberties which colonists enjoyed (see Brownhill 2009; Mamdani 1996).

16 The 1954 Tomlinson Commission was authorized to conduct an exhaustive inquiry into and report on a comprehensive scheme for the rehabilitation of the Native areas with a view to developing within them a social structure in keeping with the culture of the Natives and based on effective socio-economic planning. The commission also drew on the expertise of research specialists in economics, demography, labour matters and agricultural–environmental practices. Determined to uncover the full complexity of administration and civic life in the reserves, the commission amassed a wealth of information about Africans, their eroding 'tribal past' and their adaptation to the market economy in the white areas, and it considered ways to combat 'undesirable changes' by resuscitating the various 'tribal economies'. The far-ranging deliberations of the Tomlinson Commission report may be reduced to three primary policies that the commission regarded as interdependent: (1) the separation of farmers from nonfarmers, (2) a land rehabilitation policy and (3) the industrialization of the reserves. These were standard concerns in plans for the reserves in the segregation era. But three further points distinguished the Tomlinson Commission report from previous proposals: the vital importance that the report attached to the quantitative measurement of classes, detailed proposals that made increased agricultural productivity dependent on the large-scale removal of 'inefficient' peasants from the land, and lastly, the conviction that all plans affecting the reserves should promote tribalism in general and the Bantu Authorities model in particular. See 'The Tomlinson Commission and Bantu Authorities', archive at: https://publishing.cdlib.org/ucpressebooks/view?docId=ft2n39n7f2&chunk.id=s1.7.32&toc.depth=100&toc.id=ch7&brand=ucpress

17 Cited in Scott Everett Couper (2007), 'Chief Albert Luthuli and the Bantustan Question', *Journal of Natal and Zulu History*, 25(1): 240–267, 243 (added emphasis).

18 For an elaboration, see Lyn Ossome (2025), 'Social Reproduction and Surplus Populations of The Agrarian South', in *Handbook on Politics and Society*, Shireen Hassim and Anna Korteweg (eds.), Gloucestershire: Edward Elgar.

19 I draw here from Mezzadri's (2021) study of India's sweatshop regime, in which she methodologically draws on Barbara Harriss-White's (2003) social structures of accumulation (SSA) framework, in combination with social reproduction theory, and argues that the same social structures mediating accumulation are also central to the ways in which multiple forms of exploitation co-exist, and how labour is regenerated daily and intergenerationally as a cheap commodity, systematically paid below its reproductive cost. Exploring India's informal capital through this SSA lens, Harriss-White identifies five primary social structures of accumulation, besides the (local) state: (i) the structure of the labour force and social classes; (ii) gender; (iii) religion; (iv) caste and (v) space. Mezzadri shows how in the context of highly flexible agrarian and industrial systems, control over the labour force is realized through the manipulation of various 'non-class social identities' such as gender, caste, age and household composition, which deepens the segmentation of labour markets. Labour control here is central to the identification of the composition of the socially segmented labour force as a key SSA crucial to regenerate labour flexibility.

20 By this I mean that gendered, ethnic and caste structures are tacitly accorded leeway as surrogates of the state to exercise authority (often backed by violence) in the spheres of economic, social and political life – and in these ways provide an alibi for the liberal democratic state that allows it to retain a façade of legitimacy as far as gendered violence is concerned.

21 According to Sundstrom (2013), civic ostracism 'involves exclusion [as well as] civic banishment: those who are within the nation are regarded as not really belonging here, within the abstract, pure, or ideal nation. It is a subjective belief or affect, usually from the perspective of an individual who is, in their imagination, fully rooted in the nation, that some other person or group cannot be a part of that nation. These strangers cannot be authentic participants of the cultural, linguistic, or religious traditions of the nation they inhabit; they do not derive from soil of the nation's land or the blood of its people'. See R. R. Sundstrom (2013), 'Sheltering Xenophobia', *Critical Philosophy of Race*, 1(1): 68–85, 71.

22 Ibid., 74.

23 As Sundstrom (2013) puts it, 'since the ordering of the basic structure of society did not determine the beginning nor the progress of the life of the refugee or immigrant, then (within the constraints of ideal political theory) their life chances are not a matter of social justice. What has happened to them may be a matter of international justice, but it is not the concern of social justice, and is not a concern of "ours"' (Ibid., 74).

24 Indeed, the strong showing of former president Jacob Zuma's newly launched uMkhonto weSizwe (MK) party in KwaZulu-Natal province is indicative of this

shift. The party's support base is predominantly of Zulu ethnicity, and it received its highest share of votes (45.93 per cent) in the KwaZulu-Natal provincial elections and 14.58 per cent total national vote in the 2024 national election. Source: IEC, South Africa: https://results.elections.org.za/home/NPEPublicReports/1334/National%20Ballot/Results%20Report/National.pdf

25 Morris Szeftel (1994), 'Ethnicity and Democratization in South Africa', *Review of African Political Economy*, 21(60): 185–199, 185.

26 Furthermore, Afrikaners almost always belonged to one of the Dutch Reformed Churches, which were among the leading organs for the dissemination of National Party principles, while the English-speaking [we]re generally (though not as invariably) Anglicans.

27 Szeftel, 'Ethnicity and Democratization', 191–192.

28 Ibid.

29 Ibid., 192.

30 Morris Szeftel (1994), 'Ethnicity and Democratization in South Africa', *Review of African Political Economy*, 21(60): 185–199, 185.

31 Editorial (1984), 'Gatsha Buthelezi Thunders', *Sechaba: Official Organ of the African National Congress South Africa,* February issue, London: UK, 2 (added emphasis).

32 Roger Southall (1981), 'Buthelezi, Inkatha and the Politics of Compromise', *African Affairs*, 80(321): 453–481, 453.

33 In the book's preface I clarify my use of the term 'anticolonial' rather 'decolonial' because of what I consider as the conceptual and methodological clarity that is possible with the former. While I see this work as broadly addressing the contemporary question of decolonization, the exact meaning and framing of what it means to decolonize remains a subject of intense debate and disagreements. The choice of this concept is thus an attempt at demarcating clearer conceptual and analytical boundaries. Anticolonialism as an organizing concept is for me also useful in signalling a critique and movement *against* colonialism as well as the moral and ethical expectation t*hat its narration belongs to the colonized.* Decolonization as method has assumed wide incorporation and appropriation precisely because its narration enjoins both the colonized and the colonizer. Finally, recuperating the anticolonial for an analysis of the present also opens up the anticolonial archive in practical and material ways to which the 'decolonial' archive does not easily lend itself.

34 Ibid., 454 (original emphasis).

35 Ibid., 457. Black Consciousness leader Steve Biko too, expressed the view that Inkatha 'protected the stability [the conservative order] that older persons need' (cited in Donald Woods [1978], *Biko*, New York and London: Paddington Press, 98.

36 Southall, 'Inkatha', 457 (added emphasis).

37 Buthelezi, 27.5.77, cited in Shireen Hassim (1988), 'Reinforcing Conservatism: An Analysis of the Politics of the Inkatha Women's Brigade', *Agenda: Empowering Women for Gender Equity*, 2: 3–16, 3 (added emphasis).

38 Ibid., 5.

39 Shireen Hassim (1991), 'Gender, Social Location and Feminist Politics in South Africa', *Transformation,* 15: 65–82, 73.

40 Ibid., 75; see also Hassim 1993.

41 Shireen Hassim (1993), 'Family, Motherhood and Zulu Nationalism: The Politics of the Inkatha Women's Brigade', *Feminist Review*, 43: 1–25, 18 (added emphasis).

42 Ibid., added emphasis.

43 I borrow this formulation from Anne McClintock's (1995) insights in *Imperial Leather,* where she has argued the way, the colonial state treated factors such as religion (the ordering of time and the transcendent), money (the ordering of the economy) and sexuality (the ordering of the body) was to arrange them around the social idea of racial fetishism, thus displacing what the modern imagination (modernity) could not incorporate onto the invented domain of the primitive.

44 David Mario Matsinhe (2011), 'Africa's Fear of Itself: The ideology of *Makwerekwere* in South Africa', *Third World Quarterly,* 32(2): 295–313, 295.

45 Jason Hickel (2014), '"Xenophobia" in South Africa: Order, Chaos, and the Moral Economy of Witchcraft', *Cultural Anthropology,* 29(1): 103–127, 103.

46 Reshoketswe Mapokgole (2014), 'There Is No Black in The Rainbow (Nation): A Bikoist and Fanonian Approach to Understanding 'Xenophobic' Violence in South Africa,' Senior Theses, Trinity College, Hartford, CT 2014. Trinity College Digital Repository, http://digitalrepository.trincoll.edu/theses/425, 12. See also Andile Mngxitama, Amanda Alexander, and Nigel C. Gibson (2008), 'Biko Lives,' in *Biko Lives: Contesting the Legacies of Steve Biko*, Andile Mngxitama, Amanda Alexander and Nigel C. Gibson (eds.), New York: Palgrave Macmillan, 3.

47 Pumla Dineo Gqola (2008), 'Brutal Inheritances: Echoes, Negrophobia and Masculinist Violence,' in *Go Home or Die Here*, Shireen Hassim, Eric Worby and Tawana Kupe (eds.), Johannesburg: Wits University Press, 211.

48 Mapokgole (2014), 'There Is No Black in The Rainbow (Nation)', 12.

49 Matsinhe, 'The Ideology of *Makwerekwere*,' 295. See also Belinda Dodson (2010), 'Locating Xenophobia: Debate, Discourse, and Everyday Experience in Cape Town, South Africa', *Africa Today,* 56(3): 2–22.

50 Dodson, 'Locating Xenophobia', 12.

51 Ibid.

52 Hickel, 'Xenophobia in South Africa', 104.

53 Wendy Brown (2024), 'The Enduring Influence of Marx's Masterpiece', *The Nation,* https://www.thenation.com/article/archive/wendy-brown-marx-capital/ (accessed on 4 October 2024).

54 Lyn Ossome (2024b), 'Imperialism and Crises of Social Reproduction in Africa', *Review of African Political Economy*, 51(181): 509–524, 515; see also Amisi et al. (2011) and C. Tshitereke (1999).

55 Hickel, "Xenophobia in South Africa', 104.

56 Ibid.

57 Ibid.,106.

58 Ibid., 106–107.

59 While Gary Becker (1981), for instance, correctly showed that historically, economic considerations and market aspects have always played an important role in the institution of marriage (e.g. through the payment of dowry, marriage brokers, arranged marriages, access to land for peasants, territories for aristocrats, guild/union membership for working class men, business for capitalists), his insistence on a division of labour between women and men and argument that egalitarian couples could not maximize their wellbeing exposes the root of modern Eurocentric imaginations that conceal its requirement for structural inequality in order to produce 'efficiently' for the market. Becker further presumed individuals to be rational maximizers as each spouse supposedly specializes in what she or he does best in order to attain the largest income and greatest amount of satisfaction, and pushed for more defined traditional male and female roles following the assumption that men are more productive in the market than women and therefore earn more, and that specialization minimizes competition and conflict (within marriages). Such 'efficiency' arguments were eventually debunked by feminist economists who showed that in reality, neoclassical economics can sustain such circular explanations only by rejecting any possibility that women's lower earnings are due to discrimination: the fact that women earn less is because they acquire less human capital as they spend less time in the labour market, accumulate less labour experience, have less energy for work in the labour market because of housework. In other words, gender discrimination is original to neoclassical thinking regarding the family, as it ignores structural factors and can therefore not account for the household as both a locus of production, reproduction, as well as consumption (see also Marianne A. Ferber (2002), 'A Feminist Critique of the Neoclassical Theory of the Family', in *Women Family, and Work: Writings on the Economics of Gender*, Karine S. Moe (ed.), Wiley-Blackwell, 9–24).

60 This fact compels us to deal with the family/household as an institution and unit itself of analysis precisely because households develop strategies for labour allocation and workplace struggles based on the combined household class position and unequal gender relations inside and/or outside the home.

61 From a global north vantage point, Nancy Fraser (2016) argues that 'the 'crisis of care' is best interpreted as a more or less acute expression of the social reproductive contradictions of financialized capitalism.' Her argument is that the present strains on care are not accidental, but rather have deep systemic roots in the structure of our social order (i.e. in financialized capitalism), and is indicative of 'something rotten not only in capitalism's current, financialized form but in capitalist society per se' (2016: 99–100). My own argument has been for the need to understand the

crisis of social reproduction as much more than an economic problem. My view is that on fundamental basis, because of the complexity within social reproduction itself, the question arises regarding how to stabilize a mode of production and accumulation around a factor of production, one that is so foundational to capitalist accumulation, over which capitalists have no direct control. That is, *how does capital organise labour, which is fundamental to its stability, which it seeks to expropriate, but to whose reproduction it does not contribute*? This complexity partially arises because the reproductive economy has historically required a higher and greater level of ideological organization to make it function; here we might consider the role of patriarchal institutions, sexism, racism and devaluation of reproductive labour, which also make it harder to define and demystify the real nature of exploitation within the sector (Fortunati 1981). The organization of social reproduction outside of capital therefore lends to capitalism itself, at least in part, its volatility and vulnerability to periodic crises. The crises of social reproduction that emerge periodically must as such be understood in their social and political dimensions, as well as in relation to world historical changes in the structure of capitalism (Ossome 2024: 511–512).

62 Hickel, '"Xenophobia" in South Africa', 107 (added emphasis).

63 Ibid., 106.

64 Ibid., 107. The related literature recalls the construction of women as 'Mothers of the Nation' and their biological role as reproducers of the nation. Jayawardena and de Alwis (1996) in *Embodied Violence*, as well as Yuval-Davis and Athias (1992) in *Racialized Boundaries*, have offered influential theorising in this regard.

65 Hickel, '"Xenophobia" in South Africa', 111 (added emphasis).

66 I draw here from Kumari Jayawardena and Malathi de Alwis (1996) who have offered a significant critique of embodied violence as studied in the South Asian context. Their concern with communalism, operating within and through patriarchal structures of power, especially foregrounds its varied impositions on women's bodies, as it has legitimized the regulation of their sexuality, their interiorization and silencing and rationalized their commodification, their rape and immolation – acts describe as embodied violence. Furthermore, their argument that the reconstructed ideal woman of the ethnic and religious middle-class group during colonial times makes gender and class central categories to understanding ethnic and social exclusivism, religious fanaticism and identity politics, is important. The exigent task is that of clarifying the political form that embodied violence takes in different historical contexts.

67 I mean this in Badiou's sense of an epoch-breaking and unpredicted event, which holds the possibility of constituting new (or reconstituting) subjects, or rendering more visible, those that have been buried under the conditions that precipitate the event – and in this sense, of reshaping humanity. To Badiou, an event is a 'pure beginning', the opening of an epoch, the transformation of the relation between

the possible and the impossible (1997[2003]: 41–45). In relation to the emphasis I place on the gendered subject of Marikana, I find John Barclay's (2010) reading of Badiou's thesis to be particularly incisive: 'For Badiou, *one becomes an authentic human being (as opposed to a merely biological human animal) through total allegiance and passionate fidelity to the event.* The event becomes a truth-event through this subjective process with highly material effects (what he calls a truth-procedure), and conversely, the subject becomes a subject through fidelity to the event, in solidarity with others similarly constituted. It is crucial for Badiou that the event is always potentially a universal phenomenon, a truth destined for everyone and not just for some new sub-set of humanity' (2010: 174, added emphasis).

68 See Myles Osborne (2018), 'Reviewed Work(s): Murder at Small Koppie: The Real Story of South Africa's Marikana Massacre by Marinovich, Greg', *Africa Today*, 64(4): 115–117, 117. The Sharpeville massacre is marked annually on 21 March, the date in 1960 when South African police opened fire on an unarmed crowd of African people peacefully protesting against the pass laws. 69 people were killed and 180 wounded.

69 The June 16 1976 Uprising that began in Soweto and spread countrywide profoundly changed the socio-political landscape in South Africa. Events that triggered the uprising can be traced back to policies of the Apartheid government that resulted in the introduction of the Bantu Education Act in 1953. The rise of the Black Consciousness Movement (BCM) and the formation of South African Students Organisation (SASO) raised the political consciousness of many students while others joined the wave of anti-Apartheid sentiment within the student community. When the language of Afrikaans alongside English was made compulsory as a medium of instruction in schools in 1974, black students began mobilizing themselves. On 16 June 1976 between 3000 and 10,000 students mobilized by the South African Students Movement's Action Committee supported by the BCM marched peacefully to demonstrate and protest against the government's directive. The march was meant to culminate at a rally in Orlando Stadium. On their pathway they were met by heavily armed police who fired teargas and later live ammunition on demonstrating students. This resulted in a widespread revolt that turned into an uprising against the government. While the uprising began in Soweto, it spread across the country and carried on until the following year. Source: South African History Online: https://www.sahistory.org.za/article/june-16-soweto-youth-uprising (accessed on 6 February 2025).

70 On 9 January 1973, workers at the Coronation Brick and Tile factory, outside Durban, came out on strike. Immediately thereafter, workers from small packaging, transport and ship repairs companies also came out on strike. By the end of March 1973, close on 100,000 mainly African workers, approximately half of the entire African workers employed in Durban, had come out on strike. South Africa's Apartheid Government and its White capitalist allies were shaken by, presumably,

what looked like a spontaneous strike, which had its beginnings in the complex mix of low wages, the humiliation of pass laws, the hardship of migrant labour, forced removals and the denial of the right to organize, the denial of basic human rights and racism that was the bedrock of Apartheid legislation. Through songs and marches, Durban workers made their demands heard – the first time since the political 'stay at home' of the 1950s – and to exercise the power of factory based mass action. Source: South African History Online: https://www.sahistory.org.za/article/1973-durban-strikes (accessed on 6 February 2025).

71 Cited in Peter Alexander (2013), 'Marikana, Turning Point in South African History,' *Review of African Political Economy,* 40(138): 605–619, 605.

72 In the early 1970s there was an upsurge in workers' mobilization in the Durban area, with over 100,000 workers engaging in strike actions in 1973 alone (Hickel, 2012: 664, cited in O'Connor 2017).

73 The other two were from shop floor unions which developed a cautious policy towards political involvement, and lastly, the tradition which developed from Black Consciousness and Africanist movements, which demanded black leadership within unions. Source: South African History Online: https://www.sahistory.org.za/article/1973-durban-strikes (accessed on 6 February 2025).

74 This turn towards the state for right of participation becomes even more pronounced 'as the material bases of classic patriarchy crumble under the impact of new market forces, capital penetration in rural areas, or processes of chronic immiseration' (Kandiyoti 1988: 281).

75 This critique enjoins the patriarchal establishment across the board – not just state and capital, but also the left, including progressive social formations that while recognizing the imperative for social reproduction, do not foreground its gendered subjects.

76 Rajendra Chetty (2016), 'The Marikana Massacre,' *New Labour Forum,* 25(2): 62–70, 63. On the social reproduction question, Chetty makes a further significant observation that most miners start second families around the mines, a normal feature of the system of migrant labour – a reality that splits their salaries between two families, such that the massacre resulted in two sets of widows, contributing to disputes between the two families for the right to compensation. Providing for two families on a low salary also results in wretched living conditions, high debts and vulnerability to loan sharks. The migrant system is deeply entrenched in South Africa and has been a critical source of jobs for rural communities. The Eastern Cape is the main source for labour as it has no industries, high rates of poverty and illiteracy and a single miner is on average the breadwinner for ten people (Chetty 2016: 63–64).

77 Alexander, 'Marikana,' 611. Alexander here suggests the waning role of rural families in the social reproduction of their migrant families, an assumption that has been substantively debunked in more recent Third World agrarian scholarship

that demonstrates the enduring relevance of the peasant base to capital in its immiserating march against working people. Particularly influential in this regard have been the Agrarian South Network debates from 2005, and *Agrarian South: Journal of Political Economy* debates from 2011.

78 Much of the scholarship identifies the principal contradiction of the capitalist system in the neo-colonies as being between monopoly capital and the over-exploited masses of the periphery – or between workers and the oppressed masses on the one side and the imperialist bourgeoisie who exploit and dominate them on the other. Others identify the contradiction between colonial rule and national liberation as the most basic contradiction under imperialism (Lenin 1917; Frank 1966; Amin 1976; Tandon 1977). Furthermore, the primary contradiction between workers and the imperialist bourgeoisie 'feeds itself and determines the existence and development of other contradictions' (Tandon 1977: 109).

79 Suren Pillay (2013), 'The Marikana Massacre: South Africa's Post-Apartheid Dissensus', *Economic and Political Weekly*, 48(50): 32–37, 32 (added emphasis).

80 Pillay (2013), 'The Marikana Massacre', 32 (added emphasis).

81 Ibid., 33.

82 Ibid., 34 (added emphasis).

83 Camalita Naicker (2015), 'Marikana and the Subaltern: The Politics of Specificity', *Economic and Political Weekly*, 50(24): 99–107, 99.

84 Ibid., 100 (added emphasis). Naicker (2015) further argues that 'the families of the men who lost their lives during the strike as well as community members in the Nkaneng shack settlement in Marikana want government and London Mining (Lonmin) to construct a memorial site at the koppie, the place of the massacre. However, this process is complicated for the people at Marikana who are frequently told by their local government officials, and traditional leaders, that they must erect memorials in the Eastern Cape Province from where they come. They tell them that this land is for the Tswana people, and not for the amaXhosa. The Royal Bafokeng Traditional Authority supports this view, so does the government. Lonmin, who pays the traditional authority for mining rights on what is traditional trust land, remains silent while ethnicity becomes a way of policing and silencing democratic forms of participation in a post-apartheid society' (2015: 99).

85 Tolsi (2009), cited in Naicker (2015: 100).

86 Both Pillay (2013) and Naicker (2015) are critical of this formulation.

87 Camalita Naicker (2024), 'Gendered Boundaries', *Feminist Africa*, 5(1): 23–49, 25; see also Mamdani (1996).

88 Ibid.

89 Asanda Benya (2015), 'The Invisible Hands: Women in Marikana', *Review of African Political Economy*, 42(146): 545–560, 547.

90 Ibid.

91 Ibid., 547 (added emphasis).

92 Lyn Ossome (2018b), 'The Public Politics of Nudity', *The MISR Review*, 2: 162–173, 168.

93 Philip Frankel (2012), 'Marikana: 20 Years in the Making', *Business Report*, Sunday, 21 October 2012.

94 Ibid.

95 Ibid.

96 See, for instance, Luise White's excellent study titled *The Comforts of Home: Prostitution in Colonial Nairobi*, Chicago: University of Chicago Press (1990) of prostitution in colonial Kenya.

97 Hart (2006) sees the First/Second Economy discourses as part of an effort to contain the challenges from oppositional movements that reached their peak by 2002 and to render them subject to government intervention. What is significant about this discourse, she argues, is the way it defines a segment of society that is superfluous to the 'modern' economy and in need of paternal guidance: those falling within this category are citizens, but second class. As such, they are deserving of a modicum of social security, but 'on tightly disciplined and conditional terms'. See Gillian Hart (2007), 'Changing Concepts of Articulation: Political Stakes in South Africa Today', *Review of African Political Economy*, 111: 85–101, 96.

98 Ossome, 'Nudity', 166.

99 Karl Marx and Frederick Engels (1934), *Manifesto of the Communist Party*. London: Martin Lawrence Limited, 12.

100 Jacques Rancière (2006), *Hatred of Democracy*, London: Verso, 19.

101 Ibid.

102 Lyn Ossome (2014), 'Democracy's Subjections: Human Rights in Contexts of Scarcity', in *Decolonizing Enlightenment: Transitional Justice, Human Rights and Democracy in a Postcolonial World*, Nikita Dhawan (ed.), Frankfurt: Barbara Budrich Publishers, 290.

103 Ibid.

104 I have elsewhere (Ossome 2024a) highlighted a tension in postcolonial Africa between the domain of rights and the domain of custom, which governs the lives of so many rural and peri-urban populations. In South Africa, for instance, the resurgence of customary governance through legislation such as the Traditional Courts Bill (TCB) constitutes a reintervention by the state through a series of laws related to traditional leadership and governance that threaten localized and decolonial developments around women's access to land (Thipe 2013) and other material and social forms of access.

105 Lisa Marie Cacho (2012), *Social Death: Racialized Rightlessness and the Criminalization of the Unprotected*, New York: New York University Press, 1.

106 Ibid.

107 Hortense J. Spillers (1987), 'Mama's Baby, Papa's Maybe: An American Grammar Book', *Diacritics*, 17(2): 64–81, 65.

108 Kate Soper (1986), *Humanism and Anti-Humanism*, New York: Open Court Company, 79–95 (emphasis added).

109 Carl Schmitt (1996[1932]), *The Concept of the Political*, trans. George Schwab, Chicago: The University of Chicago Press, xv.

110 Ibid., added emphasis. In her Foreword, Tracy B. Strong persuasively argues that 'the driving force behind this argument lies in its claim that politics cannot be made safe and that the attempt to make politics safe will result in the abandonment of the state to private interests and to 'society' (ibid., xv).

Chapter 6

1 I have borrowed this phrasing from Jillian Steinhauer's (2019) piece by the same title published in *The New Republic* (https://newrepublic.com/article/155293/vivien-green-fryd-nancy-princenthal-feminist-performance-artists-book-review), in which she examines the trajectory and translatability of rape through feminist performance art.

2 This chapter is dedicated to the memory of Jyoti Singh (1989–2012) and to Baby Tshepang, and to the millions of young girls everywhere, who like them have been denied speech and the right to complete lives through brutal acts of sexual violence against them.

3 S.N. Nyeck (2020), 'Poetics: Queer Recesses of the Heart and the Spirit of Intimacy within the Africana Household', *The African Journal of Gender and Religion*, 26(2): 91–110, 101.

4 I have decided in this chapter to engage only with the literary treatment of Baby Tshepang's story, meaning that while the events depicted are factual, the names of all characters apart from Baby Tshepang are modified. I was searching, through the play, for a more nuanced reading of the histories that reproduced the play's characters, as well as seeking a greater sense of the social context in which the rape took place. I also sought a medium that could convey the rape of a child in ways that allow an exit from notions of the 'irrationality' of it, into a domain of creativity which harbours the possibility of recasting such violence beyond the limits of rationality. Lastly, I sought a universal subject and universal story in Baby Tshepang: she is of that desolate, forgotten township in South Africa, but she is also of a million other similar settlements in the Third World. There have been other treatments of this story, such as in Pumla Gqola's important book, *Rape: A South African Nightmare,* which draws on the actual reported details to elaborate her critique of child rape in Chapter 6.

5 Lara Foot Newton (2005), *Tshepang: The Third Testament,* London: Oberon Books, 7.

6 I am indebted to Lara Foot for sharing with me her reflections on the play, in a wide-ranging conversation that lent substantive form to this chapter. In all instances where the play (2018) is referenced, I have used 'Foot' as author's surname in accordance to the published reference.
7 Leslie Stones (2018), 'Tshepang: The Third Testament – Raw Trauma that Evokes Our Tears', https://www.dailymaverick.co.za/article/2018-10-22-tshepang-the-third-testament-raw-trauma-that-evokes-our-tears/
8 W.E.B. DuBois in *The Souls of Black Folk*, examined the condition of black folk through the subjectivist formulation of how it feels to be a problem – his particular insight being that groups of people are studied as problems instead of as people with problems.
9 Amilcar Cabral (1966), *The Weapon of Theory*. Address delivered to the first Tricontinental Conference of the Peoples of Asia, Africa and Latin America held in Havana in January 1966, 3.
10 Lara Foot Newton (2005), *Tshepang: The Third Testament*, London: Oberon Books, 11.
11 Ibid.
12 Ibid., 17.
13 Interview with Lara Foot on 12 March 2025 at the Baxter Theatre, Cape Town. This expression of grief does not belong to Tshepang's mother alone. A man who was like the baby's grandfather also now 'spends all of his time untangling fishing line. The peculiar thing', we are told, 'is that he never goes fishing. He's never thrown a worm in the water' (Newton, *Tshepang*,18).
14 Have sex.
15 Newton, *Tshepang*, 26.
16 The 'dop [tot] system' refers to the practice of giving wine to male farm workers at regular intervals during the working day, which was general throughout the Cape winelands by 1890. In his analysis, Gavin Williams (2016) relates the dop system with the supply and control of labour.
17 Newton, *Tshepang*, 28.
18 Ibid., 24.
19 Interview with Lara Foot on 12 March 2025 at the Baxter Theatre, Cape Town (emphasis my own).
20 Ibid.
21 That is, in relation to a subjugating structure which may be the state or capital – which may be extended to critique colonialism and imperialism.
22 Luis Guzmán (2014), 'Benjamin's Divine Violence: Unjustifiable Justice', *The New Centennial Review*, 14(2): 49–64, 52.
23 Walter Benjamin (2007), 'Critique of Violence', in *Selected Writings*, Marcus Bullock and Michael W. Jennings (eds.), Cambridge, MA: The Belknap Press of Harvard University Press, 239.
24 Newton, *Tshepang*, 13.

25 Ibid., 29 (added emphasis).

26 Ibid.

27 She had been 'raped, sodomised, disembowelled' (Newton, *Tshepang*, 40).

28 Newton, *Tshepang*, 44–45.

29 Gqola (2015), too, conveys a sympathetic stance in relation to the accused, drawing on literature which connects such violence to the structures that produce rapists of Alfred's mint. She cites a doctoral study in which the researcher interviewed ten men convicted of raping children under the age of three. All interviewees were serving lengthy jail terms at the time of interview, and they ranged in age from 19 to 61. The researcher was concerned with understanding the mentality of men such as these, and choose men who all fell into the publicly circulated profile of child rapist: unemployed at the time of raping the children, all school dropouts, three 'coloured' and seven 'black'. All the interviewees had suffered extreme institutional and personal violence as children. They all revealed stories of being beaten and verbally abused as children. Furthermore, each of these convicted child rapists had a 'heightened sexualised childhood'. In other words, the study seemed to confirm that there is a cycle of abuse and sexual violence in child rapists' lives (Gqola, *Rape*, 129–130).

30 Benjamin, 'Critique', 239 (added emphasis).

31 Newton, *Tshepang*, 48–49 (added emphasis).

32 Ibid., 53.

33 V. Geetha (2016), *Undoing Impunity: Speech After Sexual Violence*, Delhi: Zubaan Books, 61.

34 Or perhaps it could be the case that speaking violence without speaking it in the language of violence is one way in which this subject might (attempt to) escape captivity.

35 V. Geetha, *Undoing Impunity* 67 (added emphasis).

36 Ibid.

37 Ibid., 71–72 (added emphasis).

38 Babasaheb Dr Ambedkar (1990), *Writings and Speeches*, Vol 8, 243.

39 Nthabiseng Motsemme (2004), 'The Mute Always Speak: On Women's Silences at the Truth and Reconciliation Commission', *Current Sociology*, 52(5): 909–932, 910.

40 Ibid., 910–911, added emphasis.

41 Interview with Lara Foot on 12 March 2025 at the Baxter Theatre, Cape Town (emphasis my own).

42 Newton, *Tshepang*, 55.

43 In Fanon's formulation, the colonized do not speak the truth – they are *in* the truth. The lived experiences of people sufficiently speak violence without the liberal language.

44 Newton, *Tshepang*, 56 (added emphasis).

45 Blackheart Diaries (Documentary Wed 12/10/2020 – incarcerated at Leeuwkop Maximum Security Prison), Lazarus Mazingane (The Lasrec Serial Killer) has spent

the last ten years behind bars after a five-year reign of terror on Johannesburg's ethnic minority women.

46 Ibid (added emphasis).

47 Nivedita Menon (2018), 'India's Daughter in India: Old Questions, New Answers?' in *Gendered Citizenship: Manifestations and Performance*, Bishnupriya Dutt, Janelle Reinelt and Shrinkhla Sahai (eds.), Delhi: Orient BlackSwan.

48 Ibid.

49 M.L. Sharma, defence lawyer for the rapists, *India's Daughter.*

50 Ibid (added emphasis).

51 Dr. Maria Misra, Writer & Historia, Oxford University, *India's Daughter.*

52 Narrator's voice, *India's Daughter.*

53 Leila Seth, former Chief Justice and member of the Rape Review Committee, *India's Daughter.*

54 Raj Kumar, Patrolman, *India's Daughter.*

55 Jyoti's parents, Asha and Badri Singh, *India's Daughter.*

56 Pramod Kushwa, Additional Deputy Commissioner, Delhi Police, *India's Daughter.*

57 Dr. Maria Misra, Writer & Historia, Oxford University, *India's Daughter* (emphasis my own).

58 https://rsdebate.nic.in/bitstream/123456789/709243/1/IQ_251_11032020_U1959_p89_p92.pdf

59 Dr. Maria Misra, Writer & Historia, Oxford University, *India's Daughter* (emphasis my own).

60 Ibid.

61 Gopal Subramanium, Senior Advocate, Supreme Court; co-author of the J.S. Verma Committee Report, *India's Daughter* (added emphasis).

62 Leila Seth, former Chief Justice and member of the Rape Review Committee, *India's Daughter.*

63 Jyoti's mother, Asha Singh, *India's Daughter.*

64 Jyoti's father, Badri Singh, *India's Daughter.*

65 Amod Kanth, Head of Prayas, NGO for Rape Victims and Juveniles, *India's Daughter* (added emphasis).

66 Narrator's voice, *India's Daughter.*

67 Dr. Sandeep Govil, Jail Psychiatrist of the rapists.

68 One of the accused, *India's Daughter.*

69 News report, *India's Daughter,* added emphasis.

70 Puneeta Devi, wife of Akshay Thakur, one of the accused, *India's Daughter* (emphasis my own).

71 Akshay Thakur, one of the accused/driver, *India's Daughter,* original emphasis.

72 Wendy Brown (1995), *States of Injury: Power and Freedom in Late Modernity,* Princeton, NJ: Princeton University Press, 97. The source of this paradox, Brown argues, is that rights necessarily operate as an ahistorical, acultural and acontextual

idiom: they claim distance from specific political contexts and historical vicissitudes, they necessarily participate in a discourse of enduring universality rather than provisionality or partiality.

73 Jyoti's father, Badri Singh, *India's Daughter.*

74 From *The Collected Works of Langston Hughes*, vol. 2, *The Poems, 1941–1950.* University of Missouri Press. © 2001 The Estate of Langston Hughes.

75 Wendy Brown (1995) says this of the ambivalence and anxiety that flanks struggles for freedom, among which the clamour for rights has come in to occupy a liberal position, which reconstitutes power in the direction of a narrow individualism.

76 Jyoti's mother, Asha Singh, *India's Daughter.*

77 Denise Ferreira da Silva (2022), *Unpayable Debt,* Cambridge, MA: MIT Press.

78 The 'burden of proof' that accompanies the event of rape recasts as mere witnesses, the state, the police and the medical establishment, who with the help of media, move the crime from a private domain into the domain of public opinion and judgement. That burden of judgement is unevenly distributed between the survivors of violence and their caregivers. Meanwhile, the laws that authorize violence are never brought into question and are thus rendered impossible as terrains of democratic struggle, let along justice.

79 By this I do not just mean physical pain, but also the burden of care/social reproduction that has to be undertaken amidst conditions of utter immiseration and which remains marginal to the political and economic project of the postcolonial state.

80 This is not as much a claim about 'spectacular violence' which the liberal state might deploy against its male subject to justify surveillance, control and further violence, but rather to point out the silencing function which the spectacle enforces against the millions of racialized children and young girls everywhere who are raped and molested everyday but cannot on their own produce evidence of that violation because they cannot disembowel themselves.

81 James, 'The Womb of Western Theory', 258.

Epilogue

1 Rancière considers this insight as being *Marx's yet unexhausted standard of thought – see Jacques* Rancière (2014), Hatred of Democracy, trans. Steve Corcoran, London: Verso, 3 (added emphasis).

2 Dhawan (2014) writes about the 'Paradox of Modernity' as being that 'liberal values were preached to the colonized, but denied in practice . . . The construction of the West as a normative power left a trail of violent and exploitative systems in the name of modernity, progress, rationality, emancipation, rights, justice, and peace. Any non-Western individual, group, or state wanting to qualify as "civilized" and modern had to comply and imitate the European norms or risk the violence of being forcibly

"civilized" and modernized. While European norms were deemed worth emulating on the grounds of their superiority, the natives' attempts to imitate European norms could only produce "bad", "weak", or "failed" copies, which once again confirmed the authority of the European "original"' (Dhawan, 'Affirmative Sabotage', 40).

3 The postcolonial scholarship critiques the Eurocentric framework of liberal theories of global justice and 'examine the violent exclusions and elisions operating within these theories of justice'. Millan and Yıldırım (2014), for instance, 'trace the silencing and marginalization of subaltern groups, especially subaltern women, in global theories of justice. To undo subalternity demands a different practice of representation that will allow disenfranchised individuals and groups to make claims and emerge as subjects of rights' (cited in Dhawan, 'Affirmative Sabotage', 13).

4 Vijay Prasad (2023: viii) draws this from the final communique of the Asian-African conference held in Bandung, Indonesia, in 1955. Bandung Conference, argues Burke (2006), marked the 'founding moment of the Third World as a political entity' and showed 'a clear commitment to human rights among the delegates at Bandung . . . an expression of the considerable sympathy the African and Asian states had for human rights in the early post-colonial period' (Burke 2006: 948).

5 Prasad, 'Foreword', xi (added emphasis).

6 Issa Shivji (2023), *The Concept of Human Rights in Africa*, 2nd ed., Dakar: Codesria, xiv (added emphasis). Core to the idea of legitimation is the reality that indeed social struggles have been a natural response to every oppressive situation: against 'the ideology of domination . . . was a process of complex struggle producing not only slave revolts and heroes like Toussaint L'Ouverture but also its own ideologies of resistance . . . reconstructed from the elements partly "borrowed" from the ideology of domination but now turned on its head' (ibid., 23). The language of domination provides the language of critique.

7 Lyn Ossome (forthcoming, 2025), 'Decolonial Feminism', in *Handbook on Decolonizing International Affairs*, Sakiko Fukuda-Parr and Sean Jacobs (eds.), London: Routledge.

8 Patrick Wolfe (2010), 'Structure and Event: Settler Colonialism, Time, and the Question of Genocide', in *Empire, Colony, Genocide: Conquest, Occupation, and Subaltern Resistance in World History*, A. Dirk Moses, (ed.), New York: Berghahn Books, 110.

9 Dipesh Chakrabarty (2011), 'The Muddle of Modernity', *The American Historical Review*, 116(3): 663–675, 665–666.

10 Dhawan, 'Affirmative Sabotage', 64

11 Aimé Césaire (1972), 'Discourse on Colonialism', trans. Joan Pinkham, New York and London: Monthly Review Press, 4 (added emphasis)

12 Césaire, 'Discourse', 7 (original emphasis).

13 Ossome, 'Democracy's Subjections', 291, added emphasis.

14 Chinua Achebe (1958), *Things Fall Apart*, London: Penguin Books, 122.

References

Abbas, Asma (2014), 'Ressentiment', *The Encyclopedia of Political ThoughtEncyclopedia*, https://doi.org/10.1002/9781118474396.wbept0888https://doi.org/10.1002/9781118474396.wbept0888

Achebe, C. (1958), *Things Fall Apart*, London: Penguin Books.

Agamben, Giorgio (1998), *Homo Sacer: Sovereign Power and Bare Life*, trans. Daniel Heller-Roazen, Stanford: Stanford University Press.

Alexander, Peter (2013), 'Marikana, Turning Point in South African History', *Review of African Political Economy*, 40(138): 605–619.

Amadiume, Ifi (1987), *Male Daughters, Female Husbands: Gender and Sex in an African Society*, London: Zed Books.

Ambedkar, B. (1990), *Writings and Speeches*, Vol. 8 Reprint of Pakistan or the Partition of India, New Delhi: Dr. Ambedkar Foundation.

Amin, Samir (1976), *Unequal Development: An Essay on the Social Formations of Peripheral Capitalism*, New York: Monthly Review Press.

Amin, Samir (2017), 'The Agrarian Question a Century after October 1917: Capitalist Agriculture and Agricultures in Capitalism', *Agrarian South: Journal of Political Economy*, 6(2): 149–174.

Amisi, Baruti, Patrick Bond, Nokuthula Cele and Trevor Ngwane (2011), 'Xenophobia and Civil Society', *Politikon*, 38(1): 59–83.

Anthias, Floya and Nira Yuval-Davis (1992), *Racialized Boundaries: Race, Nation, Gender, Colour and Class and the Anti-Racist Struggle*, London: Routledge.

Arendt, Hannah (1951), *The Origins of Totalitarianism*, New York: Schocken Books.

Arendt, Hannah (1968), *The Origins of Totalitarianism*, New York: Harcourt.

Asiedu-Akrofi, Derek (1989), 'Judicial Recognition and Adoption of Customary Law in Nigeria', *The American Journal of Comparative Law*, 37(3): 571–593.

Badiou, Alain (1997), *Saint Paul: La Fondation de l'universalisme*, Paris: Presses Universitaires de France; translated by Ray Brassier: *Saint Paul. The Foundation of Universalism*, Stanford: Stanford University Press.

Bakare-Yusuf, Bibi (1997), 'The Economy of Violence: Black Bodies and the Unspeakable Terror', in *Gender and Catastrophe*, R. Lentin (ed.), London and New York: Zed Books, 171–184.

Barclay, John M. G. (2010), 'Paul and the Philosophers: Alain Badiou and the Event', *New Blackfriars*, 91(1032): 171–184.

Benjamin, Walter (2007), 'Critique of Violence', in *Selected Writings*, Marcus Bullock and Michael W. Jennings (eds.), Cambridge, MA: The Belknap Press of Harvard University Press.

Benjamin, Walter (2007), 'Critique of Violence', in *Reflections*, trans. Edmund Jephcott, New York: Schocken Books, 277–300.

Benya, Asanda (2015), 'The Invisible Hands: Women in Marikana', *Review of African Political Economy*, 42(146): 545–560.

Berda, Yael (2013), 'Managing Dangerous Populations: Colonial Legacies of Security and Surveillance', *Sociological Forum*, 28(3): 627–630.

Berman, Bruce, J. (1976), 'Bureaucracy and Incumbent Violence: Colonial Administration and the Origins of the "Mau Mau" Emergency in Kenya', *British Journal of Political Science*, 6(2): 143–175.

Boserup, Ester (1970), *Women's Role in Economic Development*, London: George Allen & Unwin Ltd.

Bosman, Willem (1967) [1705], *A New and Accurate Description of the Coast of Guinea*, London: Ballantyne Press.

Brown, Wendy (1995), *States of Injury: Power and Freedom in Late Modernity*, Princeton, NJ: Princeton University Press.

Brown, Wendy (2006), 'American Nightmare: Neoliberalism, Neoconservatism, and De-democratization', *Political Theory*, 34(6): 690–714.

Brown, Wendy (2024), 'The Enduring Influence of Marx's Masterpiece', *The Nation*, https://www.thenation.com/article/archive/wendy-brown-marx-capital/ (accessed on 4 October 2024).

Brownhill, Leigh (2009), *Land, Food, Freedom: Struggles for the Gendered Commons in Kenya, 1870–2007*, Trenton, NJ: Africa World Press.

Brownmiller, Susan (2002), 'Foreword', in *Japan's Comfort Women: Sexual slavery and prostitution during World War II and the US occupation*, Yuki Tanaka (ed.), London & New York: Routledge.

Burke, Roland (2006), "'The Compelling Dialogue of Freedom': Human Rights at the Bandung Conference', *Human Rights Quarterly*, 28(4): 947–965.

Cabral, Amilcar (1966), *The Weapon of Theory*. Address delivered to the first Tricontinental Conference of the Peoples of Asia, Africa and Latin America held in Havana in January 1966, https://www.jpanafrican.org/edocs/e-DocWeapon3.5.pdf

Cacho, Lisa Marie (2012), *Social Death: Racialized Rightlessness and the Criminalization of the Unprotected*, New York: New York University Press.

Césaire, Aimé (1972), 'Discourse on Colonialism', trans. Joan Pinkham, New York and London: Monthly Review Press.

Chanock, Martin (1985), *Law, Custom and Social Order: The Colonial Experience in Malawi and Zambia*, Cambridge: Cambridge University Press.

Chatterjee, Partha (1986), *Nationalist Thought and the Colonial World: A Derivative Discourse?* London: Zed Books.

Chatterjee, Partha (1993), *The Nation and Its Fragments: Colonial and Postcolonial Histories*, Princeton, NJ: Princeton University Press, Princeton.

Chatterjee, Partha (2007), *The Politics of the Governed: Reflections on Popular Politics in Most of the World*, New York: Columbia University Press.

Chatterjee, Partha (2012), *The Black Hole of Empire: History of a Global Practice of Power*, Princeton, NJ: Princeton University Press.
Chauncey, George (1981), 'Locus of Reproduction: Women's Labour in the Zambian Copperbelt, 1927–1953', *Journal of Southern African Studies*, 7(2): 135–164.
Chetty, Rajendra (2016), 'The Marikana Massacre', *New Labour Forum*, 25(2): 62–70.
Chowdhry, Prem (1996), 'Contesting Claims and Counter-Claims: Questions of Inheritance and Sexuality of Widows in a Colonial State', in *Social Reform, Sexuality and the State*, Patricia Uberio (ed.), Sage: New Delhi.
Chuku, Gloria (2009), 'Igbo Women and Political Participation in Nigeria, 1800s–2005', *The International Journal of African Historical Studies*, 42(1): 81–103.
Cooper, Frederick (2005), *Colonialism in Question: Theory, Knowledge, History*, Berkeley: University of California Press.
Couper, Scott E. (2007), 'Chief Albert Luthuli and the Bantustan Question', *Journal of Natal and Zulu History*, 25(1): 240–267.
Crenshaw, Kimberlé (1989), 'Demarginalizing the Intersection of Race and Sex: A Black Feminist Critique of Antidiscrimination Doctrine, Feminist Theory and Antiracist Politics', *University of Chicago Legal Forum*, 1(8): 139–167.
da Silva, Denise Ferreira (2022), *Unpayable Debt*, Cambridge, MA: MIT Press.
Demian, Melissa (2014), 'On the Repugnance of Customary Law', *Comparative Studies in Society and History*, 56(2): 508–536.
Dhawan, Nikita (2007), 'Can the Subaltern Speak German? And Other Risky Questions – Migrant Hybridism versus Subalternity', http://translate.eipep.net/strands/03/dhawan-strands01en/
Dhawan, Nikita (2013), 'The Empire Prays Back: Religion, Secularity, and Queer Critique', *Boundary*, 2, 40(1): 191–222.
Dhawan, Nikita (2014), 'Affirmative Sabotage of the Master's Tools: The Paradox of Postcolonial Enlightenment', in *Decolonizing Enlightenment: Transnational Justice, Human Rights and Democracy in a Postcolonial World*, Nikita Dhawan (ed.), Berlin: Barbara Budrich Press.
Dhawan, Nikita ed. (2014), *Decolonizing Enlightenment: Transitional Justice, Human Rights and Democracy in a Postcolonial World*, Frankfurt: Barbara Budrich Publishers.
Dickinson, James and Bob Russell (1986), 'Introduction: The Structure of Reproduction in Capitalist Societies', in *Family, Economy and the State: Social Reproduction Under Capitalism*, J. Dickinson and B. Russell (eds.), New York: St. Martin's Press.
Dodson, Belinda (2010), 'Locating Xenophobia: Debate, Discourse, and Everyday Experience in Cape Town, South Africa', *Africa Today*, 56(3): 2–22.
Dubois, W.E.B. (1903), *The Souls of Black Folk* (B. H. Edwards, Ed.), Oxford: Oxford University Press.
DuBois, W.E.B. (1920), 'The Damnation of Women', *Darkwater: Voices from within the Veil*, New York: Harcourt, Brace and Company.
Editorial (1984), 'Gatsha Buthelezi Thunders', *Sechaba: Official Organ of the African National Congress South Africa*, February Issue, London, UK.

Fallers, Lloyd A. and S.B.K. Musoke (1964), 'Social Mobility, Traditional and Modern', in *The King's Men: Leadership and Status in Buganda on the Eve of Independence*, L.A. Fallers (ed.), London: Oxford University Press.

Fanon, Frantz (1961), *The Wretched of the Earth*, New York: Grove Press.

Fanon, Frantz (1965), *A Dying Colonialism*, New York: Grove Press.

Fatton, Robert Jr (1990), 'Liberal Democracy in Africa', *Political Science Quarterly*, 105(3): 455–473.

Federici, Silvia (2004), *Caliban and the Witch: Women, The Body and Primitive Accumulation*, Brooklyn, NY: Autonomedia.

Ferber, Marianne A. (2002), 'A Feminist Critique of the Neoclassical Theory of the Family', in *Women, Family and Work: Writings on the Economics of Gender*, Karine S. Moe (ed.), Wiley-Blackwell.

Ferguson, Ann (2006), 'Review of Silvia Federici Caliban and the Witch: Women, the Body and Primitive Accumulation (2005, Autonomedia, NYC)', *Wagadu*, 3: 114–123.

Festa, Lynn and Carey, Daniel (2009), 'What Is Postcolonial Enlightenment?' in *The Postcolonial Enlightenment*, Daniel Carey and Lynn Festa (eds.), Oxford: Oxford University Press, 1–33.

Fortunati, Leopoldina (1981), *The Arcane of Reproduction: Housework, Prostitution, Labour and Capital*, New York: Autonomedia.

Foucault, Michel (1973), *The Birth of the Clinic: An Archaeology of Medical Perception*, trans. A. M. Sheridan Smith, New York: Pantheon Books.

Foucault, Michel (1976), *The History of Sexuality*, Vol. 1 (trans Hurley), London: Penguin.

Foucault, Michel (1984), 'What Is Enlightenment?' in *The Foucault Reader*, Paul Rabinow (ed.), New York: Penguin.

Frank, Andre Gunder (1966), *The Development of Underdevelopment*, New England: Free Press.

Frankel, Philip (2012), 'Marikana: 20 Years in the Making', *Business Report*, Sunday, 21 October 2012.

Fraser, Nancy (1997), *Justice Interruptus*, London: Routledge.

Fraser, Nancy (2016), 'Contradictions of Capital and Care', *New Left Review*, 100: 99–117.

Fraser, Nancy (2017), 'Crisis of Care? On the Social Reproductive Contradictions of Contemporary Capitalism', in *Social Reproduction Theory: Remapping Class, Recentering Oppression*, Tithi Bhattacharya (ed.), London: Pluto Press.

Geetha, V. (2016), *Undoing Impunity: Speech After Sexual Violence*, Delhi: Zubaan Books.

Goody, Jack (1973), 'Polygyny, Economy and the Role of Women', in *The Character of Kinship*, Jack Goody (ed.), Cambridge: Cambridge University Press.

Gramsci, Antonio (1971), *Selections from the Prison Notebooks*, Quintin Hoare and Geoffrey Nowell Smith (eds.), New York: International Publishers.

Gqola, Pumla Dineo (2015), *Rape: A South African Nightmare*, Johannesburg: MF Books.

Guy, Jeff (2009), 'Women in Labour: The Birth of Colonial Natal. 'Inkom' imbiw' etsheni kobelungu'', paper presented at the History and African Studies Seminar University of KwaZulu-Natal on 29 April 2009.

Guzmán, Luis (2014), 'Benjamin's Divine Violence: Unjustifiable Justice', *The New Centennial Review*, 14(2): 49–64.

Hall, Stuart (1987), *The Hard Road to Renewal: Thatcherism and the Crisis of the Left*, London: Verso.

Hart, Gillian (2007), 'Changing Concepts of Articulation: Political Stakes in South Africa Today', *Review of African Political Economy*, 34(111): 85–101.

Hartman, Saidiya (2016), 'The Belly of the World: A Note on Black Women's Labors', *Souls*, 18(1): 166–173.

Hartman, Saidiya (2021), *Wayward Lives, Beautiful Experiments: Intimate Histories of Riotous Black Girls, Troublesome Women and Queer Radicals*, London: Serpent's Tail.

Hassim, Shireen (1988), 'Reinforcing Conservatism: An Analysis of the Politics of the Inkatha Women's Brigade', *Agenda: Empowering Women for Gender Equity*, 2: 3–16.

Hassim, Shireen (1991), 'Gender, Social Location and Feminist Politics in South Africa', *Transformation*, 15: 65–82.

Hassim, Shireen (1993), 'Family, Motherhood and Zulu Nationalism: The Politics of the Inkatha Women's Brigade', *Feminist Review*, 43: 1–25.

Henry, Paget (2007), 'Review: CLR James and the Orthodoxies of John McClendon and David Scott: A Review Essay, Reviewed Work(s): CLR James's Notes on Dialectics: Left Hegelianism or Marxism Leninism? by John McClendon: Conscripts of Modernity: The Tragedy of Colonial Enlightenment by David Scott', *The CLR James Journal*, 13(1): 275–289.

Hickel, Jason (2014), '"Xenophobia" in South Africa: Order, Chaos, and the Moral Economy of Witchcraft', *Cultural Anthropology*, 29(1): 103–127.

hooks, Bell (1984), *Feminist Theory: From Margin to Center*, Boston: South End Press.

Hughes, Langston et al. (2001), *The Collected Works of Langston Hughes, Vol. 2, The Poems, 1941–1950*. Columbia: University of Missouri Press. © 2001 The Estate of Langston Hughes.

Hussin, Izra R. (2016), *The Politics of Islamic Law: Local Elites, Colonial Authority, and the Making of the Muslim State*, Chicago: The University of Chicago Press.

Jackson Lynette, A (2002), '"When in the White Mans Town": Zimbabwean Women Remember Chibuera', in *Women in African Colonial Histories*, Jean Allman, Susan Geiger and Nakanyike Musisi (eds.), Bloomington: Indiana University Press.

James, Joy (2016), 'The Womb of Western Theory: Trauma, Time Theft, and the Captive Maternal', *Carceral Notebooks*, 'Challenging the Punitive Society', 12: 255–296.

James, Joy (2021), 'Captive Maternal Love and War Stories (Ethics, Aesthetics and Feminisms)', Centre for Ethics, University of Toronto, https://www.youtube.com/embed/81W-v0UXm5A

James, Joy (2021), 'The Captive Maternal and Abolitionism', *Canadian Journal of Cultural Studies*, 43: 9–23.

James, Joy (2021), 'We Remember the Attempts to Be Free', *Millennials Are Killing Capitalism*, https://millennialsarekillingcapitalism.libsyn.com/we-remember-the-attempts-to-be-free-joy-james-on-black-august-and-the-captive-maternal

James, Joy (2022), 'Maternal (In)Coherence: When Feminism Meets Fascism', *Parapraxis I*, 145–157.

James, Joy (2022), *In Pursuit of Revolutionary Love*, London: Divided.

Jayawardena, Kumari and de Alwis Malathi (1996), *Embodied Violence: Communalising Female Sexuality in South Asia*, London & New York: Zed Books.

Jerkins, Morgan (2023), 'The Outsiders: Why Black Audiences Love Italian American Screen Icons', *Vanity Fair*, https://www.vanityfair.com/hollywood/2023/09/italian-american-film-black-audiences

Kandiyoti, Deniz (1988), 'Bargaining with Patriarchy', *Gender and Society*, 2(3): 274–290.

Kanogo, Tabitha (1987), 'Kikuyu Women and the Politics of Protest: Mau Mau', in *Images of Women in Peace and War: Cross-Cultural and Historical Perspective*, S. Macdonald, P. Holden, S. Ardener (eds.), London: Macmillan.

Kanogo, Tabitha (1988), *Squatters and the Roots of Mau Mau* by Tabitha Kanogo, Kenya: James Currey and Heinemann.

Kanogo, Tabitha (2005), *African Womanhood in Colonial Kenya: 1900–50*, Oxford: James Currey.

Katz, Cindi (2001), *Vagabond Capitalism and the Necessity of Social Reproduction*, Oxford and Malden: Blackwell Publishers.

Khanyile, Buhle (2021), 'Violences in the South African Student Movement', in *The Oxford Handbook of Global South Youth Studies*, S. Swartz, A. Cooper, C.M. Batan and L. Kropff Causa (eds.), Oxford: Oxford University Press, 185–200.

Kundera, Milan (1985), *The Unbearable Lightness of Being*, New York: Harper & Row.

Kwon, Nayoung Aimee (2015), *Intimate Empire: Collaboration and Colonial Modernity in Korea and Japan*, Durham: Duke University Press.

Lenin, Vladimir I. (1917), *Imperialism, the Highest Stage of Capitalism*, Moscow: Progress Publishers.

Levy, Jacob and Iris Marion Young (2011), *Colonialism and Its Legacies*, Plymouth: Lexington Books.

Little, Adrian and Moya Lloyd (2012), *The Politics of Radical Democracy*, Edinburgh: Edinburgh University Press.

Locher-Scholten, Elsbeth (2000), *Women and the Colonial State: Essays on Gender and Modernity in the Netherlands Indies, 1900–1942*, Amsterdam: Amsterdam University Press.

Lorde, Audre (1984), 'The Master's Tools Will Never Dismantle the Master's House', in *Sister Outsider: Essays and Speeches*, Audre Lorde (ed.), New York: Crossing Press.

Luescher, T.M., A. Wilson Fadiji, K.G. Morwe, A. Erasmus, T.S. Letsoalo and S.B. Mokhema (2022). *#FeesMustFall and Its Aftermath: Violence, Wellbeing and the Student Movement in South Africa*, Cape Town: HSRC Press.

Luongo, Katherine (2010), 'Domestic Dramas and Occult Acts: Witchcraft and Violence in the Arena of the Intimate', in *Domestic Violence and the Law in Colonial and Postcolonial Africa*, E. Burrill, R. Roberts and E. Thornberry (eds.), Athens: Ohio University Press.

Luxemburg, Rosa (1951), *The Accumulation of Capital*, London: Routledge.

MacKenzie, Fiona D. (1998), *Land, Ecology and Resistance in Kenya: 1880–1952*, Edinburgh: Edinburgh University Press.

Mahadevan, Kanchana (2002), 'Colonial Modernity: A Critique', *Indian Literature*, 46(3): 193–211.

Mahmood, Saba (2005), *Politics of Piety: The Islamic Revival and the Feminist Subject*, Princeton, NJ: Princeton University Press.

Mamdani, Mahmood (1996), *Citizen and Subject: Contemporary Africa and the Legacy of Late Colonialism*, Princeton, NJ: Princeton University Press.

Mamdani, Mahmood (1998), 'When Does a Settler Become a Native? Reflections of the Colonial Roots of Citizenship in Equatorial and South Africa', Inaugural Lecture as AC Jordan Professor of African Studies, Centre for African Studies University of Cape Town.

Mamdani, Mahmood (2001), *When Victims Become Killers: Colonialism, Nativism and the Genocide in Rwanda*, Princeton, NJ: Princeton University Press.

Mamdani, Mahmood (2012), *Define and Rule: Native as Political Identity*, Cambridge, MA: Harvard University Press.

Mamdani, Mahmood (2020), *Neither Settler nor Native: The Making and Unmaking of Permanent Minorities*, Cambridge, MA: Harvard University Press.

Mani, Lata (1998), *Contentious Traditions: The Debate on Sati in Colonial India*, California: University of California Press.

Mapokgole, Reshoketswe (2014), 'There Is No Black in The Rainbow (Nation): A Bikoist and Fanonian Approach to Understanding "Xenophobic" Violence in South Africa', Senior Theses, Trinity College, Hartford, CT, 2014. Trinity College Digital Repository, http://digitalrepository.trincoll.edu/theses/425

Marx, Karl (1934), *The Eighteenth Brumaire of Louis Bonaparte*, Moscow: Progress.

Marx, Karl (1952), *Class Struggles in France: 1848–1850*, Moscow: Progress.

Marx, Karl (1964), *Economic and Philosophical Manuscripts of 1844*, New York: International Publishers.

Marx, Karl (1971), *The Grundrisse*, edited & trans. David McLellan, New York: Harper and Row Publishers.

Marx, Karl (1971), *Writings on the Paris Commune*, H. Draper (ed.), New York: International Publishers.

Marx, Karl and Friedrich Engels (1934), *Manifesto of the Communist Party*, London: Martin Lawrence Limited.

Matsinhe, David M. (2011), 'Africa's Fear of Itself: The ideology of Makwerekwere in South Africa', *Third World Quarterly*, 32(2): 295–313.

Mbilinyi, Marjorie (1989), 'Women's Resistance in "customary" Marriage: Tanzania's Runaway Wives', *African Discourse Series*, 1: 211–254.

McClintock, Anne (1995), *Imperial Leather: Race, Gender and Sexuality in the Colonial Context*, London: Routledge.

Menon, Nivedita (2018), 'India's Daughter in India: Old Questions, New Answers?' in *Gendered Citizenship: Manifestations and Performance*, Bishnupriya Dutt, Janelle Reinelt and Shrinkhla Sahai (eds.), Delhi: Orient BlackSwan.

Merucci, Amber Noelle (2021), '"We Don't Need the Key, We'll Break In": Learning about the Occupation through Aesthetic Encounters with Three Artists', unpublished doctoral thesis, York University.

Mezzadri, Alessandra (2021), 'India's Informal Capitalism: Social Structures of Accumulation, Forms of Exploitation and Social Reproduction in the Sweatshop Regime', in *Handbook on Social Structure of Accumulation Theory*, T. McDonough, C. McMahon and D.M. Kotz (eds.), Cheltenham: Edward Elgar, 152–168.

Mies, Maria (2014), *Patriarchy and Accumulation on a World Scale: Women in the International Division of Labour*, London: Zed Books.

Millan, Anna and Ali Can Yıldırım (2014), 'Decolonizing Theories of Global Justice', in *Decolonizing Enlightenment: Transitional Justice, Human Rights and Democracy in a Postcolonial World*, Nikita Dhawan (ed.), Frankfurt: Barbara Budrich Publishers, 195–210.

Mitra, Durba (2020), *Indian Sex Life: Sexuality and the Colonial Origins of Modern Social Thought*, Princeton, NJ & Oxford: Princeton University Press.

Motsemme, Nthabiseng (2004), 'The Mute Always Speak: On Women's Silences at the Truth and Reconciliation Commission', *Current Sociology*, 52(5): 909–932.

Motsemme, Nthabiseng (2007), '"Loving in a Time of Hopelessness": On Township Women's Subjectivities in a Time of HIV/AIDS', in *Women in South African History*, Nomboniso Gasa (ed.), Cape Town: HSRC Press.

Muthu, Sankar (2003), *Enlightenment against Empire*, Princeton, NJ: Princeton University Press.

Muthu, Sankar (2012), *Empire and Modern Political Thought*, Cambridge: Cambridge University Press.

Naicker, Camalita (2015), 'Marikana and the Subaltern: The Politics of Specificity', *Economic and Political Weekly*, 50(24): 99–107.

Naicker, Camalita (2024), 'Gendered Boundaries', *Feminist Africa*, 5(1): 23–49, 25.

Nengwekhulu, Ranwedzi H. (1986), 'Race, Class and Ethnicity in South Africa', *African Journal of Political Economy / Revue Africaine d'Economie Politique*, 1(1): 29–39.

Newton, Lara Foot (2005), *Tshepang: The Third Testament*, London: Oberon Books.

Nielsen, Emily H. (2007), 'Manifestation of a Lack: Capitalism, Democracy, and the Christian Identity Movement', Master's Thesis: Graduate College of Bowling Green State University.

Nietzsche, Friedrich (1954), 'Twilight of the Idols', in *The Portable Nietzsche*, W. Kaufmann (ed.), Viking: New York.

Nyeck, S.N. (2020), 'Poetics: Queer Recesses of the Heart and the Spirit of Intimacy within the Africana Household', *The African Journal of Gender and Religion*, 26(2): 91–110.

O'Connor, Francis (2017), 'The Marikana Massacre and Labour Protest in South Africa', in *Global Diffusion of Protest: Riding the Protest Wave in the Neoliberal Crisis*, D. della Porta (ed.), Amsterdam: Amsterdam University Press, 113–136.

Oduol, Wilhemina A. (1993), 'Kenyan Women in Politics: An Analysis of Past and Present Trends', *Transafrican Journal of History*, 22: 166–181.

Osborne, Myles (2018), 'Reviewed Work(s): Murder at Small Koppie: The Real Story of South Africa's Marikana Massacre by Marinovich, Greg', *Africa Today*, 64(4): 115–117.

Ossome, Lyn (2014), 'Integrating Sexual and Economic Justice: Challenges for Queer Feminist Activism against Sexual Violence in South Africa', in *Global Justice and Desire: Queering Economy*, Nikita Dhawan, Antke Engel, Christoph Holzhey, Volker Woltersdorff (eds.), London: Routledge.

Ossome, Lyn (2018a), *Gender, Ethnicity and Violence in Kenya's Transitions to Democracy: States of Violence*, New York, Lexington Books.

Ossome, Lyn (2018b), 'The Public Politics of Nudity', *The MISR Review*, 2: 162–173.

Ossome, Lyn (2023), 'Intersectionality from the Margins: Historical Subjects/ Subjectivation in the Global South', in *The Routledge Handbook on Intersectionality Studies*, Kathy Davis and Helma Lutz (eds.), London: Routledge.

Ossome, Lyn (2024a), "The Colonial State and Postcolonial Feminist Predicaments," *Feminist Africa*, 5(2): 42–62.

Ossome, Lyn (2024b), 'Imperialism and Crises of Social Reproduction in Africa', *Review of African Political Economy*, 51(181): 509–524.

Ossome, Lyn (forthcoming, 2025), 'Decolonial Feminism', in *Handbook on Decolonizing International Affairs*, Sakiko Fukuda-Parr and Sean Jacobs (eds.), London: Routledge.

Ossome, Lyn and Sirisha Naidu (2021), 'The Agrarian Question of Gendered Labour', in *Labour Questions in the Global South*, Praveen Jha, Walter Chambati and Lyn Ossome (eds.), New Delhi: Springer.

Oyěwùmí, Oyèrónkẹ́ (1997), *The Invention of Women: Making an African Sense of Western Gender Discourses*, Minneapolis: University of Minnesota Press.

Ozban, Esra L. (2014), 'The Politics of Archive and Counter-archival Practices: The Case of Geziparkarsiv', MA Film and Screen Studies. Goldsmith College, University of London.

Paterson, Orlando (1985), *Slavery and Social Death: A Comparative Study*, Cambridge, MA: Harvard University Press.

Patnaik, Utsa (2012), 'Some Aspects of the Contemporary Agrarian Question', *Agrarian South: Journal of Political Economy*, 1(3): 233–254.

Paton, Alan (1948), *Cry, The Beloved Country*, New York, Penguin Books.

Peele, Stanton and Stanley J. Morse (1974), 'Ethnic Voting and Political Change in South Africa', *The American Political Science Review*, 68(4): 1520–1541.

Pillay, Suren (2013), 'The Marikana Massacre: South Africa's Post-Apartheid Dissensus', *Economic and Political Weekly*, 48(50): 32–37.

Pitts, Jennifer (2005), *A Turn to Empire: The Rise of Imperial Liberalism in Britain and France*. Princeton, NJ: Princeton University Press.

Plaatje, Sol (2007), *Native Life in South Africa*, Northlands: Picador Africa.

Prasad, Vijay (2023), 'Foreword to the Second Edition', in *The Concept of Human Rights in Africa*, I. Shivji (ed.), 2nd ed., Dakar: Codesria.

Presley, Cora Ann (2003), *Kikuyu Women, the Mau Mau Rebellion, and Social Change in Kenya*, Baltimore: Inprint Editions.

Ranchod-Nilsson, Sita (1992), "Educating Eve": The Women's Club Movement and Political Consciousness among Rural African Women in Southern Rhodesia, 1950–1980', in *African Encounters with Domesticity*, Karen T. Hansen (ed.), New Jersey: Rutgers University Press.

Rancière, Jacques (2014), *Hatred of Democracy*, trans. Steve Corcoran, London: Verso.

Richards, Audrey I. (1964), 'Authority Patterns in Traditional Buganda', in *The King's Men: Leadership and Status in Buganda on the Eve of Independence*, Lloyd A. Fallers (ed.), London: Oxford University Press.

Richards, Audrey I. and P. Reining (1954), 'Report on Fertility Surveys in Buganda and Buheya, 1952', in *Culture and Human Fertility*, Lorimer, F. (ed.), Zurich: UNESCO.

Robertson, Claire C. (1997), *Trouble Showed the Way: Women, Men and Trade in the Nairobi Area, 1890–1990*, Bloomington: Indiana University Press.

Said, Edward (1992), *The Question of Palestine*, New York: Vintage Books.

Santoru, Marina E. (1996), 'The Colonial Idea of Women and Direct Intervention: The Mau Mau Case,' *African Affairs*, 95: 253–267.

Schiff, Stacy (2015), *The Witches: Suspicion, Betrayal, and Hysteria in 1692 Salem*, New York: Black Bay Books.

Schler, Lynn (2004), 'Writing African Women's History with Male Sources: Possibilities and Limitations', *History in Africa*, 31: 319–333.

Schmidt, Elizabeth (1990), 'Negotiated Spaces and Contested Terrain: Men, Women and the Law in Colonial Zimbabwe, 1890–1939', *Journal of Southern African Studies*, 16(4): 622–648.

Schmitt, Carl (1996[1932]), *The Concept of the Political*, trans. George Schwab, Chicago: The University of Chicago Press.

Schoenbrun, David Lee (1998), *A Green Place, A Good Place: Agrarian Change, Gender and Social Identity in the Great Lakes Region to the 15th Century*, Portsmouth, NH: Heinemann.

Scott, David (2004), *Conscripts of Modernity: The Tragedy of Colonial Enlightenment*, Durham: Duke University Press.

Sekyi-Otu, Ato (2018), *Left Universalism, Africacentric Essays*, London: Routledge.

Shadle, Brett L. (2006), *'Girl Cases': Marriage and Colonialism in Gusiiland, Kenya, 1890–1970*, London: Heinemann.

Sheeba, K.M. (2002), 'Modernity in Social Reform Discourse: The Women Question in Colonial Kerala', *Proceedings of the Indian History Congress*, 63: 931–938.

Shivji, Issa (1983), 'Seven Theses on Reform and Revolution', *Journal of African Marxists*, 4: 45–53.

Shivji, Issa (2023), *The Concept of Human Rights in Africa*, 2nd ed., Dakar: Codesria.

Shula Marks and Richard Rathbone (eds.) (2023), *Industrialisation and Social Change in South Africa: African Class, Culture and Consciousness, 1870–1930*, London and New York: Longman.

Snyder, Francis (1988), 'Review Article: Rethinking African Customary Law' Reviewed works: *Law, Custom and Social Order: The Colonial Experience of Malawi and Zambia*, by Martin Chanock, Cambridge: Cambridge University Press 1985', *The Modern Law Review*, 51: 252–258.

Soper, Kate (1986), *Humanism and Anti-Humanism*, New York: Open Court Company.

Southall, Roger (1981), 'Buthelezi, Inkatha and the Politics of Compromise', *African Affairs*, 80(321): 453–481.

Spillers, Hortense, J. (1987), 'Mama's Baby, Papa's Maybe: An American Grammar Book', *Diacritics*, 17(2): 64–81.

Spinoza, B. (1958), *The Political Works*, London: Oxford Press.

Spivak, Gayatri Chakravorty (1988[1993]), 'Can the Subaltern Speak?' in *Marxism and the Interpretation of Culture*, Cary Nelson and Lawrence Grossberg (eds.), London: Macmillan.

Spivak, Gayatri Chakravorty (1994), 'Bonding in Difference', in *An Other Tongue: Nation and Ethnicity in the Linguistic Borderlands*, Alfred Arteaga (ed.), Durham: Duke University Press, 273–285.

Spivak, Gayatri Chakravorty (1995), 'Supplementing Marxism', in *Whither Marxism*? Steven Cullenberg and Bernd Magnus (eds.), New York: Routledge.

Spivak, Gayatri Chakravorty (2007), 'Feminism and Human Rights', in *The Present as History: Critical Perspectives on Global Power*, Nermeen Shaikh (ed.), New York: Columbia University Press.

Steinhauer, J. (2019), 'The Art of the Unspeakable', *The New Republic*, https://newrepublic.com/article/155293/vivien-green-fryd-nancy-princenthal-feminist-performance-artists-book-review (accessed on 20 May 2020).

Stichter, Sharon (1977), *Women and the Labour Force in Kenya, 1895–1964*, Nairobi: IDS.

Stoler, Ann Laura (2002), *Carnal Knowledge and Imperial Power: Race and the Intimate in Colonial Rule*, Berkeley: University of California Press.

Strobel, Margaret (1979), *Muslim Women in Mombasa, 1890–1975*, New Haven: Yale University Press.

Sundstrom, Ronald R. (2013), 'Sheltering Xenophobia', *Critical Philosophy of Race*, 1(1): 68–85.

Szeftel, Morris (1994), 'Ethnicity and Democratization in South Africa', *Review of African Political Economy*, 21(60): 185–199.

Tanaka, Yuki (2002), *Japan's Comfort Women: Sexual Slavery and Prostitution during World War II and the US Occupation*, London & New York: Routledge.

Tandon, Yash (1977), 'Review: Whose Capital and Whose State?' *The African Review: A Journal of African Politics, Development and International Affairs*, 7(2): 104–124.

Thipe, Thuto (2013), 'Defining Boundaries: Gender and Property Rights in South Africa's Traditional Courts Bill', *Laws*, 2(4): 483–511.

Thomas, Lynn M. (1997), 'Regulating Reproduction: State Interventions into Fertility and Sexuality in Rural Kenya, c. 1920–70', PhD. dissertation, University of Michigan.

Thomas, Lynn M. (2003), *Politics of the Womb: Women, Reproduction and the State in Kenya*, Berkeley: University of California Press.

Tosh, John (1978), *Clan Leaders and Colonial Chiefs in Lango: The Political History of an East African Stateless Society, c.1800–1939*, Oxford: Clarendon Press.

Touraine, Alain (2005), 'The Subject Is Coming Back', *International Journal of Politics, Culture, and Society*, 18 (3/4): 199–209.

Tshitereke, Clarence (1999), 'Xenophobia and Relative Deprivation', *Crossings*, 3(2): 4–5.

Tzanelli, Rodanthi (2012), 'Resentment and Ressentiment', *The Wiley-Blackwell Encyclopedia of Globalization*, https://doi.org/10.1002/9780470670590.wbeog498

Udwin, Leslee (2014), *India's Daughter: The Story of Jyoti Singh*, https://archive.org/details/indias-daughter-2015

Umoren, Uduakobong E. (1995), 'The Symbolism of the Nigerian Women's War of 1929: An Anthropological Study of an Anticolonial Struggle', *African Study Monographs*, 16(2): 61–72.

Vahabzadeh, Peyman (2007), 'The Conditions of Subalternity: Reflections on Subjectivity, Experience and Hegemony', *Socialist studies/Études socialistes*, 3(2): 93–113.

Vinogradoff, Paul (1924), 'The Juridical Nature of the State', *Michigan Law Review*, 23(2): 138–153.

wa Thiong'o, Ngugi (1964), *Weep Not, Child*, Nairobi: Heinemann.

Wells, Julia C. (1982), 'The History of Black Women's Struggle against Pass Laws in South Africa 1900–1960', unpublished PhD thesis, Graduate School of Arts and Social Sciences, Columbia University.

White, Luise (1990), *The Comforts of Home: Prostitution in Colonial Nairobi*, Chicago: University of Chicago Press.

Williams, Gavin (2016), 'Slaves, Workers, and Wine: The "Dop System" in the History of the Cape Wine Industry, 1658–1894', *Journal of Southern African Studies*, 42(5): 893–909.

Williams, Patricia J. (1991), *The Alchemy of Race and Rights: Diary of a Law Professor*, Cambridge, MA: Harvard University Press.

Wolfe, Patrick (2006), 'Settler Colonialism and the Elimination of the Native', *Journal of Genocide Research*, 8(4): 387–409.

Woods, Donald (1978), *Biko*, New York and London: Paddington Press.

Yuval-Davis, Nira (1997), 'Women and the Biological Reproduction of the Nation', in *Gender and Nation*, N. Yuval-Davis (ed.), London: Sage.

Index

Note: Page numbers followed by "n" refers to the endnote, e.g., 20 n.1 refers to endnote 1 on page 20